ML
3561
.J3
B245

ML
3561
.J3
B245

Humber College
Lakeshore Campus

D0801706

319

996 05 14

Due

OCT 17 1983
OCT 6 1983
SEP 18 1985
SEP 13 1985
OCT 05 1990
SEP 24 1990
SEP 25 1993
SEP 18 1993
DEC 04 1996
DEC 02 1996

MAR 18 2000
MAK 24 2000

HUMBER COLLEGE L. R. C. (LAKESHORE)

HUMBER COLLEGE
LAKESHORE CAMPUS
LEARNING RESOURCE CENTRE
3199 L. KESHORE BLVD., WEST
TORONTO, ONTARIO   M8V 1K8

IMPROVISING

IMPROVISING

Sixteen Jazz Musicians and Their Art

WHITNEY BALLIETT

HUMBER COLLEGE
LAKESHORE CAMPUS
LEARNING RESOURCE CENTRE
3199 LAKESHORE BLVD., WEST
TORONTO, ONTARIO   M8V 1K8

New York
OXFORD UNIVERSITY PRESS
1977

FOR WILLIAM SHAWN

Copyright © 1977 by Whitney Balliett
Library of Congress Catalogue Card Number: 76-42635

Printed in the United States of America

Most of the material in this book appeared in somewhat different form in *The New Yorker* magazine.

NOTE

This book was written over the course of the past fifteen years. "The Blues Is a Slow Story," "Sunshine Always Opens Out," "Out Here Again," and "Even His Feet Look Sad" were brought out in *Such Sweet Thunder*, which has long been out of print. "Super-Drummer" appeared as a little book of its own, *Super-Drummer: A Profile of Buddy Rich*, with photographs by the late Fred Seligo, and it, too, is out of print—although there is some question that it was ever *in* print, for I have never met anyone who has seen it, let alone heard of it. "The Music Is More Important" and "Like a Family" are part of *Ecstasy at the Onion*, which continues in print but, like the Rich book, is a well-kept secret. "For the Comfort of the People," "Back From Valhalla," "Big Sid," "You Must Start Well and You Must End Well," "The Answer Is Yes," and "The Westchester Kids" have never been in book form.

There are good reasons for bringing all these remarkable people together here. Their lives, in intertwining and overlapping, form a scattershot history of the music, not as outsiders have reconstructed it, but as they themselves have lived it, which is an altogether different vision. The history of jazz is its music, of course, but it is also the Andy Kirk band playing roadside baseball in a corn field; Sid Catlett and Johnny Williams sitting on a railroad observation-car platform in the thirties and digging the train rhythms; Red Norvo and Mildred Bailey having at it for no good reason in their celebrated house in Forest Hills—the house where they helped give birth to the Benny Goodman Trio and where they entertained and instructed such as Bessie Smith and Fats Waller and Alec Wilder; and Jess Stacy listening to the gophers munching his irises in his Hollywood Hills yard. Another reason for gathering these musicians—aside from the obvious benefit of having their stories in one place at last—is that they are (or were) all good improvisers, and improvisation, as Alec Wilder points out in *Alec Wilder and His Friends* (in print), is a "lightning mystery." He continues: "In fact, it's *the* creative mystery of our age, and I wonder how many people know that. I wish to God that some neurologists would sit down and figure out *how* the improviser's brain works, *how* he selects, out of hundreds of thousands of possibilities, the notes he does and at the speed he does—*how*, in God's name, his mind works so damned fast! Any why, when the notes come out right, they *are* right. Maybe we'll just have to go on thinking of it on the folk level as a series of secrets paraded in public. Musicians *talk* to one another when they improvise, and they say things they wouldn't *dare* say in words. It's all a terrific act of confession." Each musician here—with the exception of King Oliver and Sid Catlett, both long beyond the bar—peers into the mysteries of improvisation. Some appear almost shocked, as if it were an indecent thing to do. Some are baffled and driven into inarticulateness. And some, like Pee Wee Russell and Stéphane Grappelli and Jim Hall and Bob Wilber, are eloquent and fascinating. But no one blows the mists completely away, and no one, I suspect, ever will.

New York, N.Y.   W. B.
January 1977

CONTENTS

THE BLUES IS A SLOW STORY

Red Allen, who died in 1967 at the age of fifty-nine, was something of a wonder in jazz. He was, along with Zutty Singleton and Louis Armstrong, one of the great New Orleans musicians, and he was the only New Orleans musician who, barring a few stops and starts, continued to develop. His playing became increasingly subtle, and there were suggestions in it of Miles Davis and Art Farmer. His style was fully formed by 1930. Armstrong hovered in its background, but Allen's originality dominated it. It was an elegant and primitive and fearless style, and it was perfectly balanced. His full, often declamatory tone was suitably crimped by growls or piercing high notes; his basically legato approach was enlivened by rushes of on-the-beat notes; his seemingly straightforward melodic content was enriched by long, sagacious phrases and by a daring choice of notes. Allen was particularly striking at slow tempos. He would linger over his notes, holding them far longer than any other trumpeter, and he would bend them and press them, coloring them with a distinct and disturbing melancholy. His slow solos were often requiems. But this sadness, which lifted at faster tempos, was invariably toughened and guided by a subtle, leashed power. By 1934, he had become a full-fledged innovator; indeed, in the recordings he made with Fletcher Henderson he is a one-man avant-garde—a credit only recently granted him. His solos are full of long, roving lines, unexpected off-notes, and free rhythmic turns. It is the sort of crossing-the-bar-lines improvising that was perfected five or six years later by Lester Young and Charlie Christian and that still sounds absolutely fresh. Some of Allen's solos with Henderson had such completeness and authority that they were studied a few years later by Harry James when he was with Benny Goodman, and several were scored for whole sections of the Henderson band. Allen's playing changed in the forties. It became brassy and harsh, and his unevenness, theretofore occasional, became pronounced. He would start a solo with a beautiful, languorous phrase, pause, lose the impetus of it, and wander off into an entirely different mood. But this uncertainty began to lessen in the early fifties, and in 1957 he made a startling recording for Victor. It included several long ballads, and Allen converted each into a massive lullaby. He flowed around his horn (lower-register notes—almost trombone notes—would be planted beside soft, high flutters), and the blues underlay almost every passage. He made equally good recordings after that, and gorgeous patches appeared in every solo he took in night clubs or at concerts, no matter how hard he was blowing. Allen had much in common with Pee Wee Russell. Both appeared to be inimitable and both had long been lumped with the wrong musical schools—Russell with the Chicagoans and Allen with New Orleans jazz. Both were, in reality, advanced swing musicians who played best in fast, original company.

For the last twenty-seven years of his life, Allen lived with his wife, Pearlie May, and assorted children and grandchildren on the fifth floor of a yellow-brick walk-up on Prospect Avenue in the east Bronx. Jobs were scarce in the year or two before he died, and he welcomed visits from friends.

Allen was tall and he had gotten portly, but he took the stairs in his apartment house at a fast pace, and he was not winded when he reached his floor. He pushed his doorbell and there was a thumping sound inside. A muffled voice said, "Is that you, Allen?"

"I'm here, Pearlie May. Open up." There were more confused sounds and the word "doing" came through the door. Allen chuckled. "She's putting the dog away. He's a big white German shepherd that we call White Fang after another White Fang we had, and he'll jump all over you, cover you with hair. But he's a fine watchdog. When I come in late, I ring the bell downstairs and Pearlie May lets him out and he runs down to meet me."

A chain rattled and the door opened. Mrs. Allen, who is short and plump and has a round, pretty face, was fastening the top button of a house dress. "Lord, that dog is so *curi*ous," she said. "Wants to see what everybody looks like comes in the house, and then sits all over them. I put him in the bathroom, where he won't bother anyone."

Mrs. Allen stepped back, and Allen led the way down a

short, dark hall and past a small, cheerful kitchen. An impressionistic painting of Allen hung by the kitchen door, and farther along, on the opposite wall, there was a large photograph of a thin, young, smooth-faced Allen dressed in a dapper double-breasted suit and holding an extremely long trumpet. A small room with a day bed and a television set and a couple of chairs was at the end of the hall, and opening out of the hall to the left, behind glass doors, was a larger room. "This is the front room, which is what we call the parlor," Allen said. The room had a small green sofa, several red chairs, and two end tables. A silver tea service and a pair of tall orange china swans were on one of the tables. A dark abstract painting hung on one wall, and another painting of Allen across from it. On the wall near the doors were two plates, one with the message "God Bless This Allen Home." The venetian blinds at the only window were down, but the slats were open. The room was in pleasant half-light.

Allen sat down heavily in one of the chairs, his legs spread wide, his toes pointing in. His face was a study in basset melancholy. He had a high, narrow forehead and thin, dark hair. A single, ironbound furrow ran across the lower part of his forehead, and it seemed to weigh on his eyes, which were heavily lidded and slanted down at their outer corners. Two deep furrows bracketed his generous nose and his mouth, and he had a cleft chin. His cheeks were heavy but firm. His smile was surprising; it easily lifted and lit the mass around it. His speech resembled the odd, watered-down version of the Brooklyn accent that is found in New Orleans and St. Louis. He was apt to start sentences with "der"—in the manner of the French "*donc*"—or to use it to fill a pause. Moreover, words like "rehearsal" and "bird" he pronounced "rehoisal" and "boid." Allen yawned, tweaked his nose, and rested his thick, square hands on his thighs. "My first visit to New York was when King Oliver called for me to come and meet him," Allen said. "I was leery of leaving New Orleans. I'd heard of too many New Orleans musicians getting stranded up in the North. But I went because Oliver had worked in my dad's brass band. I lived in a boarding house with Omer Simeon and Barney Bigard and Paul Barbarin, New Orleans friends and all in Oliver's band, before I moved in with Oliver and his sister. Oliver's teeth had gone bad by then and he wasn't playing much, so I'd take most of the solos at the Savoy, where we were appearing, and pretty soon people started calling me King Oliver. Then Oliver was supposed to go into the Cotton Club, but somebody brainwashed him about the money, telling him he should get more, so he didn't take the job. Duke Ellington, who was just starting out, did, and that was the beginning of *that* story. Oliver's band was booked into a park in Baltimore, but we had rough luck there with weather, and that job didn't work out, either. When we got back to New York, I couldn't take it anymore. I made my first record—with Clarence Williams—and the next day I took off for home. I'd saved my fare money—kept it in my shoe—so I didn't have to send to my father for money. I was only gone two months and I was happy to get back. Even the coffee was bad in New York. In New Orleans it was so strong it stained the cup, but I drank so much of it I got headaches if I didn't drink it. In New York I drank the same amount, but the headaches just got worse, so I gave it up. And I don't drink much of it to this day, unless I'm in New Orleans on a visit."

There was a commotion in the hall, and White Fang appeared outside the glass doors. Mrs. Allen grabbed him by the collar and started pulling him back toward the kitchen. Allen laughed. "Let him be, Pearlie May!" he shouted. "Just put that chair against the door so's he can't get in." Mrs. Allen wedged a chair under the door handle. She shook a finger at the dog, and said, "You want to come out, you act like a grown boy." The dog sat down, his nose pressed against the glass. He stared at Allen, and then he jumped up on the chair and resumed his vigil.

"I joined Fate Marable's band when I got back," Allen said. "Fate worked the riverboats on the Streckfus line, and during the winter we'd stay in New Orleans and play one-nighters. Go up the river a little way and turn around and come back. When it warmed up, we'd head for St. Louis and stop at towns along the way and dock and play dances on the boat. We stayed in St. Louis about three months, and though we played on the boat we lived in the city. You had to go out and find a room—which was called every tub on its bottom, or being on your own. There were some rough places in St. Louis. The Chauffeurs' Club was so bad they built a fence of chicken wire around the bandstand to protect the musicians when fights broke out. In 1929, I started getting letters and wires from New York. Luis Russell, who had been with Oliver when I was and who had the band now, wrote me to join him, and Duke Ellington wired me. I knew most of the people with Russell. Pops Foster, who'd been a longshoreman with my father, was on bass; Charlie Holmes was on alto; and old Paul Barbarin, who had instigated my joining Oliver in 1927, was on drums. I knew about J. C. Higginbotham, on trombone, and I'd heard of Bill Coleman and Otis Johnson, who were on trumpets. So I told Russell yes, and turned down Ellington. Barney Bigard was the only person I knew in his band. I believe he hired Cootie Williams instead. Fate Marable said O.K., I could go. He also said, 'Red'—that was a nickname given me because I was light-skinned and my face got red when I blew—'Red, if you see my man Jelly Roll Morton, tell him hello. He used to work for me, you know.' The first time I ran into Jelly in New York, I gave him the message. Well, Jelly Roll had a lot of posing and hot air in him, always saying thinks like 'My car is so long I got to go over to Central Park to turn it around,' and he just stood there and looked around and after a while he said, 'Oh, Fate *Mar*able. He had this big old band that wasn't doing *nothing* and so one time I let him use my name to help him out.'" Allen laughed and rubbed his hands together. White Fang was on the hall floor, asleep.

"That first week back in New York was scary," Allen went on. "Teddy Hill, who played tenor for Russell, met me at the train and took me straight to the Roseland Ballroom, where the band was playing. I was to learn it was the kind of band that hung out like a family. It had brotherly love going. It was also the most swinging band in New York. It put the audiences in an uproar. One of the reasons was rhythm. Ellington had switched from tuba to bass and from banjo to guitar, and so had Russell. All the New York bass players were taking lessons from Pops Foster, and they even began carrying their basses on their shoulders, like the New Orleans men. Before that, you'd see them in the street carrying that fiddle in front of them in their arms like a baby. Russell did most of the arrangements, and whenever you took a solo there was a lot of fire up and down the band. But it wasn't Russell that made me nervous that first week. It was the after-hours jam sessions. I'd heard a lot about them and about the 'cutting' contests and I didn't know if I'd make it or not. I couldn't look to alcohol or tobacco for support, either. My father had never allowed me to drink or smoke, and I obeyed him. I don't believe I took my first strong drink until the forties, and I still don't smoke. I hadn't been in New York but a day or two when Alphonse Steele, who was a drummer, began taking me to the sessions at the Rhythm Club, on a Hundred and Thirty-second Street. He used to be a Paul Revere, sending around the news of sessions and announcing a new man in town. They would have trumpet nights and trombone nights and saxophone nights at the Rhythm Club. The first sessions I went to, every trumpeter was there—Cootie Williams, Rex Stewart, Ward Pinkett, Freddy Jenkins, Sidney de Paris. I don't believe Joe Smith showed up, but I learned later that when he did you were really in the lion's mouth. Whoever was on piano decided on the key and set the tempo, and then everyone soloed. If you wanted extra choruses, you stomped your foot. The applause decided the winner." Allen laughed. "I guess I did all right, because I'm still in New York. But those sessions were more than just outblowing someone. They were the only way of getting noticed, they were our publicity. If you made a good appearance, stood on your own, the word got around, and that's where the jobs come from. If you lost out too often, you just wouldn't make it. There were challenges all the time. One night, Big Green challenged Higginbotham. It was late, so Big Green went back to the Saratoga Club, where he was working, to get his horn and had to break down the door, which was locked. He came on back and I believe Higgy took care of him. Another time, the St. Louis clarinettist Thornton Blue—'the reputed Blue,' he called himself—took on Prince Robinson and Omer Simeon and Buster Bailey. When Buster got going on 'Tiger Rag,' that sealed it up. I heard Rex Stewart and Bix Biederbecke battle, but, all due respect for the dead, Rex must have been in better form that night. And of course the bands battled all the time—at the Roseland and the Savoy and the Renaissance. And white musicians came up from downtown to sit in or listen: Jack Teagarden and the Dorseys and Krupa and Red Nichols and Goodman and Bunny Berigan. And there were breakfast dances at Small's Paradise, which began around four or five in the morning and went on half the day. I'd developed a strong embouchure on the riverboats, where the hours were long, so I could stand it."

There was muffled barking, and two little girls in school uniforms appeared outside the doors. "Oh, that's nice," Allen said, and smiled. "Here's the grands, home from school. Their address is with my son and his wife, who are only four blocks away, but they practically live here. They come by every day to do their homework and spend the night. They only go home Saturdays, but their parents stop in most every day, too. That way we get to see them. The grands call Pearlie May 'Mama' and me 'Papa.' " The taller girl opened one of the doors and came in and kissed Allen. "This is Alcornette," Allen said. "She's eleven. Pearlie May's maiden name is Alcorn, and of course there had to be some mention of a trumpet or cornet. And this is Juretta. She's named after my mother. She's six. They go to a Catholic school nearby. Go change your clothes and get on that homework. Alcornette, ask Mama can I have some ice and glasses. And close the door. We'll have a little taste, a little Scotcherini.

"I stayed with the Russell band until 1933, when I got a telegram from Fletcher Henderson asking me to meet him at a drugstore uptown. Russell Smith, who played trumpet with him, mainly persuaded me to join. I didn't like leaving the Luis Russell band, which was my home. But I guess Henderson offered me more money, and it was *the* band. Most of the arrangements were by Fletcher or Horace, his brother, and they were in difficult keys—D natural and the like. I'd learned all the keys in New Orleans by playing along with records set at every different speed. Each speed would put the music in a new key. I'd try all kinds of things with Fletcher, loafing through the channel of a number like 'Yeah Man,' with the result that Horace liked what I'd done so much he wrote it out for the brass. Horace would just sketch out the chords for new numbers and you could skate on that. I got accustomed to him. Take my thirty-one bars, or whatever, and get out. I was with the band for a year, and during that time Coleman Hawkins left and Lester Young replaced him. He only stayed a couple of weeks. He had a light tone and it just didn't fit with the arrangements, which called for a rich, deep sound. But I was happy for Lester to be in the band, because his father and my father had played together in New Orleans. Ben Webster took his place. I got ninety dollars a week when I joined, and I made something on the side with small-band dates for Brunswick. They paid a hundred dollars a date. I picked the men— mostly from Henderson's band—and we made popular things like 'Red Sails in the Sunset' and 'If I Could Be Twins' and 'Boots and Saddle.' They sold very well in Europe. Fletcher always had money, even when he said he didn't. It seems he had these special pockets—a two-dollar pocket, a five-, a ten-. Because whenever you asked him for a slight advance he'd go to such-and-such a pocket and bring out just the amount. In 1934, things got bad. Henderson couldn't find work. The Mills Blue Rhythm Band, which was fronted by Lucky Millinder, was having trouble, too, but when

Lucky sent for Higgy and Buster Bailey and me, we went. Irving Mills made the proposition of making me the leader of the Blue Rhythm Band, but I couldn't see cutting in on Lucky. I was satisfied to be what I was. Every band I'd been in I'd been featured. I got good money and didn't have the headaches. It's not so easy to relax when you're the leader. Imagine, you have fifteen or sixteen minds going you have to control. I joined Louis Armstrong's big band in 1937, which was like coming home again, because it was still the old Russell band, but expanded. Higgy came with me. Louis was very good to me. He gave me little solo parts here and there. In fact, it was just the other month Louis and Lucille Armstrong climbed these five flights to come and see me. They'd heard something had happened to me, but it was only rumor. We had a fine dinner together."

Mrs. Allen put a bowl of ice, Old-Fashioned glasses, and a bottle of Scotch on a table. "You hungry, Allen?" Mrs. Allen asked. "I got something coming up in a few minutes." She leaned into the next room, where Juretta and Alcornette were. "Now hurry up and change those clothes," she said. "And, Alcornette, when you finish, set up that card table in the front room."

"I eat around two o'clock in the evening and after work," Allen said. He poured a little water in his glass and took a sip and coughed. "Even though I got to be a leader, the forties were all right for me. John Hammond arranged for me to see Barney Josephson, the owner of Café Society Downton. We weren't doing all that much work with Louis, so I formed my own group in 1940, with Higgy and Edmond Hall. We were at Café Society a year with people like Pete Johnson and Billie Holiday and Art Tatum and Hazel Scott and Lena Horne, who was in the chorus at the Cotton Club in 1934, when I played there. I took the band to Boston from Café Society for a long gig at the Ken Club. Sidney Bechet played with us. Don Stovall replaced Edmond Hall, and Kenny Clarke came in on drums, and later Paul Barbarin. We had another long stay at the Down Beat Room in Chicago, where we worked with Billie again. She missed a lot of shows and so we'd use a girl named Ruth Jones, who was always hanging around waiting for the chance to sing. I'd announce her—burlesque style—as Dynamite Washington, which later became Dinah when she joined Lionel Hampton. I added Ben Webster to the band. Later, we worked in San Francisco, and in Salt Lake City and at the Onyx and Kelly's Stable on Fifty-second Street, and back to Chicago and to Boston. They were all long engagements. I went into the Metropole in 1954. I had Higgy and Buster Bailey and Cozy Cole, and I took Claude Hopkins out of deep freeze and put him on piano. It was a seven-year gig. The owners of the Metropole were very good to me. *They* didn't make us play loud. It was the people. We'd try a soft number or two, and they'd say, 'Now what's the matter with you, Red? You sick or something?' And we'd go up again."

Juretta sidled into the room and handed Allen some schoolwork papers. He held them at arm's length, read through them slowly, and handed them back. He smiled. "That's just fine, darlin'. Lovely. You go and finish now." Alcornette brought in a card table, and Allen heaved himself to his feet and helped her set it up. Then he walked around the room, peered through the venetian blind, and went back to his chair.

Mrs. Allen called from the kitchen, "Alcornette, put on that white tablecloth that's in the chest in your room! And set some plates and glasses and napkins, please!"

"You got some peppers, Pearlie May?" Allen called.

"I got them right here, Allen," she replied.

"The most influence Louis Armstrong had on me was on the records he made in the twenties—the 'Savoy Blues,' 'Cornet Chop Suey.' We used to learn those numbers from the recordings in New Orleans. And I'd hear Whiteman recordings that Mr. Streckfus brought back from New York with him. I also listened to people in New Orleans like Buddy Petit and Chris Kelly, who never recorded. And to Kid Rena and Punch Miller. Rena was the first trumpeter I ever heard play high. Those things worked together to make my style, and the rest was me. When you play, so many things work together. You have your brain. You have your fingers. You have your breathing. You have your embouchure. Playing, it's like somebody making your lip speak, making it say things he thinks. I concentrate a couple of bars ahead at all times. You have to have an idea of where you are going. You have more expression of feeling in the blues. And you have more time. The blues is a slow story. The feeling of the beautiful things that happen to you is in the blues. They come out in the horn. You play blues, it's a home language, like two friends talking. It's the language everybody understands. You can inject into people with the instrument, I think. I've had nights when it was better than others, but I've been a little fortunate in my loving to play so much."

Mrs. Allen brought in a platter of fried chicken and a dish of boiled cabbage. She put a jar of pickled hot peppers between them. Allen grunted, pulled his chair up to the table, and helped himself. "Bring some of that Rheingold, please, Pearlie. We call these hot peppers birds' eyes. My aunt just sent them from New Orleans. It's what they make Tabasco Sauce from. People live on hot peppers and mustard and garlic in New Orleans."

"You eat them with every meal, you get used to them," Mrs. Allen said. She was standing arms akimbo. Juretta stood beside her, staring at the chicken. "All right, a *small* piece," Mrs. Allen said. "Otherwise, you'll ruin your supper. And don't chew all over the carpet."

"I visit my mother and my aunt in New Orleans every year," Allen said. "My mother is eighty-two and spry. She still lives in the house where I was born, at 414 Newton Street, in Algiers, which is to New Orleans what the Bronx is to New York. My father passed in 1952. He was seventy-five. He was born in Lockport, Louisiana. Everyone was in his brass band at one time or another—Punch Miller, Papa Celestin, King Oliver, Louis Armstrong, Sidney Bechet. My father played trumpet. His brother Samuel was a bass player, and a younger brother, George, played drums. The band generally had two trombones, three trumpets, a bass horn and a baritone horn, a peck horn, a clarinet, and two drummers. The trombones marched in front, so they wouldn't hit anybody in the back. The bass and the baritone came next, then the clarinet and the peck horn, the trumpets, and then the drummers—bass drum to the left and snare drum to the right. The bass drummer played his drum and a cymbal attached to it, and the other drummer played snares. The two of them got a sound like a regular set of drums. The horn players needed strong embouchures. The roads were rough, and if you stepped into a hole you had to hold on to that horn to not break your notes. Maybe that was the reason King Oliver never marched with the band but always next to it, on the sidewalk, where it was smoother. There were generally parades on Sundays, and of course when there was a decease and for special occasions, like house-buildings and the regular outings of the social clubs. I don't know how many social clubs there were—the Money Wasters, the Square Deals, the Bulls, the West Side Friends of Honor. You paid dues and when you passed, your club paid for a band and for putting you away. The big men belonged to four or five clubs and they'd have four or five bands. My father had six when he passed. If you wasn't a member of any club, they put a saucer on your chest while you lay in the front room, and pretty soon there'd be enough for the proper arrangements. Each club had its own colors and its own banner. In parades, the two men who carried the banner got twenty-five cents apiece, and the man who carried the American flag got fifty cents. And each club had its own button—black on one side and its colors on the other. You'd wear the colors for regular parades and the black for funerals. The men who played in the bands were stonemasons or slaters or plasterers and such, and their jobs would let them off for a funeral. These funerals went according to the Bible—sadness at birth and rejoicing at death. If the deceased belonged to several clubs, he'd generally stay on view in the front room for three or four days to give all his brothers time to pay their respects. If you were very sacred, you'd stay with the deceased some while, then you'd go

through to the kitchen, where they'd have a bousin [pro-
nounced "boozeanne"], which is a Creole term for a party.
There would be gumbo and ham salad and burgundy and
sangaree, a kind of punch." Allen helped himself to another
piece of chicken and more cabbage.

"On funeral days, the club and the band assembled at the
deceased's house and then they'd march to the church," he
said. "The band played very slow, very slow. The snare was
taken off the snare drum, giving a kettle effect. When the
deceased went by, everyone in the street would stop talking
and moving and take off their hats and put them over their
hearts, and then go back to what they were doing. While
everyone was in the church, the musicians sometimes went
to a saloon nearby, and it was my job when I was little to
run from the church to the saloon when the service was
over and get the musicians together. We'd march to the
cemetery, and the band would stand in the road and wait
until the moans and cries went up, which meant that the
preacher was saying 'Ashes to ashes, dust to dust' and throwing the dirt on the coffin. Then the drums rolled like thunder
and the band would break into a fast 'Oh, Didn't He Ramble' and march back. On a wide avenue, when there was
more than one band, the first band would split in half, one
half lining up on one side of the avenue and the other on
the other side, and the band right behind would march between these lines. The bands would be playing different
tunes. Then the second band would split open and the first
one would form up again and march through *them*. You
could tell by the applause of the onlookers who was best,
and the winner would go a roundabout way to the house of
the deceased and play there up on the gallery, really swinging, for ten or fifteen minutes, and then go inside and enjoy
the bousin. Pearlie May, let me have one more beer!" After
shouting to the kitchen, Allen pushed himself back from the
table and took a bite of a red pepper the size of his finger.

"Of course, we played at dances, too," he said. "The men
in the band would get three dollars apiece and the leader
four, and there was a dollar allowed for phone calls and

such. And there were building parties. When a man decided to build himself a house, it was like the pioneering days. The members of his club and his neighbors would all gather on a weekend on his plot—wives and children, too. The men would put down the foundation and get the frame up. There would be a few kegs of beer or some home brew— Sweet Lucy or Son Kick Your Mammy—and a band to play. They'd build and eat and build and drink and build and laugh and have a fine bousin. The man whose house was being put up would turn around next time a house had to be built and help with that. At Mardi Gras, musicians got scarce in New Orleans, and a week or so before, my father would hitch up a sulky and travel maybe a hundred miles into the country to round up musicians he'd heard or heard about. He took me when I got big enough. The roads were poor, and we never went too fast for fear the horse's legs might get stoved up or swollen. We'd stop and visit every few miles and spend the night with relatives or friends."

Mrs. Allen cleared the table and brought more beer. Then she went to the window and looked out, her hands clasped behind her. The room was darker and Allen switched on a lamp.

"I started on the violin. My mother preferred it because most of the boys who took up the trumpet got balls in their cheeks and necks from all that blowing. But I'd practice on my father's trumpet, and he'd keep telling me to tell my mother it would be all right, I wouldn't get those balls in my cheeks, and finally she said yes. From the age of eight I played the upright alto—the peck horn—in my father's band. He'd carry me in parades some of the way and then put me down on a corner and I'd play and a little crowd would gather and he'd tell everybody 'Sonny's got it, Sonny's got it.' My first teacher on trumpet was Manuel Manetta, but my father taught me to read. I did pretty nice in school. I had to—my father signed the report cards. He was a serious man, a strict man. I had to obey the New Orleans curfew, which was nine o'clock. It was sounded by a cal-

liope on one of the riverboats. Come nine every evening,
you'd see nothing in the streets but children running, this
way, that way, like mice. I also indulged in track in high
school, and I set up a few records in the cross-country. My
father was never rich, but he tried to give me everything I'd
think of. At one time, I even had a couple of horses—a pacer,
which puts down two feet at a time, and a racker, which
puts down one foot at a time. We were building a neighbor's house once, and I was sent over the canal into the
woods to drag back a cross-stile, which was made of six-
by-twelve beams, and when my horse got on the bridge
over the canal he balked. He wouldn't *move*. I blew a
whistle and rang this bell I had, and all of a sudden that
horse moved. He moved right into the canal, cross-stile and
all, everything mired down in mud. Sometimes I'd go to
auctions where they were selling horses and watch the pep
man. He stood kind of backstage, and before the horse—it
was usually an old nag—came out of the chute to where the
people was, the pep man would take a rag soaked in turpen-
tine and whap the horse right across his rump end and that
horse would come shooting out of the chute, head up, pranc-
ing and looking like a colt, and then, after somebody had
bid and bought, he'd sag and his head would go down and
he'd look like the used-up horse he was. Some afternoons
after school, when my father was still at work, I'd take my
horse and ride over to the poolroom—Louis Kohlman's poolroom—and tie him up outside. The horse got so used to the
route that once when my father asked me to ride him over
to the ferry to New Orleans, the horse got to the corner
near the poolroom, and instead of going straight to the ferry
he turned the corner, with me pulling and straining at him,
and headed right for the poolroom and stopped dead in
front of it. My father looked at me and I didn't say anything. He said, 'Sonny, I thought you didn't hang around
here.' Then he smiled, and I knew I was off the hook. My
father wanted me to be a musician and nothing else, so I was
already working in brass bands and in cabarets when I was
in my teens. You weren't allowed to wear long pants until

you were eighteen; just short pants—knickers they were. Leonard Bocage would bring me home at night, or my father would come and get me. He got so set in the habit that when I visited him not long before he passed and went out somewhere and didn't get home until three or four in the morning, I found him in the front room waiting up for me—and me not a junior anymore but a grown man."

Mrs. Allen was sitting in a chair, her head resting on one hand, watching Allen. "You used to try and get him to stop playing when he got old, Allen."

Allen smiled. "That's right, but you said I was wrong. 'Let him play,' you said. 'It's good for him. He'd suffer without it.' He played right up to the end."

"My father died when I was but fourteen," Mrs. Allen said, "and my mother when I was two. I was born a Creole—the last of three children. My father was a slater. New Orleans was famous for its slate steeples, and most of the roofs were slate, too. I went to public schools and then to New Orleans University. My parents were gone, but I had thirteen people on each side of the family, and they contributed to put me through. I took a general course, and then I went to Guillaume College for a business course for two years, and then went to work teaching in Utica, Mississippi, for a year. I was working for an insurance company in New Orleans when I met Allen. He was playing at the Pelican, a ballroom, and I sold tickets there at night. We were married in New York in 1930, and my son Henry—he's our only child—was born in 1931."

"He's been with the New York police for eight or nine years," Allen said. "Before that, he was an M.P. in the Marines in Korea. He plays trumpet, too, and he's good. Pearlie May and I have never been apart much. If I was on the road more than a week, Pearlie May would come and stay. If I was away and had a couple of days off, I'd come home for a quick visit. We're rare ones. Most of the others have been divorced and married three or four times. Pearlie May knows how to carry things on. She's very good brainwise.

All my flexible brains are musicwise. She pays the bills and does the taxes. I get the loot."

"If I can close myself up in my room, really get my brain to it, the taxes don't take too long," she said.

"We have relations in Chicago and Michigan and New Orleans, and we have a tremendous phone bill," Allen said.

"A letter's something you keep putting off," Mrs. Allen said. "I'm gonna write, I'm gonna write, I'm gonna write, and then you never do."

"If you do, then you call up the person on the phone and say, 'Oh, here's something I forgot to say in my letter.'"

"We have plans to move out of this neighborhood some-day. We've been in this apartment since 1940. Before that, we lived at St. Nicholas Place, around a Hundred and Forty-eighth Street."

"One day, my boy got tagged up there with a brick," Allen said. "Kids in the street called him out and then dropped a brick on his head from the roof. We lived on the ground and we were robbed a couple of times."

"That's why we live on the fifth floor. I like it here. I know everyone in the neighborhood and they know me. People'll carry your groceries up for you and things like that. Allen can leave his car unlocked, and if he's parked on the wrong side of the street someone calls up and tells him he better move, the policeman's coming."

"I love to play; that horn is good for me. So when I pass is when I'll retire. When I'm not working, I sit in front of the television when there is a decent musical show and play along with it. Or I go and sit in at Jimmy Ryan's. A couple of weeks ago, I played with Tony Scott at the Dom on St. Marks Place. I think those young cats were a little surprised."

"When Allen's on television, the children and I watch. Even that dog sits and watches, turning his head from side to side. When he finishes, we applaud."

"Jobs are scarce now," Allen said. "But this isn't the first time."

"In 1934, Allen told me, 'Let's pull in the belts and tighten up a little.' " Mrs. Allen laughed, showing perfect teeth. "You get a few nickels together in the good times and you survive the bad ones."

"Nineteen-thirty-four was with Fletcher," Allen said. "We'd been booked to go to Europe and before that we were supposed to go into Connie's Inn. We never made either scene. In fact, I didn't get to Europe until 1959." He took a sip of his beer. "They ask me what I've done, I don't have any regrets. Pearlie May is happy. She has her grands. I've raised my family, even if I don't have a mansion. If I was anyway fixed financially, I would still want to play the music on my way out, all the way. The only thing gets to me once in a while is the dropouts, the guys that are gone. Just yesterday I was listening to a record I made with Lionel Hampton in 1939—'Haven't Named It Yet.' It shook me some when I looked at the label. Sid Catlett gone, Artie Bernstein gone, Charlie Christian gone, Earl Bostic gone, Clyde Hart gone. Just Higgy and Hampton and me left. But I guess we carry on for them. Least, that's the way I like to look at it."

FOR THE COMFORT OF THE PEOPLE

two

In the late thirties and early forties, when jazz was still a newly settled provincial enclave (the music had been recorded for no more than twenty years), with its paranoia (the supposed condescension of "classical" musicians), its internecine warfare (the moldy figs versus the moderns), its hagiographers and apologists, and its sense of musical grandeur, real and imagined, one kept on course by attending one's heroes (in the flesh and/or on records, both endeavors being cheap and easy) and by adding an occasional reverential brick to the shrine that housed the music's three great legendary figures—King Joe Oliver, Bessie Smith, and Bix Beiderbecke. That world has grown up, its heroes have become aged or have died, and its legends have at last been tested in biographies and in extensive, critically equipped reissues and have been declared human—all except Joe Oliver, who, mysterious, almost primeval, remains enshrined.

Oliver was born in or near New Orleans in 1885, or earlier, and was raised by his sister Victoria Davis. Bunk Johnson said that Oliver was a slow musical student, but by the turn of the century he was working in marching bands and in cabarets. He was also a butler in a house still standing in the Garden District. His musical career in New Orleans lasted at least twenty years, and by the time he moved to Chicago, in 1918, he had been nicknamed King by Kid Ory, even though he was probably already past his prime. Except for brief forays to California (1921-22) and New York (1924, 1927), Oliver stayed in Chicago for ten years, leading the Creole Jazz Band and the later and larger Dixie Syncopators. In 1928, he at last committed himself to the exodus to New York, where, the year before, he had made a disastrous decision. Two successful weeks at the Savoy Ballroom had led to an offer to open the new Cotton Club with his group as the house band. But the New Orleans evil, a local affliction made up equally of hubris and perversity, took hold, and Oliver decided he was not being paid enough. He turned down the job, and a newcomer named Duke Ellington took it. But Oliver had been wrongheaded before. He had had lucrative offers from New York for years but had stubbornly stayed in Chicago—so long, indeed, that when he moved to New York he discovered that his music had already been accepted, absorbed, and filed away. During the next three years, Oliver, whose gums and teeth had begun to trouble him, subsisted by making records, writing occasional music, and taking whatever gigs were offered him. Then, in 1931, he put together a good band and went on the road. It was his last mistake. He never got back to New York or Chicago or New Orleans (partly because of the New Orleans evil), and by 1936 he had landed in Savannah, where he spelled out his final days selling fruit and vegetables and sweeping out a pool parlor. He died in Savannah, on April 10, 1938. His body was brought to New York and buried in Woodlawn Cemetery in an unmarked grave.

Within two years, Oliver was enshrined by Frederic Ramsey in the book *Jazzmen*, and by the New Orleans revival movement, which would have put him on Easy Street again. Ramsey made Oliver a tragic, put-upon figure, and quoted several letters that Oliver wrote from Savannah to his niece and sister in New York:

> *Dear Niece,*
> I receive your card, you don't know how much I appreciate your thinking about the old man. . . . I am not making enough money to buy clothes as I can't play any more. I get [a] little money from an agent for the use of my name and after I pay room rent and eat I don't have much left. . . . I've only got one suit and that's the one sent me while I was in Wichita, Kansas. So you know the King must look hot. But I don't feel downhearted. I still feel like I will snap out of the rut some day.
>
> Well, the old man hasn't got the price of Xmas cards so I will wish you all a Merry Xmas and Happy New Year . . . Love to the entire family including the bird dog and cat.
>
> *Sincerely,*
> Uncle

In 1922, Oliver set Louis Armstrong up in business by summoning him from New Orleans to Chicago to play second horn in the Creole Jazz Band. Armstrong borrowed wisely and liberally from Oliver's style, and revered him the rest of his life. He told Richard Meryman, in 1966, what his last visit with Oliver had been like: "So Joe winds up in little cheap rooming houses, landladies holding his trunk for rent. In 1937 my band went to Savannah, Georgia, one day—and there's Joe. He's got so bad off and broke he's got himself a little vegetable stand selling tomatoes and potatoes. He was standing there in his shirtsleeves. No tears. Just glad to see us. Just another day. He had that spirit. I gave him about a hundred and fifty dollars I had in my pocket, and Luis Russell and Red Allen, Pops Foster, Albert Nicholas, Paul Barbarin—all used to be his boys—they gave him what they had. [If all this is true, Oliver, despite his melancholy protestations that he could not scrape train fare together, could easily have gone North.] And that night we played a dance, and we look over and there's Joe standing in the wings. He was sharp like the old Joe Oliver of 1915. He'd been to the pawn shop and gotten his fronts all back; you know, his suits and all—Stetson hat turned down, high-button shoes, his box-back coat. He looked beautiful."

When Oliver set out from New York, in 1931, everything went well for a time. The bookings were good, and the band travelled in style through the West and Southwest. The trombonist and singer Clyde Bernhardt was in the band, and he has said, "I joined Oliver's band on March 1, 1931, and left it in Topeka, Kansas, on November 10th, when I found out he didn't have any intention of coming back to New York again. We played mostly white places—big ballrooms like the Coliseum, in Tulsa—and we didn't have any trouble with whites. In fact, we were treated so nice in Texas and Louisiana that we got scared. These judges and doctors and people like that would ask us to their homes, and we were scared to go and scared not to go. We travelled in a bus that would hold twenty people. The driver, Roy Johnson, was white, and he was our road manager and collected the money and such. Oliver was a Christian-hearted man, but he didn't have no business sense. He couldn't even find himself a place to sleep at night. In those times, we'd stay with families in their houses. The colored hotels was

small and very often couldn't put up all fifteen, sixteen of us.
I always made a neat appearance, and I'd walk in the colored
neighborhood and find this real nice house and I'd talk to
them and they'd take me in and Joe Oliver, too. He ate as
much as four men, and he always paid double for his food.
He'd sit down with me—I was a slow eater, and so was he—
and he'd eat a chicken and a whole apple pie. He didn't
drink, but he smoked a lot of cigarettes, so I gave him a pack
of cigarettes on his birthday, in May, and he was so pleased.
'The rest of them didn't give me a damn thing,' he said, 'but
you did, and that feels good to an old man of fifty-four.' So
he was older than anybody thought he was—older by eight
years, which would have put him in his sixties when he died.

"Those New Orleans musicians were funny. They had
strong likes and dislikes. But I was lucky. Oliver knew some
of my family in New York, and he treated me as his son. He
was very easygoing, and he loved to talk—at least, he liked to
talk to me, so much sometimes that he aggravated me. It
would go this way:

"oliver: Why the hell don't you say something!
"bernhardt: I ain't got nothin' to say.
"oliver: Well, I'm going to make you sing tonight if you
    don't open your mouth now.
"bernhardt: Who is?
"oliver: Who's talkin' to you?

"And on like that. Joe didn't look his age because he was so
dark. He was really comical about color. If he spotted someone as dark as he was, he'd say, 'That son is uglier than me.
I'm going to make him give me a quarter.' Or he'd light a
match and lean forward and whisper, 'Is that something
walking out there?' He wouldn't hire very black musicians.
I suggested several who were very good players, but he told
me, 'I can stand me, but I don't want a whole lot of very
dark people in my band. People see 'em and get scared and
run out of the place.'

"He had a dental plate by then, and he could play for an
hour and a half before his gums would get to aching. Then

he'd take down and go off the bandstand and let his other trumpet players go. When his teeth weren't bothering him, he had a strong, piercing tone you could feel right through you."

During 1934 and 1935, the saxophonist Paul Barnes kept a log of the band's ceaseless, swaybacked swings across the South. (In 1932 or 1933, Lester Young, then in his early twenties, joined the band; it was Genesis and Revelation under the same roof.) Here is Barnes' log for the first two weeks of March, 1935. The date is at the left and the money paid each man at the right. (Oliver presumably got double, and there were occasions in his career when his men accused him of shortchanging them.) "N" means a black audience and "W" a white one. "B" means a radio broadcast:

1	Gadsden, Ala.	N	.50
3	Columbus, Ga.		
	(Liberty Theatre)	N	.25
4	Columbus, Ga.		
	(Army camp) B	N	3.00
5	Moultrie, Ga.	N	1.00
6	St. Augustine, Fla.	N	1.50
7	Daytona Beach	N	3.00
8	Lakeland	N	3.00
9	Tampa	N	1.00
11	St. Petersburg	N	2.00
12	Sanford	N	1.50
13	Melbourne	N	1.00
14	Miami	N	3.71
15	West Palm Beach	N	3.00
16	Vero Beach		
	(Firemen's Ball)	W	3.53

Only nine years before, Jess Stacy, just arrived in Chicago from Missouri, had gone to see the famous Oliver in the Plantation Café, at Thirty-fifth and Calumet. Stacy recalls: "The first time I ever went to hear Oliver he was playing 'Ukelele Lady,' and he was playing the fool out of it, and he took five or six choruses in a row. He played sitting down, and he didn't play loud. He knew his instrument. He wasn't spearing for high notes; he stayed right in the middle register. His chord changes were pretty and his vibrato just right—none of that Italian belly vibrato. You could hear that both Louis and Bix had learned from him. In fact, Bix was nuts about him, and one of the things he liked was that Oliver played open horn a lot. Which reminds me of what Eddie Condon said of those days in Chicago when there was so much music: 'You could take a trumpet out of its case and it would blow by itself.' Oliver's band worked from nine to six—I know, because I was often there—and what with the shows to play for and the dancing, it took an iron lip."

Two or three years earlier, the Creole Jazz Band was still intact and was playing at the Dreamland Café. (Oliver and Armstrong, cornets; Johnny Dodds, clarinet; Honoré Dutrey, trombone; Lil Hardin, piano; Bill Johnson, bass; and Baby Dodds, drums.) Here are three scenes. The first is by Lou Black, the banjoist with the fine white New Orleans Rhythm Kings; the second is from Armstrong-Meryman; and the third was told to Larry Gara by Baby Dodds:

BLACK: "We were at the Friar's Inn for a couple of years, and when we'd finished work, or when there were no more customers to play for, we'd go over to the Dreamland and sit in with Pop Oliver and Louis Armstrong. You know why he was called Pop? When he played, his right eye came almost out of the socket from the force of his blowing. . . . He had enormous lips, too, and his cornet mouthpiece would disappear right inside them. Once in a while he'd stand up there in front of the band, cradle the cornet on its valves in a handkerchief in his left hand, put his right hand in his pocket, and play ten or eleven choruses of 'Tiger Rag' or 'Dippermouth Blues' without ever touching the valves with his right hand and without repeating himself."

ARMSTRONG-MERYMAN: "In those days the bands sat in chairs, and Joe, with his big wad of chewing tobacco in his cheek, would go *pa-choo* into a brass cuspidor, then he'd start beating his foot on top of that cuspidor, setting the tempo, and *blow!* And whatever Mister Joe played, I just put notes to it, trying to make it sound as pretty as I could. I never blew my horn over Joe Oliver at no time unless he said, 'Take it!' Never. Papa Joe was a creator—always some little idea—and he exercised them beautifully. I hear them phrases of his in big arrangements and everything right now. And sitting by him every night, I *had* to pick up a lot of little tactics he made—phrases, first endings, flairs. I'll never run out of ideas. All I have to do is think about Joe and always have something to play off of."

DODDS-GARA: "We had the sort of band that, when we played a number, we all put our hearts in it. Of course that's why we could play so well. And it wasn't work for us, in those days. . . . We took it as play, and we loved it. I used to hate when it was time to knock off. I would drum all night till about three o'clock, and when I went home I would dream all night of drumming. . . . We worked to make music, and we played music to make people like it. The Oliver band played for the comfort of the people. Not so they couldn't hear, or so they had to put their fingers in their ears. . . . Sometimes the band played so softly you could hardly hear it. . . . [It] played so soft that you could hear the people's feet dancing."

Clyde Bernhardt's belief that Oliver was eight years older than people thought explains a good deal—why his teeth and gums and embouchure began to weaken in the mid-twenties, when he was supposedly just forty (Dizzy Gillespie is fifty-nine, Harry Edison is sixty, Roy Eldridge is sixty-three, and Doc Cheatham is seventy, and all play with clarity and ease); why he repeatedly called himself an "old man" in his letters to his niece and sister; why he was so slow to adapt to the new music around him; why his bands played what they did. Oliver—tall, fat, secret, solemn—was old-fashioned and formal, and so was his music, particularly when he had the Creole Jazz Band. It played the sort of contrapuntal ensemble jazz that probably reached perfection in New Orleans around 1915. The musical difference between Louis Armstrong-Earl Hines in 1928 and Oliver just five years before is too great; Oliver must have been mirroring a music at least ten years older. Oliver was summarizing New Orleans jazz with intelligence, wit, honesty, and great cool. The summary, insofar as the Creole Jazz Band is concerned, was not complete, however. Its recordings have few solos, and for good reason: there wasn't time, and tried-and-true ensembles (most were partly written) were safer than improvised solos in the perilous confines of an acoustical recording studio. But Stacy and Lou Black tell us that Oliver soloed often and at great length in the flesh. No matter the tempo, the Creole Jazz Band swung steadily and easily. It beckoned but never shouted, it pointed but never pushed. The ensemble passages were controlled, dense, and full of marvellous four-way counterpoint. Each voice was skilled enough to speak comfortably and to blend with the other voices without fault or interference. It was a band completely at ease with itself and its materials. Musicians of greater or lesser skill would have destroyed its fabric. The Creole Jazz Band offered many pleasures: Armstrong, and Oliver's clean, neat unison playing in "High Society"; the great cornet duet breaks in "Sobbin' Blues" (Armstrong-Meryman: "While the rest of the band was playing, Oliver'd lean over to me and move the valves of his cornet in the notes he would play in the next breaks or a riff he'd use. So I'd play second to it"); the steady, enveloping drive, the slow-motion *galloping* of "Dippermouth Blues," "Chattanooga Blues," "Buddy's Habit," "Riverside Blues," and "I Ain't Gonna Tell Nobody"; Armstrong's brilliant-kid solo in "Riverside"; and Oliver's serene and miraculous three-chorus solo in "Dippermouth," a solo that reverberated throughout jazz for twenty-five years.

Oliver was a classic player. His tone was strong and even, and his vibrato was controlled. He loved the middle and low register, and he was a first-rate melodic embellisher. He liked to play behind the beat, and he never wasted a note. And he had *presence*. Cootie Williams is the third link in the chain begun by Joe Oliver and Bubber Miley, and Oliver at this period sounded the way Williams does now—stripped down, primitive, and majestic.

In many ways some of the records Oliver made with his later Dixie Syncopators and in New York are more absorbing. Electronic recording had come in, and one can hear Oliver clearly. Also, he was heroically trying to catch up with what had happened in jazz while he was molting in Chicago. The Dixie Syncopators sides have arrangements and a saxophone section, and they have the sound of pioneer big bands. Much the same is true of the New York recordings Oliver made for Victor between 1928 and 1931, although Oliver plays only occasionally on them. The New York recordings have an eerie quality. They are very much of their time and place, with their soupy saxophones, one-legged rhythm sections, and often halting solos. But Oliver's statements, particularly his muted ones, have a special long-ago sweetness and directness and simplicity. New Orleans musicians were Arcadian no matter where they went. Red Allen, who was Oliver's last protégé, described his arrival in New York in 1927 this way: "It was my first time away from home. I was an only child and I'd had a lot of care. I wasn't accustomed to taking things to the laundry and making my own bed. I couldn't get used to it. Then I moved in with Oliver and his sister. Oliver and I stayed together like father and son. I used to kid with him all the time and imitate the grand marshal in one of the parades back home, and he'd laugh so hard he'd cry."

SUNSHINE ALWAYS OPENS OUT

three

ate in the winter of 1964, Earl "Fatha" Hines gave a concert at the Little Theatre, on West Forty-fourth Street,
that is still mentioned with awe by those fortunate enough
to have been there. The obstacles Hines faced that night
were formidable. He was fifty-nine, an age when most jazz
musicians have become slow-gaited; he had, except for a
brief night-club appearance, been absent from New York
for ten years, and the occasional recordings that had floated
east from Oakland, where he had settled, had done little to
provoke demands for his return; and he had never before at-
tempted a full-length solo recital—a feat that few jazz pianists, of whatever bent, have carried off. He met these hin-
drances by first announcing, when he walked on stage, that
he was not giving a concert but was simply playing in his
living room for friends, and by then performing with a bril-
liance that touched at least a part of each of his thirty-odd
numbers. Not only was his celebrated style intact, but it had
taken on a subtlety and unpredictability that continually
pleased and startled the audience. Even Hines' face, which
has the nobility often imparted by a wide mouth, a strong
nose, and high cheekbones, was hypnotic. His steady smile
kept turning to the glassy grimace presaging tears. His eyes—
when they were open—were bright and pained, and his
lower lip, pushed by a steady flow of grunts and hums,
surged heavily back and forth. He made quick feints to the
right and left with his shoulders, or rocked easily back and
forth, his legs wide and supporting him like outriggers. Between numbers, that smile—one of the renowned lamps of
show business—made his face look transparent. It was exem-
plary showmanship—not wrappings and tinsel but the gift itself, freely offered.

Not long after, Hines took a small band into Birdland for
a week, and he stayed at the Taft Hotel. The Birdland gig
had upset him: "Man, that's a hard job at Birdland," he said
quickly and clearly. "It's ten to four, which I'm not used to
anymore, and it wears me out. I got to bed at seven yesterday, but I had to be up and downtown for my cabaret card,
then to a booking agency, then to a rehearsal for the Johnny
Carson show. I didn't get to bed until six-thirty this morning, and then some damn fool called me at nine and said [his

voice went falsetto], 'Is this Earl Hines, and did you write "Rosetta"?' I won't say what I said. So I'm a little stupid. I'm *breathing*, but I don't feel like jumping rope."

Hines was stretched out on his bed in his hotel room watching an old Edward G. Robinson movie on television. He had on white pajamas, a silver bathrobe, and brown slippers. A silk stocking hid the top of his head. The room was small and hot and cluttered with suitcases, and its single window faced a black air shaft. Hines' eyes were half shut and there were deep circles under them. "I haven't eaten yet, so I just ordered up some chicken-gumbo soup and a Western omelette and plenty of coffee and cream. It'll probably come by suppertime, the way room service goes here. Yesterday, I asked for ham and eggs for breakfast and they sent a ham steak and candied sweets and string beans and rolls, and when I called down, the man said he was two blocks from the kitchen and how could he help what the chef did?" Hines laughed—or, rather, barked—and rubbed a hand slowly back and forth across his brow. "I mean, I don't know what has caused New York to tighten up so. All the hotels—including this one—want musicians to pay in advance. My goodness, it's almost dog-eat-dog. Pittsburgh, where I'm from, is a country town compared to New York, where it takes every bit of energy to keep that front up. The streets are all littered up, and last night I go in the back door at Birdland and three guys are laying there, sick all over theirselves. Next time, I go in the front door, and two guys want a dime, a quarter. I've been all over this country and Canada and Europe, and how clean and nice they are. I'd be ashamed to tell people I was from New York. Maybe I been away from home too long. It's three months now. I finish this recording date I have with Victor tomorrow and the next day and—boom!—I'm off. Stanley Dance—he's the jazz writer and an old friend from England—set up the Victor date. He's coming by around now with tapes of some records I made with my big band in the late thirties that Victor is bringing out again. He wants me to identify a couple of the soloists. My man Stanley."

There was a knock, and a portly, mustached man walked briskly in. He was carrying a small tape recorder. "Hey, Stanley," Hines said, and sat up straight.

"Did you get a good sleep?" Dance asked, in a pleasant Essex accent.

"Oh, people start calling at eight or nine again, but I'll sleep later, I'll rest later. I'm not doing *nothing* for a month when I get home."

"If it's all right, I'll play the tapes now, Earl." Dance put the machine on a luggage stand and plugged it in.

Hines stood up, stretched, and pummelled his stomach, which was flat and hard. "I haven't been sick since I was twelve years old. In the thirties, when we were on tour in the East, I'd work out with Joe Louis at Pompton Lakes. We'd sit on a fence a while and talk, and then we'd throw that medicine ball back and forth. That's why my stomach is so hard today." He sat down next to the tape recorder, crossed his ankles, clasped his hands in his lap, and stared at the machine. Dance started the tape. The first number, "Piano Man," was fast and was built around Hines' piano.

Hines listened attentively, his head cocked. "I haven't heard that in I don't know *how* long," he said. "That was a big production number in the show at the Grand Terrace, in Chicago, where I had my band from 1928 to 1940. I played it on a white grand piano and all the lights would go down, except for a spot on me and on each of the chorus girls, who were at tiny white baby grands all around me on the dance floor. When I played, they played with me—selected notes I taught them. Just now at the end I could picture the girls going off. Gene Krupa came in a lot, and he used that number for *his* show number—'Drummin' Man.' He just changed the piano parts to drum parts. I told him he was a Tom Mix without a gun." Hines laughed. "What's that?" he asked when the next number began.

" 'Father Steps In,' " Dance said.

Hines hummed the melody with the band. A trumpet soloed. "That's Walter Fuller. He was my work horse." An alto saxophone came in. "That's Budd Johnson, my Budd.

He'll be down at Victor tomorrow. He usually played tenor." Hines scat-sang Johnson's solo note for note. "He sounds like Benny Carter there."

"G. T. Stomp," "Ridin' and Jivin'," and " 'Gator Swing" went by. "The only trouble with this record, Earl, is there are so many fast tempos," Dance said.

"It was a very hot band. That's why the people were all so happy in those days. Nobody slept at the Grand Terrace. When we went on the road, the only band we had trouble with in all the cutting contests there used to be was the Savoy Sultans, the house group at the Savoy Ballroom, in Harlem. They only had eight pieces, but they could swing you into bad health. They'd sit there and listen and watch, and when you finished they'd pick up right where you'd left off and play it back twice as hard. We had a chance, we ducked them. *Everybody* did."

A waiter rolled in a table and placed it beside the bed. "Am I glad to see you, even if it is almost suppertime!" Hines barked, and he sat down on the bed. "Stanley, could we finish that after I've had something to eat? I only eat twice a day, and never between meals, and I get hungry. Take some coffee. Did they bring enough sugar? I like a lot of sugar and cream." He opened a suitcase beside the night table and took out a two-pound box of sugar. "I never travel without my sugar bag. I learned that long ago." Hines filled a soup bowl from a tureen and buried the soup under croutons. Dance sipped a cup of coffee and watched Hines. "Earl, you were talking a bit the other day about what it was like to be the leader of a big band."

Hines looked up from his soup and put his spoon down. He wiped his mouth with a napkin. Then he picked up his spoon again. "An organization is no bigger than its leader, Stanley. You have to set an example—let them know *you* know what you're doing. An animal will fear you if you're leading, but you let down and he'll get you. Same thing with handling a big band. For that reason, I used to stay a little apart from the band, so there wouldn't be too much familiarity. But I had to be an understanding guy, a psychologist.

I had to study each man, I had to know each man's ability. I'd be serious with one, joke with another, maybe take another out for a game of pool. Once in a while I'd give a little dinner for the band. But I was very strict about one thing. The band had to be on time, particularly on the road. There was a twenty-five-dollar fine if you missed the curtain in a theatre, and a dollar a minute after that. It cost five dollars if you were late for the bus, and a dollar a minute after that. We even fined the bus driver if he was late. The fines worked so well, after a while I could take them off. As I said before, I've always stayed physically in condition. The band knew I'd fight at the drop of a hat, even though I had an even disposition. I believe the only time I lost my temper was on the road when a trombonist I had was bugging me and I picked him up and had him over my head and would have thrown him off the bus if the boys hadn't stopped me.

"The Grand Terrace was very beautifully done—a big ballroom with a bar in the back and mirrors on the walls, with blue lights fixed here and there on the glass. Those mirrors were like looking at the sky with stars in it. The bandstand was raised and had stairs coming down around both sides for the chorus girls and the show. The dance floor was also elevated. The Grand Terrace was the Cotton Club of Chicago, and we were a show band as much as a dance band and a jazz band. We worked seven days a week, and how we did it I don't know. There were three shows a night during the week and four on Saturday. The hours were nine-thirty to three-thirty, except on Saturday, when we worked ten to five. The chorus girls—we had fourteen or sixteen of them—were very important. They were ponies—middle-sized girls who were not overweight and could dance. Or they were parade girls, who were taller and more for just show. The chorus line, coming down the stairways, opened the show. Then there was a vocalist, he or she. A soft-shoe dancer or ballroom team came next. Then maybe a picture number, with fake African huts and a big fire and such. The highlight of the show was a special act, like the four Step Brothers or Ethel Waters or Bojangles, and then everyone on for the finale. Sometimes a comedian like Billy Mitchell took the dancers' spot. He had a trick of turning one foot all the way around, so that that foot pointed one way and the other the other way, and he'd walk along like it was nothing and bring down the house. It was always a good hot show, with everything jumping. The girls were its heart, and they really danced. They'd come off the floor wringing wet. They spent a lot of money on their costumes, and we always had two women backstage to put on buttons and fasten snaps and adjust new costumes that sometimes didn't arrive until half an hour before show time. I was a stickler for the boys in the band dressing, too, and we had a costume fund. One cause of my feeling for clothes was George Raft. I'd visit him in his hotel room when he was in town and he'd have three trunks of clothes. He'd tell me not to buy expensive suits—just suits that looked good—and to have plenty of them and change them all the time and that way they'd last. I had shoes made to fit my suits from the Chicago Theatrical Shoe store. They were dancers' shoes—sharp-looking, with round toes, and soft, so that they fitted like a glove. Wherever I went, they'd send a new pair if I needed them, because they had my measurements. A valet took care of my clothes, and there was another valet—a band valet—for the boys."

Hines emptied the tureen into his soup bowl. "The Grand Terrace was always an orderly place. The audiences were mixed. Segregation never crossed anyone's mind. Friday nights we had college kids and we had to learn the college songs. Saturdays we got the office and shop people. Sunday was 75 per cent colored, and Mondays were tourists. On Wednesdays we got elderly people and played waltzes. The racketeers owned 25 per cent of the Grand Terrace, and they always had four or five men there—floating men. They never bothered us. 'We're here for your protection, boys,' they'd say. If they were going to run some beer from Detroit to Chicago, they'd figure the job out right in the kitchen. I'd be sitting there, but it was hear nothing, see nothing, say nothing if the cops came around. There was pistol play every night during prohibition. No shooting; just waving guns around. I was heading for the kitchen one night and this guy went pounding past and another guy came up behind me and told me to stand still and rested a pistol on my shoulder and aimed at the first guy and would have fired if the kitchen door hadn't swung shut in time. Some of the waiters even had pistols. The racketeers weren't any credit to Chicago, but they kept the money flowing. My girl vocalist might make fifteen hundred a week in tips for requests, and she'd split it with the boys, and they'd put it in the costume fund. The racketeers owned me, too, and so did the man who controlled the other 75 per cent of the Grand Terrace. This was something I didn't fully realize until late in the thirties. We were always paid in cash—one hundred and fifty a week for me and ninety apiece for the boys in the band. I couldn't complain. The Grand Terrace was our seat nine months of every year, and we had a nightly coast-to-coast radio hookup, which gave us solid bookings for the two or three months we were on the road. I couldn't afford to hire stars for the band, so I had to *make* my stars. In this way, I brought along Ivie Anderson, the singer, and Ray Nance, the trumpet player. Duke Ellington took both of them from me. And I developed other singers, like Ida James and Herb Jeffries and Billy Eckstine and Sarah Vaughan, and I had musicians like Trummy Young and Budd Johnson and Dizzy Gillespie and Charlie Parker."

Hines exchanged his soup bowl for the Western omelette and poured more coffee. He chewed carefully. "We had a doctor at home, Dr. Martin, and he always said all your sickness derives from your stomach. I've never forgotten that. I was a wild kid in the twenties and thirties and I drank a lot, but what saved me was I always ate when I was drinking. The music publishers had something to do with my drinking. After we had our radio hookup, they'd come around every night, trying to get me to play this tune or that." Hines shifted into falsetto again: " 'I got a little tune here, Earl, and I wish you'd play it and blah blah blah,' and then he'd buy me a drink and another publisher would buy me a couple of more drinks and I'd end up drinking all night and then I'd have to drink some more, if we had a record session early the next day, to keep going. I'd forget where I left my car, and I got so tired sometimes I'd put on shades and play whole shows asleep, with George Dixon, my sax man, nudging me when I was supposed to come in. I never considered myself a piano soloist anyway, so I was happy to just take my little eight bars and get off. It's the public that's pushed me out and made me a soloist. Then one night the owner of the Grand Terrace said, 'Earl, you're drinking yourself to death.' I thought about that and I decided he was right. When we went on the road soon after, I quit. I was all skin and bones. I bought a camera and took a picture of every pretty girl I saw to pass the time, and when I came back to Chicago I weighed one hundred and eighty-five. I only drink now after I'm finished work. But people *still* are after me to buy me drinks, and you hate to keep saying no. It almost agitates you."

Hines pushed his plate away and lit a big cigar. He arranged a couple of pillows against the headboard, leaned back, and swung his feet onto the bed. He puffed quietly, his eyes shut. "The excitement of the Grand Terrace days was something you couldn't realize unless you were there," he said, in a low voice. "It was a thrill when that curtain went up and us in white suits and playing and you knew you'd caught your audience. I bought my way out of the Grand Terrace in 1940 after I finally learned about all the money I was making and wasn't seeing. I kept the band together until 1948. By then it had twenty-four musicians and strings. But things were changing, with the entertainment tax and higher prices and fewer and fewer bookings in theatres and ballrooms. I saw the handwriting on the wall, and I disbanded and went with Louis Armstrong's All Stars. I didn't care for being a sideman again after all the years I'd spent building my reputation. Play some more of that tape, Stanley. Let me hear that band again."

Midway in the fourth or fifth number, Dance looked

over at Hines. His cigar was in an ashtray on the night table, his eyes were shut, and his mouth was open. He was asleep.

Hines' view of himself as reluctant soloist was surprising, for although Hines has spent a good part of his career as a leader of big and small bands, he is valued chiefly as a pianist. When he came to the fore in Louis Armstrong's celebrated 1928 recordings, the effect he created was stunning. No one had ever played the piano like that. Most jazz pianists were either blues performers, whose techniques were shaped by their materials, or stride pianists, whose oompah basses and florid right hands reflected the hothouse luxury of ragtime. Hines filled the space between these approaches with a unique, almost hornlike style. He fashioned complex, irregular single-note patterns in the right hand, octave chords with brief tremolos that suggested a vibrato, stark single notes, and big flatted chords. His left hand, ignoring the stride pianists' catapult action, cushioned his right hand. He used floating tenths and offsetting, offbeat single notes, and he sometimes played counter-melodies. Now and then he slipped into urgent arhythmic passages full of broken melodic lines and heavy offbeat chords. Hines and Louis Armstrong became the first jazz soloists to sustain the tension that is the secret of improvisation. Each of Hines' solos—particularly any that lasted several choruses—had a unity that was heightened by his pioneering use of dynamics. He italicized his most felicitous phrases by quickly increasing his volume and then as quickly letting it fall away. He gave the impression of a dancer repeatedly moving toward and receding from the listener, or of distant sounds being bandied about by the wind. At the same time, he retained the emotional substance of the blues pianists and the head-on rhythms of the stride men. His earliest recordings still sound modern, and they must have been as shocking then as the atonal musings of Ornette Coleman first were. In time, his followers included Mary Lou Williams, Teddy Wilson, Billy Kyle, Jess Stacy, Nat Cole, Eddie Heywood, Erroll Garner, and Art Tatum.

That night at Birdland, Hines sat down at the piano ten minutes before the first sit. The bandstand was dark and Hines unreeled a progression of soft, Debussy chords. He finished, and a couple of spotlights went on, but the illumination seemed to come from Hines himself. He was immaculate; his smile was permanently in place for the evening, and he was wearing a dark suit and a white shirt and dark shoes. His jet-black hair was flat and combed straight back, and he appeared as limber as a long-distance swimmer. Stanley Dance had pointed out that the group Hines happened to have at the moment was the sort of ingenuous, good-time, doubling-in-brass outfit that used to be a part of the stage show at the Apollo Theatre. It was, Dance had said, a surprising group—for Hines and for Birdland. It had a drummer and an organist, a male vocal trio, and a female alto saxophonist who sounded like Charlie Parker and who also sang. The next forty-five minutes were totally unpredictable, and Hines' assemblage soon seemed twice its actual size. The vocal trio sang together and separately; the organist soloed and sang a couple of numbers; the lady saxophonist not only emulated Charlie Parker but sang by herself or with the trio; the drummer took over for a long spell; and Hines, after eight-bar sips here and there, played a fifteen-minute solo medley. All this was executed with the precision of a Grand Terrace show, and when it was over, Hines was soaking wet. "I'm trying something nobody else is," he said, mopping himself. "I've had this group six months and I want to reach young and old. You play Dixieland, you get the old and drive away the young. You play modern, you get the young and keep away the old. A girl asked me last night, 'Are you Earl Hines' son? My mother used to listen to your dad at the Grand Terrace in 1930.' The young don't believe I'm me and the old are too tired to come and see. But I want both, and the manager has told me he's seen types of people in here all week he's never seen before. People have also said I'm crazy to have such a group, that the public wants to hear my piano, and that's why I put that medley in every show. This band is a kind of variation of what I was trying to do in my own club in Oakland, which opened last December. It had an international tinge. I had Irish and Chinese dancers and Italian and Japanese vocalists. I had Negro and Chinese and white waiters. I had Jewish musicians. I had Mexican and Chinese comedians. Then I found out one of my partners wasn't international and that the other didn't know much about show business, and I got out."

Hines ordered coffee, and lit a cigar. He was quiet for a while, then he said: "I don't think I *think* when I play. I have a photographic memory for chords, and when I'm playing, the right chords appear in my mind like photographs long before I get to them. This gives me a little time to alter them, to get a little clash or make coloring or get in harmony chords. It may flash on me that I can change an F chord to a D-flat ninth. But I might find the altering isn't working the way it should, so I stop and clarify myself with an off-beat passage, a broken-rhythm thing. I always challenge myself. I get out in deep water and I always try to get back. But I get hung up. The audience never knows, but that's when I smile the most, when I show the most ivory. I've even had to tell my bass player I'm going into the last eight bars of a tune because he wouldn't know where the hell I was. I play however I feel. If I'm working a pretty melody, I'll just slip into waltz time or cut the tempo in half. My mind is going a mile a minute, and it goes even better when I have a good piano and the audience doesn't distract me. I'm like a race horse. I've been taught by the old masters—put everything out of your mind except what you have to do. I've been through every sort of disturbance before I go on the stand, but I never get so upset that it makes the audience uneasy. If one of my musicians is late, I may tell the audience when he arrives that I *kept* him off the stand because he needed a little rest. I always use the assistance of the man upstairs before I go on. I ask for that and it gives me courage and strength and personality. It causes me to blank everything else out, and the mood comes right down on me no matter how I feel. I don't go to church regularly, because I'm generally too tired from the hours I have to keep. I'd only fall asleep, and I don't believe in going just to say, yes, I go to church every Sunday. One Easter Sunday, I played in the Reverend Cobbs' church in Chicago—a standing-room-only church, he's so popular with his parishioners. I played 'Roses of Picardy.' They had three hundred voices in the choir. I played the first chorus; the choir hummed the second behind me and sang the lyrics on the third. Good God, it shook me up, the sound of those voices. I was nothing but goosepimples, and I stood right up off the piano stool. It was almost angelic."

Hines looked fresh and eager the next day. He was smoking a pipe and watching television, and he was wearing a black silk suit, a striped tan sports shirt, and pointed shoes trimmed with alligator leather. He had on a dark porkpie hat and dark glasses. Stanley Dance was telephoning. "He's checking Budd Johnson to make sure he's left for the studio," Hines said. He pointed to his glasses. "I wear these to shut out those photographers who turn up at every record session and seem like they're popping pictures of you from right inside the piano."

"Budd's on his way," Dance said. "And Jimmy Crawford and Aaron Bell are definite for drums and bass."

"Fine, fine. Stanley, bring that fake book, please, in case they ask me to play something I recorded forty years ago. Everybody but me remembers those tunes."

Hines leaned back in the cab and tilted his hat over his eyes. It was drizzling and the traffic was heavy. "Coming down in that elevator puts me in mind of Jack Hylton, the English bandleader, and the time he came to Chicago in the thirties. He was staying at the Blackstone and asked me if I'd come and see him. When I got there, the elevator man told me to take the freight elevator around back. Like a delivery boy. That upset me and I refused and pretty soon the assistant manager and the manager and Hylton's secretary and Hylton himself were all there and it ended in my going up in the front elevator. I don't say much about race, but it's always in the back of my head. I've tried to handle it by thinking things out up front and avoiding trouble if it can be avoided—like when I bought my house in Oakland four or five years ago. It has four bedrooms, a maid's room, family room, kitchen, parlor, and a fifty-foot patio in back. It's almost too much house. It was a white neighborhood before my wife and I and our two girls came, and I knew there might be trouble. The house belonged to a guy down on his luck and it was a mess inside and out. It's in an area where people keep their lawns nice, so before we moved in I painted the outside and installed a watering system and hired a Japanese gardener. I painted the inside and put in wall-to-wall carpets and drapes. When it was the best-looking place around, we moved in. We haven't had any trouble. But I've learned those precautions the long, hard way, beginning when we were the first big Negro band to travel extensively through the South. I think you could call us the first Freedom Riders. We stayed mostly with the Negro population and only came in contact with the Caucasian race if we needed something in a drug or dry-goods way. On our first tour, in 1931, we had a booker named Harry D. Squires. He booked us out of his hat, calling the next town from the one we'd just played and generally using his wits, like once when we got stopped for speeding. Squires told us before the cop came up, 'Now, we'll just tell him we're a young group and haven't had any work. So get out all your change and put it in a hat to show him what we're worth.' And that's just what we did. The cop got on the bus and we all sat there, looking forlorn and half starved and he looked in the hat, which had ten or twelve dollars in it, and he let us go. That was our first acting duty. Going South was an invasion for us. We weren't accustomed to the system, being from the North, and it put a damper on us. Things happened all the time. They made us walk in the street off the sidewalk in Fort Lauderdale, and at a white dance in Valdosta, Georgia, some hecklers in the crowd turned off the lights and exploded a bomb under the bandstand. We didn't none of us get hurt, but we didn't play so well after that, either. Sometimes when we came into a town that had a bad reputation, the driver would tell us—and here we were in our own chartered bus—to move to the back of the bus just to make it look all right and not get anyone riled up. We pulled into a gas station early one morning and a trombonist named Stevens got out to stretch his legs. He asked the gas-station attendant was it O.K., and he said, "Go ahead, but I just killed one nigger. He's layin' over there in the weeds. You don't believe me, take a look for yourself.' Stevens got back on the bus quick, and the next day we read about the killing in the papers. They had a diner at another gas station, and my guitarist, who was new and very, very light-skinned, ducked off the bus and went right into the diner. He didn't know any better and we didn't see him go in. When we'd gassed up, I asked our road manager, a Jewish fellow who was swarthy and very dark, to get us some sandwiches. The counterman took one look at him and wouldn't serve him, and my road manager glanced up and there was my guitarist at the counter, stuffing down ham and eggs. We never let that manager forget. It was a happening we kept him in line with the rest of the trip."

Hines laughed quietly and looked out of the window. It was raining heavily and the cab was crawling through Twenty-eighth Street. "We played a colored dance somewhere in Alabama and it worked out there was a gang of white people sitting back of us on the stage because there wasn't any more room on the floor. They'd been invited by the Negro who was giving the dance, since he worked for one of the whites. We'd only been playing fifteen minutes when along came this old captain, this sheriff man, and told me, 'You can't have those white people up there. You get them off that stage.' I said I didn't know anything about it. Fifteen minutes more and that cap'n was back. 'You and these niggers get out of here and out of this town. You have half an hour.' He escorted us personally to the town line. I found out later he knew all those white people, but they were the cream in the town and he was afraid to say anything to them, except to tell them after we'd gone that one of my boys had been looking at a white woman and that was why he drove us out. But I had me a victory in Tennessee. I went into a dry-goods store to buy some shirts. The clerk said, 'You want something, boy?' I told him. He took me to the cheapest section. I told him I wanted to see the best shirts he had. 'Where you from, boy, to ask for things like that?' I pointed at some ten-dollar silk shirts. 'Give me five of those,' I said. 'You want five of *those*?' He started to laugh and I showed him a fifty-dollar bill. After that, that man couldn't get enough of me. Money changed his whole attitude. Money shamed him. I spent close to eighty-five dollars, and when I came out all these local colored boys were looking in the front window, noses on the glass. They said, 'You go in *there*? Don't *no one* go in there!' Well, those were the days when if you were a Negro and wanted to buy a hat and tried it on it was *your* hat whether it fitted or not.

"But there were good times, too. We were always seeing new territory, new beauty. In those days the country was a lot more open and sometimes we'd run into another band and just park the buses by the road and get out and play baseball in a field. We travelled by train also, but buses were only twenty-eight cents a mile and you kept the same bus and driver throughout a whole tour. There was always a little tonk game on the bus at night. The boys put something for a table across the aisle and sat on Coke boxes and hung a flashlight from the luggage rack on a coat hanger. I generally sat on the right side about four seats back of the driver, where I kept an eye on things. They played most of the night, and it was amusing and something to keep you interested if you couldn't sleep. Our radio broadcasts made us well known after a while and sometimes we felt like a Presidential party. People would gather around the bus and say, 'Where's Fatha Hines? Where's Fatha Hines?' Fatha was a nickname given to me by a radio announcer we had at the Grand Terrace, and one I'd just as soon be shut of now. I had a kiddish face then and they expected an *old* man from my nickname, so I'd just slip into the hotel and maybe go into the coffee shop, but when these people found out who and where I was they'd come in and stand around and stare at me. Just stand and stare and not say anything, and if I looked up they'd pretend to be looking away in the distance."

Hines is greeted at the R.C.A. Victor recording studio, which is on East Twenty-fourth Street, by Brad McCuen, an a.-and-r. man of Sydney Greenstreet proportions. Hines goes immediately into the studio, which is bright and chilly and thicketed with microphones. Jimmy Crawford is setting up his drums and Aaron Bell is putting rosin on his bow.

HINES (*in a loud, happy voice*): O solo mio, o solo mio. Hey, Craw, man. And Aaron. A *long* time, a *long* time. (*All shake hands warmly.*) We're going to do something today. But just leave all the doors open so we can git out when everything goes wrong.

CRAWFORD: You look wonderful, Earl. Just wonderful.

HINES: I feel like a million dollars. (*He takes off his coat and and sits down at a grand piano and rubs his hands together and blows on them. McCuen leaves a list of prospective tunes and a large gold ashtray beside Hines, who lights a cigar. McCuen is followed into the control room by Dance, still carrying the fake book. A round, genial man enters the studio. He is dressed all in brown and has an Oriental face.*) My Budd. Budd Johnson. (*The two men embrace and laugh and pound one another. Hines returns to the piano and plays ad-lib chords, which gradually crystallize into a slow "It Had to Be You." Crawford and Bell join in. Hines has already vanished into what he is doing. His mouth is open slightly and his lower lip moves in and out. His face, disguised by his hat and glasses, looks closed and secret. A photographer comes out of the control room, lies down on the floor near Hines, and starts shooting pictures. Hines finishes two choruses and stops.*) Hey, Mr. Camera Man, would you mind waiting on that? You're getting me all nervous. (*The photographer retreats into the control room.*) You ready, Budd? Tenor would be nice for this. Rich and slow and warm. *Pretty* tenor.

I'll take the first two choruses and you come in for one.
I'll come back and you come in again for the last sixteen
bars.

MCCUEN (*in a booming voice over the control-room microphone*): Ready to roll one, Earl?

HINES: Let's do one right away. (*After the last note dies
away, Hines jumps up, laughs, snaps his fingers, and spins
around.*) Ooooo-wee. Budd, how'd you like that ad-lib
ending? I couldn't do that again to save my life. I didn't
know if I was going to get out alive or not. Shoo, man.

MCCUEN: We'll play it back.

HINES: No, let's do another real quick. I feel it. Here we go.
(*The second take is faster and the ending more precise.*)
All right, let's hear *that*. (*The music comes crashing out
of two enormous loudspeakers. Hines gets up and moves
over beside the nearest wall. His hands hang loose at his
sides. He throws back his head, opens his mouth, and listens. He is even more concentrated than when he plays.
He doesn't move until the number ends. Then he does a
little dance and laughs.*) I'll buy it. I'll buy it. Beautiful,
Budd. Just beautiful. You can shut those doors now.
(*During the next couple of hours, the group does "I've
Got the World on a String," "A Cottage for Sale," "Linger
Awhile," and a fast original by Hines. Two or three takes
suffice for each tune. Hines wastes no time, and after each
play back he starts playing again.*)

HINES: "Wrap Your Troubles in Dreams." Budd, you rest
on this one. We'll do about four choruses. (*The first take
is indifferent, but on the second one Hines suddenly
catches fire, moving with extraordinary intensity into the
upper register in the third chorus and shaping the fourth
chorus into a perfect climax.*)

MCCUEN: Let's try another, Earl. That opening wasn't quite
right. (*Hines looks surprised, but immediately makes another take. After the playback, he shakes his head.*)

HINES: I don't know. Let's go again. (*In all, twelve takes, including false starts, are made. Each is slightly faster, and
each time Hines appears less satisfied. The last take is re-
played. Hines is leaning on an upright piano in the center
of the studio, Bell and Johnson flanking him.*) You know,

I don't *feel* it, I'm not *inside* that tune. I'm not bringing it *out*.

BELL: Earl, you know it's getting faster and faster?

HINES: Yeh? I didn't notice.

JOHNSON: Earl, you were *cookin'*, man, way back there on that second take, and they never did play it back for you.

HINES (*looking puzzled*): That right? Hey, Brad, can you play that *second* take for me. You never did, and I can't recall it. (*It is played, and slowly Hines' face relaxes. Johnson snaps his fingers and Bell nods his head.*) Budd, you got it, man. You were right. *That's* it, and we wasting all that time when the *good* one is just sitting there waiting to be heard. Man, I feel *young* again.

(*It is now almost six o'clock, and McCuen suggests that they meet again the next day. He thanks the musicians. Hines moves to the center of the studio, lights a fresh cigar, and stretches his arms wide. Crawford and Bell and Johnson fall into a loose semicircle before him.*)

HINES: Thank you, Craw, and Aaron. Just fine, man. Just fine. Budd, I haven't heard that baritone of yours in I don't know how long. You take Harry Carney's job away he doesn't look out. (*Johnson beams.*) The piano they got here makes it feel good, too. You play on a bad instrument and you want to take just eight bars and get out. *So* many clubs now have cheap pianos. It's the last thing the owners think of. They wouldn't put a well behind their bars and dip water out of it, instead of having faucets, so why do they have pianos that are cheap and out of tune?

JOHNSON: That's right, Earl.

BELL: Yeah, Earl.

HINES: In the forties, we played a place in Texas and they had a *miserable* piano. It was even full of water from a leak in the roof first night we were there. When the job was finished, Billy Eckstine and some of the boys decided to take that piano apart. Man, they clipped the strings and loosened the hammers and pulled off the keyboard and left it laying all over the floor. (*All laugh.*) I just finished four weeks in Canada, and the owner of that club must have had a hundred-dollar piano, it was so bad. And he had this fancy bandstand with a great big Buddha sitting on each side of it and they must of cost a *thousand* dollars apiece.

I asked him, "Man, why do you spend all that money on Buddhas and decorations and not on a piano?," and he answered blah blah blah, and got mad. Now, that's crazy.

CRAWFORD: Well, you told him, Earl.

HINES: It's the same thing nowadays with dressing rooms. No place to put on your makeup or rest and change your clothes between sets. (*Hines' voice has slowly grown louder and he is almost chanting. His listeners intensify their responses.*) They got one room down at Birdland, one small room, man, and we can't use it when Vi Redd— she's my saxophonist—goes in there, and when she's finished there's no time left anyway. I have to go back to the hotel between every set and change clothes. It's only a couple of blocks and I don't mind, but what if it snowing or raining and I catch my death?

JOHNSON: Earl, I was down to the Copa a while ago and it's the same there. You got to go out and walk the sidewalk.

HINES: That's what I mean. That's what I mean. You remember the old days all the theatres had good dressing rooms and places to sit down? Of course, these young musicians don't dress anyway, so maybe it doesn't matter. The band opposite me at Birdland, led by that young trumpet player —what's his name?

BELL: Byrd? Donald Byrd?

HINES: Yeh. Well, the first night they all dressed in different clothes and have scuffy shoes and no neckties. We come on, all spruced and neat—ties, of course—and you watch, the next night they got on ties and suits and their hair combed and they look *human*. And those young musicians don't know how to handle themselves before an audience. Never look at the audience or tell it what they're playing or smile or bow or be at all gracious. Just toot-toot-a-toot and look dead while the other guy is playing and get off. No wonder everybody having such a hard time all over. No one—not even Duke or Basie—raising any hell anymore. They just scuffling to keep the payroll going. That's why I have this different group, to reach the young people and teach them the old ways, the right ways, not the rock-and-roll ways. I've always helped the young people along, developed them, showed them how to dress and act and carry themselves properly. I've been at it so

long I couldn't stop. Well, man, all we can do is be exam-
ples. A man can't do no more than that.
JOHNSON: Amen, Earl. Amen.

The rain had stopped, and Hines found a cab on Third Avenue. He was still wound up from his oration and the recording session, and he sat on the edge of his seat, puffing at his
cigar. "Why didn't somebody tell me I still had these dark
glasses on? I wondered why I couldn't see anything when I
came out of that building. The reason I've always looked
out for the young people, I guess, is because my dad always
looked out for me. I don't think there was anyone else in the
world who brought up their children better than my mother
and dad. We lived in Duquesne, where I was born, and my
mother was a housewife. My dad started on a hoisting machine—or histing machine, as they called it—on the coal
docks and worked his way up to foreman. He was a loosely
type fellow. He never chastised me for the medium things,
and I didn't have over four solid whippings from him. I
never was brought in at night at the time the average kid in
my neighborhood was, and it looked like I was let run
helter-skelter and my dad was criticized for that, but he de-
fended himself by saying if you don't chastise your child
continually he will confide in you. When I was twelve, he
sat down with me one night at evening table after my
mother had gone out and told me I was too old to whip anymore and how to conduct myself. 'I'm not a wealthy man,'
he told me. 'So I can't get you out of serious trouble.' He
told me *everything* that night—about all the different kinds
of women and men I'd come up against, and how to tell the
good from the bad, about thinking you're outsmarting someone else when he's probably outsmarting *you*, about staying
on lighted streets at night, and such as that. It gave me the
confidence that's always guided me. A lot of the children
of strict parents where I grew up ended in jail. The excep-
tions were far and few.
    "My family was very musical. My mother was an organist
and my dad played cornet. My uncle knew all the brass in-

struments and my auntie was in light opera. My dad was also
the leader of the Eureka Brass Band, which played for pic-
nics and dances and outings. I was nine or ten when I was
taken on my first outing. We travelled from McKeesport
about twelve miles in four open trolleys, which were chartered. The band rode the first trolley and played as we went.
After the picnic there was dancing in a hall and the children who were allowed to stay were sent up to a balcony,
where they had a matron to watch us. Some of the kids
roughhoused, but I just leaned over the rail and listened and
watched. It was such a pretty thing to see all those people
dancing and flowing in one direction. The men seemed so
pleasant to the women and the women back to the men. My
mother started teaching me the piano when I was very
young. I also tried the cornet, after my dad, but it hurt me
behind the ears to blow, so I gave it up. I had my first outside piano lessons when I was nine, from a teacher named
Emma D. Young, of McKeesport. My next teacher, Von
Holz, was German and pretty well advanced. I was studying
to be a classical artist. I loved the piano and I was always
three or four lessons ahead in my book. My auntie lived in
Pittsburgh, and when I went to Schenley High School,
where I majored in music, I lived with her. I was interested
in conducting and watched the directors of pit orchestras
every chance I got. And I memorized all the music I heard,
some of it even before the sheet music came out. When I
was about thirteen, my life changed. I had a cousin and an
uncle who were play-time boys and they used to take me
downtown to the tenderloin section with them. I was tall
and they fitted me out in long trousers. The first time they
took me to the Leader House, which had dancing upstairs
and a restaurant downstairs, I heard this strange music and
I heard the feet and the beat and so much laughter and hap-
piness I asked my uncle and cousin could I go upstairs and
listen. They put a Coca-Cola in my hand and I did. Pittsburgh was a wide-open town and there wasn't such a ban
then on children going into clubs. A hunchback fellow
named Toadlo was playing the piano. He was playing

'Squeeze Me,' and singing. His playing turned me around completely. It put rhythm in my mind, and I went home and told my auntie that that was the way I wanted to play. In the meantime, I was shining shoes and had learned barbering and for the first time I had enough money to get around. I formed a little trio, with a violinist and a drummer, and then Lois B. Deppe, who was a well-known Pittsburgh singer and bandleader, hired me and my drummer for his band at the Leader House. It was summer and I talked to my dad and he said it was all right and I went to work. Fifteen dollars a week and two meals a day. Toadlo still worked there, and so did a pianist named Johnny Watters. He was dynamic. He was more advanced than Toadlo. He could stretch fourteen notes with his right hand and play a melody at the same time with his middle fingers. He liked Camels and gin and in the afternoons I'd buy him a pack of cigarettes and a double shot of gin and we'd go upstairs at the Leader House, and he would show me. Then, at a party, I heard a piano player named Jim Fellman playing tenths with his left hand, instead of the old oompah bass. It was so easy and rhythmic. *He* liked beer and chewed Mail Pouch, so I got him upstairs at the Leader House, too, and he showed me those tenths. I got my rhythmic training from a banjoist named Verchet. He was a musical fanatic. He tried to make his banjo sound like a harp, and he had all these nuts and bolts for tightening and loosening the strings, only the damn thing always fell apart when he played. His instrument case was full of tools and he sounded like a plumber when he picked it up. But he was a heck of a critic of tempo. He'd sit there, strumming like lightning and rocking back and forth in half time, and if I got away from the beat, he'd say, 'Watch-it-boy, watch-it-boy.' So I began to form my little style. I still had the idea of the cornet in my head and I would try things that I might have played on the cornet—single-note figures and runs that were not ordinary then on the piano. And I hit on using octaves in the right hand, when I was with a band, to cut through the music and be heard."

The cab stopped in front of the hotel. Upstairs, Hines ordered a bottle of Scotch and ice and glasses. Then he took off his hat for the first time that afternoon and flopped down on the bed. He looked tired but pleased. "That Budd Johnson is something, isn't he, Stanley? He was a playing fool today. He was in my big band almost ten years. But I've always been lucky in my musicians. I formed my first band in 1924 and Benny Carter played baritone in it and his cousin Cuban Bennett was on trumpet. He was a *great* trumpet player, but nobody remembers him. We went into the Grape Arbor, in Pittsburgh, and stayed there several months. Eubie Blake used to come through town once in a while, and the first time I met him he told me, 'Son, you have no business here. You got to leave Pittsburgh.' He came through again while we were at the Grape Arbor, and when he saw me, he said, 'You *still* here? I'm going to take this cane'—he always carried a cane and wore a raccoon coat and a brown derby—'and wear it out all over your head if you're not gone when I come back.' I was. That same year, I went to Chicago to the Elite No. 2 Club, an after-hours place. Teddy Weatherford, the pianist, was *it* in Chicago then, and soon people began telling him, 'There's a tall, skinny kid from Pittsburgh plays piano. You better hear him.' Teddy and I became friends, and we'd go around together and both play and people began to notice me. They even began to lean toward me over Teddy. Louis Armstrong and I first worked together in the Carroll Dickerson orchestra at the Sunset. Louis was the first trumpet player I heard who played what *I* had wanted to play on cornet. I'd steal ideas from him and he'd steal them from me. He'd bend over after a solo and say way down deep in that rumble, 'Thank you, man.' Louis was wild and I was wild, and we were inseparable. He was the most happy-go-lucky guy I ever met. Then Louis and I and Zutty Singleton, who was also with Dickerson, formed our own group. We were full of jokes and were always kidding each other. We drove around in this old, broken-down automobile we had, and when we got home after work we'd leave it parked in the middle of the street or in front of someone else's house. But there wasn't *that* much work and we like to starve to death, making a dollar or a dollar and a half apiece a night. So we drifted apart, and I worked for Jimmie Noone for a year, and then I went to New York to make some QRS piano rolls. I had a little band rehearsing at the same time, and it was then I got a call to come and open up the Grand Terrace."

The whiskey and ice and glasses arrived. Dance gave Hines a brandy from a bottle on the dresser and poured himself a Scotch-and-water. Hines lifted his glass in the air. "This is for Stanley. If it hadn't been for him, I'd probably be out of this business now. I was ready to quit about a year ago. In fact, my wife and I were talking about opening a little shop out on the Coast. But Stanley kept after me on that long-distance phone, and persuaded me to come here last winter, and then he set up the record session. I was down low again when I got here last week. But something *good* happened today, and it's going to happen tomorrow. I try never to worry. The greatest thing to draw wrinkles in a man's face is worry. And why should I be unhappy and pull down my face and drag my feet and make everybody around me feel that way too? By being what you are, something always comes up. Sunshine always opens out. I'll leave for the Coast day after tomorrow in my car, and I'll stop and see my mother in Duquesne. My sister, Nancy, and my brother, Boots, still live with her. I'll see my mother-in-law in Philadelphia and she'll give me a whole mess of fried chicken. I'll put that on the seat beside me, along with those cigars and my pipe and pipe tobacco and a map and a gallon jug of water. I'll open the window wide and keep my eye on the road. Stanley, let me have a little more of that brandy, please."

OUT HERE AGAIN

Mary Lou Williams at the Hickory House, after a long period of semiretirement: Dressed in a black sleeveless gown, cut low in the back, she looked extremely pretty. Her black hair was arranged in a loose helmet, and on her right arm she had a watch with a wide gold strap. She sat straight, her body motionless and her elbows brushing her sides, as if she were pouring tea. Her head and her face, however, were in steady, graceful motion. Sometimes she shut her eyes and tilted her chin up, so that the light from a spot bounced off her high, prominent cheekbones. Sometimes, her eyes still shut, she moved her head counterclockwise in an intense, halting manner, punctuated with rhythmic downward jabs. When she was pleased by something her bassist or her drummer did, she rocked gently back and forth, partly opened her eyes, and smiled. She never looked at her long, thin fingers, which lay almost flat on the keys.

The triumph of Mary Lou Williams' style is that she has no style. She is not an eclectic or an anthologist or a copyist; she is a gifted and delicate appreciator who distills what affects her in the work of other pianists into cool, highly individual synopses. The grapes are others', the wine is her own. In the late twenties and early thirties, echoes of Jelly Roll Morton and Fats Waller and Earl Hines hurried through her work. The mountainous shadow of Art Tatum passed over around 1940, and by 1945 she had become an expert bebop pianist. Since jazz piano—the otherworldly convolutions of Cecil Taylor aside—has not moved very far since then, she is now a post-bebop performer, her chords and single-note melodic lines applauding such juniors as Bill Evans and Red Garland. But while discreetly judging her peers she often scoops them. In the forties, she advanced certain dissonant chords that became part of Thelonious Monk's permanent furniture. She also outlined the sort of Debussy impressionism that no modern pianist confronted by a number like "Polka Dots and Moonbeams" would be caught without. In the thirties, she perfected an airy, slightly joshing form of boogie-woogie that pointed a way out of the mechanized morass that that singular music had sunk into. Mary Lou Williams' present work is an instructive history of jazz piano —a kind of one-woman retrospective of an entire movement.

Her technique is faultless, and she has Art Tatum's touch. Fragments of boogie-woogie basses—in six-eight, rather than four-four or four-eight, time—frequently appear in her introductions. These are relieved by muted left-hand figures and right-hand chords that abstract the melody. Spare single-note lines surface in the right hand; their arpeggios are mere serifs, and they include generous rests. These melodic lines, strung between the chords of the tune like telephone wire, soon thicken, and she moves on to intense chords, often in double time or placed off the beat. Things begin to rock insistently and lightly, and after a few cloudlike melodic statements she returns to the six-eight introduction. Along the way, a Waller stride bass or an Ellington dissonance drifts by; a Basie aphorism is struck; big-interval Hines chords leap up and down the keyboard; a serpentine Bud Powell figure is carefully unspooled. But uppermost are a delicacy and wit and lofty invention that imply absolute knowledge. Rarely conscious of tempo, one is simply carried along at speeds that suggest wings and plenty of space.

The music stopped. Mary Lou Williams, having announced the intermission pianist, got down from the stand, and, after speaking a few words to a group of well-wishers, retired to a booth at the rear of the room. A waiter brought her a cup of coffee.

"I never could drink," she said. "When I was with the Andy Kirk band, back in the thirties, the boys had what they called the Hot Corn Club—named for the corn liquor they bought—and they were always trying to get me to drink. Backstage during a tonk game, somebody would make me a drink and I'd take one sip, and when I wasn't looking they would refill the glass, so I always thought I hadn't had but a taste. Once I was back at the piano, it would go right to my head, and I'd almost faint, and sit there woozy, saying 'Oh, my heart! Oh, my heart!,' and that broke the boys up." Miss Williams laughed—a low, tumbling, girlish chuckle in the quick flow of her talk—and lit a cigarette. The smoke closed her eyes, which are brown and slanted and heavy-lidded.

"I was off yesterday and I'm as stiff as a board," she said. "My fingers get stuck in the cracks. And that bass player of mine—if he'd only play jazz! He plays the bass like a guitar, with all those slurs, and he runs high notes when I'm trying to play funk. He's not with me, and it makes me mad. I'm going to call him tomorrow and nail his foot right to the floor and tell him he should go with the symphony." She shook her head, and laughed again.

"The madder I am, the more I smile," she went on. "And when I stomp my foot on the beat, it means nothing is happening. I'm dry. When I stop, it's like Erroll Garner said—'When Mary keeps her leg still, look out. Something is starting to *build*.' But all I've been doing tonight is bang my foot. Sometimes you get cold, you freeze up, but you just play until the inspiration comes. You play what you know, and play it as well as you can, and then the feeling starts. A bad audience or a waiter dropping a tray can take your inspiration. If you have a dead rhythm section, you shut it out of your mind, and you learn this the hard way. If you make a mistake, you work something good out of that mistake. We were doing 'How High the Moon' a while ago, and I hit a wrong note in a chord, and what I did was go off immediately on a different tack and work that wrong note into a pattern that fitted. It sounded way out, but it was all right. You have to be on your tiptoes every minute. No one can put a style on me. I've learned from many people. I change all the time. I experiment to keep up with what is going on, to hear what everybody else is doing. I even keep a little ahead of them, like a mirror that shows what will happen next. One reason I came out here again is the sounds I hear in modern jazz. They're disturbed and crazy. They're neurotic, as if the Negro was pulling away from his heritage in music. You have to love when you play. Lord, I've talked talked talked music to young musicians, but they don't listen. So I've decided to show them, make them *hear* the soul." Mary Lou Williams ground out her cigarette and took a sip of coffee. "Young musicians—and old ones, too—are coming in every night, and they're listening," she said. "Too many young musicians learn from records, and copy wrong chords and wrong notes and don't know it. I can hear them, because I have perfect pitch. I'm going to stay out here and teach them."

She looked at her watch and rose.

"I've got to talk to my stepbrother," she said. "He's due in now. Tomorrow morning I'm going up to Elmsford to my dressmaker. She moved up there recently from New York. I've grown fat since I last played, and I have to have all my dresses let out. Joe Wells—he owns Wells' Restaurant, up on Seventh Avenue—is going to drive me. At ten o'clock."

Several sets later, the bassist was running high notes, Mary Lou Williams was smiling, and it was obvious from the posting motions of her skirt that she was banging her foot.

Mary Lou Williams is one of the few first-rate female musicians in an unsentimental and peculiarly male music. There is little about the life of a jazz musician to attract women. The hours are long and topsy-turvy, the living conditions on the road are strikingly uncongenial for the traditional feminine pursuits, and most women lack the physical equipment—to say nothing of the poise—for blowing trumpets and trombones, slapping bass fiddles, or beating drums. Those female instrumentalists who have cropped up in jazz in the past thirty or forty years have decorated pianos, harps, guitars, or vibraphones, and, in the main, they have dropped quickly out of sight. (Since jazz is predominantly an instrumental music, the great female jazz singers, like Bessie Smith and Billie Holiday, form a separate conclave.) But Mary Lou Williams has survived. She is also one of the few jazz musicians, male or female, who have survived the swing era, which she graced as a pianist, arranger, and composer with the Andy Kirk band.

Taken together, the big swing bands resembled an iceberg. In plain view were the Goodmans, Shaws, Jameses, and Hermans; partly above water were the Basies and Ellingtons and Luncefords; and below were countless unknown, though often excellent, groups. A considerable number of these subsurface bands came from the Midwest and the Southwest, including, among others, those of Kirk, Jay Mc-Shann, Harlan Leonard, Jap Allen, Troy Floyd, and Jeter-Pillars. They formed, along with Count Basie's band, the so-called Kansas City school of jazz, playing a loose, easy, blues-based music that, through such graduates as Lester Young and Charlie Christian, assisted at the birth of bebop in New York in the early forties. In some ways, the Kirk band was better than the Basie band; its personnel remained almost unchanged throughout the twelve years Mary Lou Williams was with it, and it had a casual precision that Basie's band, with its stellar iconoclasts, often lacked. Moreover, the Kirk band had a calmness and obliqueness that set it apart from the Kansas City bands; it implied what its peers shouted. Part of this was due to its best soloists—Mary Lou Williams, Dick Wilson, Shorty Baker, and Ted Donnelly—and to its drummer, Ben Thigpen. Donnelly was a serene, thoughtful trombonist in the style of Benny Morton, and Wilson was a subtle, big-toned tenor saxophonist who had the fleetness of Chu Berry but none of his garrulity, and who also shared Lester Young's adventurous harmonies and rhythms. Baker was an economical and legato trumpeter, whose solos had a lyric slow-motion quality. Mary Lou Williams' own solos—she was distilling Hines and Tatum much of the time—were graceful and meditative. Ben Thigpen (the father of the drummer Ed Thigpen) had a light, flexible touch and perfect time, and certain of his methods presaged modern drumming. Part of the Kirk band's unforced assurance also came from Mary Lou Williams' arrangements, which were uncluttered and advanced. She used clarinet trios to spell out her attractive blues melodies; she opened and closed numbers simply, with a soloist and the rhythm section; her improvised-sounding saxophone passages suggested the creamy writing of Benny Carter; and there were odd, beautifully constructed background harmonies, often played by the saxophones and trombones. Her best arrangements had a small-band compactness. They also had an almost schoolmarm purpose, and unfailingly pointed up both the tunes and the frequent solos.

Mary Lou Williams left Kirk in 1942 (the band petered out several years later) and joined the remarkable collection of singers, instrumentalists, dancers, and comedians that travelled back and forth between Café Society Downtown and Café Society Uptown during the Second World War. This informal repertory company was brought together by Barney Josephson, and at various times it consisted of the bands of Teddy Wilson, James P. Johnson, Frankie Newton, Edmond Hall, Red Allen, and Eddie Heywood; comedians like Imogene Coca, Zero Mostel, and Jimmy Savo; the Kraft Sisters, who were dancers; such singers as the Golden Gate Quartet, Joe Turner, Mildred Bailey, Billie Holiday, and Josh White; and pianists such as Mary Lou Williams, Meade Lux Lewis, Albert Ammons, Pete Johnson, and Hazel Scott. Mary Lou Williams worked this attractive circuit until 1947, and then, having been visible for the greater part of seventeen years, abruptly became a ghost. Jazz itself had turned transparent. The big bands had been replaced by esoteric small groups that played bebop or cool jazz. Dancing—and the musicians who played for it—had been obliterated by a 30 per cent wartime cabaret tax. Fifty-second Street, which had cradled jazz since the thirties, was being taken over by the office buildings. Jazz musicians—particularly those weaned on swing—had not felt so put upon since the early days of the Depression. Mary Lou Williams played at occasional concerts and in night clubs, and in 1952 she went to Europe for two years. She found things pretty much the same on her return, and, with the exception of a recording date, she lay low. Then, in 1957, the reasons for her disappearance changed; she was received into the Catholic Church, and entered a period of religious fervor. Rumor had it that she had quit music for good. Her admirers, long accustomed to her jack-in-the-box ways, mourned but waited.

Mary Lou Williams lives alone in a two-and-a-half-room apartment on the second floor of a yellow brick building on

Sugar Hill, near 144th Street and St. Nicholas Avenue. A small, cheerful kitchen faces the front door. To its left is a living room, crowded with an upright piano, a sofa, a couple of cabinets, a portable phonograph, an aluminum worktable, and a glass-topped coffee table. The top of the piano is covered with religious statues. There are three bright windows. Mary Lou Williams appeared, carrying a shopping bag filled with clothes. She had on a brown nutria coat, a brown woollen dress, and tan leather boots. Her hair was in mild disarray, and her eyes were puffy with sleep.

"Mornin'," she said.

"My, my. You ready?" Wells asked. He is short, solid, and nattily dressed, and he was wearing horn-rimmed glasses and smoking a cigar.

She replied by opening the front door. Wells trooped downstairs after her. "We used to have a doorman years ago," she said in the foyer. "But he wouldn't let *anybody* in, so we got rid of him."

It was raining outside, and Wells' car, a new tan Buick, was pebbled with water. "You get in back," Wells ordered Mary Lou Williams. "No sense jamming the front. Now, where's this Elmisford, Mary?"

"Elmsford," Miss Williams said. "Elmsford, New York." She pulled a slip of paper from her pocket. "Get on the Major Deegan and the Thruway, and get off at Exit 8. Then I'll tell you where."

Wells crossed the 149th Street bridge and worked his way onto the Deegan through the Bronx Terminal Market.

"How far is this Elmsford?" he asked.

"She said about twenty-five miles. A half hour."

"Lord! I've got a twelve-o'clock appointment—with a lady. And I make it a rule never to keep a lady waiting."

"You kept me waiting plenty of times. Get over in the middle lane, Mr. Wells."

"Cool and easy. I've never had an accident in my life."

"Well, I've had two. It's the people who have had the accidents are the good drivers. It gives them mother wit on the road."

Rain, wiping at the car from all sides, erased conversation, and no one spoke for several minutes.

"I've been driving since I was twelve," Miss Williams said eventually. "When I was eighteen, I was driving one of the cars the Kirk band travelled in. My first husband, John Williams, who played alto and baritone, had been with Kirk about six months—the band was still led by T. Holder then—and I'd been jobbing around Memphis waiting for him to send for me. I wasn't playing regularly with the band yet. I'd wait outside ballrooms in the car, and if things went bad and people weren't dancing, they would send somebody to get me and I'd go in and play 'Froggy Bottom,' or some other boogie-woogie number, and things would jump. The regular pianist, Marion Jackson, was a wanderer, and I replaced him around 1930. My, what a band that was! It was a happy band, a good-looking band, an educated band. We had love for each other. There was a lot of love among musicians in the thirties—not like it is now, with everyone out for himself. We had the type of boys that even if a woman they met didn't respect herself, they did. I was never allowed to go around by myself. My husband or two or three of the boys were always with me. I was well sheltered. But we had a hard, hard time at first. We were stranded all over —in Buffalo and Chicago and Cincinnati and Greeley, Colorado. When Kirk came backstage after a job with his head down, we'd know he hadn't been paid, and one of the trumpet players would take out his horn and play the 'Worried Blues,' and we'd all laugh. I made a little extra by manicuring the boys' nails. They paid me a nickel, and I'd take it out of the money they made from cards, which I held for them. In Greeley, we stayed next to a cornfield, and I ate corn right up to the farmer's back door. The boys played a little semi-professional baseball there. It was hot summertime, and I carried water for them. Stumpy Brady, the trombonist, nearly got himself killed chasing balls he couldn't see. It seems you've got to starve a little before you can get on. Else you get that swelled head. My husband never let me get one. He trained me. Once, I developed an introduction I liked so much that I played it and played it until he finally knocked me right off the piano stool: 'You don't play the piano that way. Just because you did that "Twinklin' " '—that was another of my numbers—'you think you're something.' He said unbelievable things to me, but they worked. I was learning to arrange all this time. Don Redman was my model. I could hear my chords in my head but didn't know how to write them. Kirk helped me—he was a good musician—and I learned. I was very high-strung and sensitive. When the boys fooled around at rehearsals with what I wrote, I got mad and snatched the music off their stands and began to cry and went home to bed. I'd discovered I had perfect pitch, and I couldn't stand hearing wrong notes, any more than I can now. But I could expand with that band, and try all sorts of things. We played everything—ballads, jump tunes, novelties, slow blues, fast blues—and they were all different. We even extracted things from Lombardo records to play at ofay college dances. Exit 4, Mr. Wells."

"I see it, Mary."

"When we weren't on the road, we spent most of our time around Kansas City, and there were after-hours sessions every night. They were something else. A good one went right through the next day. Style didn't matter. What mattered was to keep the thing going. I'd stop in at a session after work, and they would be doing 'Sweet Georgia Brown.' I'd go home and take a bath and change my dress, and when I got back—an hour or more later—they'd still be on 'Georgia Brown.' Ben Webster came and threw some gravel on the window screen one night and woke me and my husband up and asked my husband if I could come to a session, because they were out of piano players. I went down, and Coleman Hawkins was there—Fletcher Henderson was in town—and he was having a bad time. He was down to his undershirt, and sweating and battling for his life against Lester Young and Herschel Evans and Ben, too. But they weren't cutting sessions. I recall Chu Berry sitting out front at a session and listening and not moving. When he got on the stand, he repeated note for note the last chorus the man before him had played—just to show how much he admired it—and then he went into his own bag. Whenever we were in Cleveland, I stayed close to Art Tatum, who worked there—he came from Toledo—when he wasn't in New York. When I had a day or two off, we played pinball in the afternoons, and at night we went to Val's, a little after-hours place, where we sometimes stayed until eleven in the morning. Tatum played, and they gave him fifty dollars. Then I played—usually some boogie—and they gave me five dollars. Tatum taught me how to hit my notes, how to control them without using pedals. And he showed me how to keep my fingers flat on the keys to get that clean tone. Of course, he didn't *show* me anything. He just said, 'Mary, you listen.' But once I showed *him* something. Buck Washington—of Buck and Bubbles—had given me a little run in Pittsburgh, which I used one night at Val's. Tatum said, 'What's that run, Mary? Where'd you get that? Play it for me again, please.' I did, and he developed that run—it covered just about the whole keyboard—and used it until the end of his life. Around 1940, something went wrong between me and the Kirk band. I don't think it was jealousy—or I don't like to think it was, anyway. He had hired several new people, and maybe I wasn't getting as much attention as I used to, and little things upset me—untuned pianos, pianos with nine or ten keys that didn't work. I began to feel my time was up, and one night, in Washington, D.C., I just left. God must have got the ball rolling to move me somewhere else. Exit 6, Mr. Wells."

The rain was heavier, and it had got chilly. Dark escarpments on both sides of the road turned the air gray. Miss Williams shivered, and hunched down in her coat.

"You have a little heat, Mr. Wells? I'm cold. I was so upset when I left Kirk I decided to leave music, and I went home to my mother's, in Pittsburgh. But Art Blakey kept coming over to the house and pestering me to form a group. So I finally did. We worked a park in Cleveland, and then went into Kelly's Stable, on Fifty-second Street. Shorty Baker—he was my second husband—had left Kirk by this time, and he came with us. Then John Hammond persuaded me to go to Café Society. We were kind of a family there, and Barney Josephson thought of us that way. Josh White was around a lot, and I loved to hear him laugh. He had one of those laughs that come right from the stomach. I was feeling low after work one night, and I didn't want any more of the teasing that was always going around. So I flounced out with some dresses I had to get cleaned. Josh said, 'Where you going, Pussycat?'—which is what they called me. 'We'll take you home.' I said, 'I'm going home by myself. I'm tired of all this mess,' and went and got a cab. About halfway up the West Side Drive, we had a flat tire. It was near zero and blowing hard, and after a while I stepped out and saw another cab coming. It slowed down, and it looked like Josh and some of the others in it. I hollered with all my might, and it must have sounded like 'josSSHHhh' as they went by. The cab stopped, and somebody got out and walked back. It was Josh. 'Is that *you*, Pussycat?' he said. He started laughing, and he laughed so hard he fell down on the road and lay there, hawing and holding himself. I used to be very quiet in those days—a zombie. When people talked to me, I looked at them and nodded, but in my mind I was writing an arrangement or going over a new tune or thinking about something I had played the last set. And I never smiled while I was playing, so Josh would stick his head out of the curtain backstage and make a face, and that would break me up, and I'd smile. I came closest to getting a swelled head at this time. People would tell me, 'Mary, you're the greatest girl pianist in the world,' and 'Mary, you're the greatest *pianist* in the world,' and for a while I believed it. But I remembered what John Williams used to tell me. So I discarded those compliments, and it's never happened since. After I left Café Society Downtown, I worked on Fifty-second Street with Mildred Bailey. She was a wonderful, big, salty person. She always had dachshunds, and she'd walk from her living room to her kitchen to get a drink, rock, rock, rock"—Miss Williams swung stiffly from side to side and tramped with her boots in time—"with these little dogs all around her, and back into the living room, rock, rock, rock, the dogs still there. She joked all the time. People said you couldn't get along with Mildred, but I got along with her fine. All during this time, my house was kind of a headquarters for young musicians. I'd even leave the door open for them if I was out. Tadd Dameron would come to write when he was out of inspiration, and Monk did several of his pieces there. Bud Powell's brother, Richie, who also played piano, learned how to improvise at my house. And everybody came or called for advice. Charlie Parker would ask what did I think about him putting a group with strings together, or Miles Davis would ask about his group with the tuba—the one that had John Lewis and Gerry Mulligan and Max Roach and J. J. Johnson in it. It was still like the thirties—musicians helped each other, and didn't just think of themselves. Exit 8, Mr. Wells."

Mary Lou Williams fished her instructions from her pocket. "First light, turn left, go past Robert Hall. Turn left on Payne Street. It's the yellow house at the top of the hill."

Robert Hall swung by, and Payne Street appeared, on our right.

"Payne Street, Mary," Wells said.

"She said it was on the left. Maybe that's it down the road by that garage."

Wells obligingly drove down a narrow, winding road through a rubbish-filled field.

"Now, isn't this disappointing?" Miss William said. "I was expecting a nice house with a view. That's how she described it."

The road ended in a mountain of old tires, and Wells turned around. "Let's go back and try the other Payne, dollin'," he said. "Somebody's mixed up."

The other Payne went up a steep hill, and near the top was a small yellow house. A tall woman in a sweatshirt and blue jeans opened the door, with two miniature white poodles dancing around her feet.

Miss Williams apologized for being late.

"That's all right, honey," the dressmaker said. "There's nobody here at the moment. You come in and we'll get right to work. Mr. Wells, make yourself comfortable in the living room. We won't be too long."

Wells sat down on a wrought-iron love seat. A dining alcove with more wrought-iron furniture was at one end of the room and a giant picture window at the other. The walls and ceiling were soft violet. A clump of plastic lilies and a stand containing brass fire irons flanked a raised fireplace. A photograph of a handsome young woman, done in the peekaboo mode of décolleté eighteenth-century portraits, hung over the mantel. A Pollock-type abstraction, full of racing reds and blacks, faced it.

Wells crossed his legs and lit a fresh cigar, and looked out at the rain. "Eleven-fifteen," he said. "I'll never make my twelve-o'clock. And I have an appointment at one, and another at two-twenty. I get very upset when I miss appointments. It tightens my stomach. But I'll do anything for Mary. I've known her since the early forties, and we've had little deals off and on through the years. Right now I'm pushing that record she just made—'St. Martin de Porres,' about the Negro saint. It has a chorus of voices, and she plays. Very lovely. She's the most brilliant woman I know. A little nervous, maybe, but brilliant."

A steady hum of talk came from the next room, and Wells, occasionally jumping up to flick ashes into the fireplace, delivered a discourse on the restaurant business, which, he said, was very good. Then it was noon, and Miss Williams appeared. She looked wide-awake and pleased, as if she were already in one of her altered dresses.

Wells drove back to the Thruway hunched over, the minutes ticking away almost audibly in his head.

Miss Williams began chanting in time to the windshield wipers: "Watch out. Watch out. Watch out. Da de-da, da de-da," and hummed a little tune, using the same rhythm. "This weather reminds me of the time I got stranded about fifteen miles outside of Pittsburgh. I wasn't more than twelve, and I'd played a job with a union band, and when it was over they wouldn't pay us. We walked all the way home. We moved to Pittsburgh from Atlanta, where I was born, when I was five or six. I've had a lot of names. I was born Mary Elfrieda Scruggs, and later I was Mary Lou Winn and Mary Lou Burley, after stepfathers. I don't know where the Lou came from, but I got the Williams when I was married. I don't remember seeing my father until twelve years ago, when I went to Atlanta. I said to him, 'I bet you don't know who I am," and all he could say was 'What have you brought me?' I said, 'You have the nerve, after all these years of doing nothing for your children!' But my mother was a good person. She worked most of the time, and my sister, Mamie, and my stepbrother, Willie, took care of me. My mother told my sister she'd kill her if anything happened to me. Of course, things did. I swallowed a pin once, and another time a Great Dane who was rabid bit me and they took me to the hospital for those shots. We had a cousin who could dance, and he and my sister dared me to jump over a box with a lighted candle on top. I did, and I tripped and broke my arm. I was so scared of what my mother would think that I crawled under my bed, with that broken arm, and stayed there for over an hour, until I finally came out crying. People shouldn't say things like 'I'll kill you' to their children. I used to stutter—I still do when I get upset—but I broke myself of the habit. My mother's almost eighty now, and has a heart condition. She played the organ, and she used to hold me on her lap when I was three, and I'd play. She wouldn't allow for a music teacher to come into the house, but she invited different musicians, and I'd listen. By the time I was six or seven, I was playing the piano in neighbors' houses all afternoon and evening—my cousin or sister taking me—and sometimes I came home with twenty or thirty dollars wrapped in a handkerchief. All I bought was shoes. My mother was a size two and a half, and I was already a five. Up to then, I used to wear her shoes to school, and they hurt so much I had to walk home barefooted. I got to be known all over our part of Pittsburgh. Miss Milholland, the principal of the Lincoln School, took me to afternoon teas at Carnegie Tech, where I played light-classical things. She also took me to the opera, but I guess I was too young, because I still don't like it. I played a home-talent show in on old theatre out in East Liberty, and did all this clowning with my elbows on the keys. One time, the Mellon family sent their chauffeur in a big car into our district looking for a Negro pianist for one of their parties. Somebody told him about me, and that night he drove me and a friend to this mansion, and I played the party. They gave me a check for a hundred dollars. My mother was very upset, and called to see if there was a mistake, but there wasn't. The first pianist who made an impression on me was Jack Howard. He played boogie so heavy he splintered the keys. I also heard a woman pianist in a theatre I went to with my brother-in-law. I can't recall her name. She sat sidewise at the keyboard with her legs crossed and a cigarette in her mouth, and she was wonderful. Earl Hines was a Pittsburgh boy, and, of course, I listened to him every chance I got."

A truck slammed past us, throwing up a curtain of water that landed with a thump on the windshield. Some of it flew in at Wells' window and sprayed Mary Lou Williams.

"That went right on me," she said, and dabbed at her face with a sleeve. "Close your window, please, Mr. Wells, and I'll open mine a crack."

"You open yours a crack and you'll give me a crick," Wells replied.

She laughed. "That's what an old man gets for driving around on a day like this," she said.

"Listen, dollin'. I'm just thinking about getting myself en-gaged. Old man!" said Wells.

Mary Lou Williams laughed again. The rain was letting up, and there was blue sky over a hump of woods. "My first real professional job was with the union band I got stranded with," she said. "My next was with a vaudeville group, The Hottentots. They had a pianist who was an addict, which in those days was about as familiar as going to the moon. He

disappeared, and they sent someone to find me. I was playing hopscotch in the yard. When this man saw me, he said,
'Oh, man! Why did they send me all the way out here? This
a *baby!*' We went inside, and he hummed a couple of tunes,
and I played them back perfectly. I joined the show for the
summer. I was about twelve or thirteen, and a friend came
with me. We toured carnivals and such, and it was an animal life. The *worst* kinds of people. I was a good student,
but I quit high school in my first year and went with another vaudeville group, Seymour and Jeannette. I was in the
band, and so was John Williams. They had a trombonist
who worked his slide with his foot, or danced the Charle-
ston when he played. After Seymour died, we came to New
York, and I sat in for a week with Ellington's Washing-
tonians in a theatre pit. I remember Sonny Greer and Tricky
Sam Nanton. Tricky Sam drank whiskey out of a big jug
held over one shoulder. I met Fats Waller at that time—that
was about 1926—and I played for him, and he picked me up
and threw me in the air. I didn't weigh more than eighty or
ninety pounds. He played organ for the movies at Lincoln
Theatre, and people screamed, he was so good. Then John
Williams formed a group, and we gigged around the Midwest until he joined T. Holder. I took over the band after
he left. One of the people I hired was Jimmie Lunceford. I
had some rough times with gangsters, and the like, and in a
roadhouse I worked near Memphis without the band, this
white farmer from Mississippi came in every night and sat
out front and stared at me. It shook me. Then the cook told
me the farmer said he'd give him fifty dollars if he helped
him take me to his farm in Mississippi. When I heard that, I
never went back."

The car was rolling along beside the Harlem River, and
the sun had come out.

"You want to go back to your house, Mary?" Wells
asked.

"Take me down to my thrift shop, please, Mr. Wells. I
got to pay the rent. It's on Twenty-ninth Street, right near
Bellevue."

Wells shook his head. "I'm going to miss my one-o'clock, too."

"I started this thrift shop to help get my Bel Canto Foundation going," Mary Lou Williams said. "The idea for the Bel Canto came to me in 1957. It's a plan to help jazz musicians in trouble with drugs or alcohol. If I ever raise the money, I'll buy a house in the country. I'll only take a small number of patients, and I'll have doctors and nurses and soundproof rooms where the musicians can meditate and play. But they'll work, too—hard physical work. I'm not an organizer, but I *know* musicians. I've worked with them all through the years. Almost everybody has come to me at one time or another. I put the worst cases in a room down the hall from my place I rent cheap from a neighbor. They stay a couple of weeks, and I talk to them and pray with them and help them get a job. But I can be very hard in my charity, and sometimes I tell them, 'You've got to be a *man*. Stand up and go downtown and get a job. No use lying around Harlem and feeling sorry for yourself.' Sometimes they come back in worse shape and ask for money, and sometimes they get on their feet. One boy I've been helping has a job at Gimbels, and he's doing just fine. I've also sent musicians to the Graymoor Monastery, near Garrison. Brother Mario there has been a lot of help to me. I gave a benefit concert at Carnegie Hall to get the Bel Canto started, but it used up more money than it made. Then I tramped all over downtown until I found this place for a thrift shop. I fixed it up, and people in and out of music sent thousand-dollar coats and expensive dresses. I worked twelve hours a day collecting stuff and running the shop. In the evening, I went over to Bellevue to visit with musicians who were there. I raised money, but it went to rent and musicians I was helping. I was living mostly on royalty checks from records and arrangements, and then in 1960 *I* ran out of money and had to go to work at the Embers. I couldn't find anybody I could trust to run the shop. It's been closed off and on almost a year now, but I'm still working on money for the foundation. Some club ladies in Pittsburgh are very interested."

Wells turned into Twenty-ninth Street and pulled up in front of a modest store.

"I won't be long, Mr. Wells."

Wells turned around, his eyes wide, and said, "Mary dollin', I've already missed *two* appointments. You take a cab home, please."

"O.K., and thank you," Mary Lou Williams said.

The car roared away. Mary Lou Williams unlocked the shop door. On the floor were a couple of Con Edison bills and a letter addressed to her. The walls were covered with paintings by amateurs, whose enthusiasm ranged from Grandma Moses to Picasso. Two handsome evening dresses hung in the windows, and around the shop were odd pieces of china, a sewing machine, a butcher's mallet, a rack of clothes covered with a plastic sheet, a cue stick encased in a fancy scabbard, serving trays, a tin lunchbox, rows and rows of shoes, assorted lamps, vases, and pitchers, and a cut-glass bowl. In the back, behind a partition, were piles of books and records, and two automobile tires in good condition. Everything was peppered with New York grit.

"Lord, this place is dirty," Mary Lou Williams said. "I've got to come down next Monday and clean. Those new-looking moccasins are from Duke Ellington—and this alpine hat, too. Here's a drawerful of shirts from Louis Armstrong, and those dresses are from Lorraine Gillespie, Dizzy's wife."

She opened her letter. "It's from a convict upstate—I don't know him," she said. "He says he's about to get out, and wants to know if I can help him get a job. He saw a piece in the *Christian Science Monitor* about Bel Canto. I'll write him and tell him to pray and call me when he gets here. I receive letters like this all the time."

Mary Lou Williams put her Con Edison bills in her bag, and sighed.

"You know, I'm tired," she said. "I only slept four or five hours last night. There's a kosher butcher around the corner who has the best ground beef in New York. I'll cook a hamburger at home."

Miss Williams bought the meat and, at a fish market across the street, picked up a filet of sole for supper. She hailed a cab. It was after two-thirty when she reached her apartment.

"I'm not used to running around like this," Mary Lou Williams said in her living room after lunch. "If I didn't have my prayers, they'd have to put me in a straitjacket." She laughed, and lit a cigarette. "My life turned when I was in Europe. I played in England for eleven months, and spent money as fast as I made it. But I was distracted and depressed. At a party given by Gerald Lascelles—he's an English jazz writer and a member of royalty—I met this G.I. He noticed something was wrong, and he said, 'You should read the Ninety-first Psalm.' I went home and I read *all* the Psalms. They cooled me and made feel protected. Then I went to France, and played theatres and clubs, but I still didn't feel right. Dave Pochonet, a French musician, asked me to his grandmother's place in the country to rest. I stayed there six months, and I just slept and ate and read the Psalms and prayed."

The living room had settled into twilight. Mary Lou Williams' face was indistinct. She stood up and stretched. Then she knelt on the sofa and, cupping her chin in her hand, looked out the window at St. Nicholas Avenue. It was a little girl's position. "When I came back from Europe, I decided not to play anymore," she said. "I was raised Protestant, but I lost my religion when I was about twelve. I joined Adam Powell's church. I went there on Sunday, and during the week I sat in Our Lady of Lourdes, a Catholic church over on a Hundred and Forty-second Street. I just sat there and meditated. All kinds of people came in—needy ones and cripples—and I brought them here and gave them food and talked to them and gave them money. Music had left my head, and I hardly remembered playing. Then Father Anthony Woods—he's a Jesuit—gave Lorraine Gillespie and me instruction, and we were taken into the Church in May of 1957. I became a kind of fanatic for a while. I'd live on apples and water for nine days at a time. I stopped smoking. I shut myself up here like a monk. Father Woods got worried, and he told me, 'Mary, you're an artist. You belong at the piano and writing music. It's *my* business to help people through the Church and your business to help people through music.' He got me playing again. The night before I opened at the Hickory House, I had a dream, and it was filled with dead musicians, all friends of mine. Oscar Pettiford was in it, and Pha Terrell and Dick Wilson from Kirk's band. They were all rejoicing on this kind of stage, and there was a line of showgirls dancing and singing. Oscar was very happy because I was coming out again. It was a good sign."

EVEN
HIS FEET LOOK SAD

The clarinettist Pee Wee Russell was born in St. Louis, Missouri, in March of 1906, and died just short of his sixty-third birthday in Arlington, Virginia. He was unique—in his looks, in his inward-straining shyness, in his furtive, circumambulatory speech, and in his extraordinary style. His life was higgledy-piggledy. He once accidentally shot and killed a man when all he was trying to do was keep an eye on a friend's girl. He spent most of his career linked—in fact and fiction—to the wrong musicians. People laughed at him—he *looked* like a clown perfectly at ease in a clown's body—when, hearing him, they should have wept. He drank so much for so long that he almost died, and when he miraculously recovered, he began drinking again. In the last seven or eight years of his life, he came into focus: his astonishing originality began to be appreciated, and he worked and recorded beautifully with the sort of musicians he should have been working and recording with all his life. He even took up painting, producing an ample series of seemingly abstract canvases that were actually accurate chartings of his inner workings. But then, true to form, the bottom fell out. His wife Mary died unexpectedly, and he was soon dead himself. Mary had been his guidon, his ballast, his right hand, his helpmeet. She was a funny, sharp, nervous woman, and she knew she deserved better than Pee Wee. She had no illusions, but she was devoted to him. She laughed when she said this: "Do you know Pee Wee? I mean what do you *think* of him? Oh, not those funny sounds that come out of his clarinet. Do you *know* him? You think he's kind and sensitive and sweet. Well, he's intelligent and he doesn't use dope and he is sensitive, but Pee Wee can also be *mean*. In fact, Pee Wee is the most egocentric son of a bitch I know."

No jazz musician has ever played with the same daring and nakedness and intuition. His solos invariably arrived—but not always at their original destination. He took wild improvisational chances, and when he found himself above the abyss, he simply turned in another direction, invariably hitting firm ground. His singular tone was never at rest. He had a rich chalumeau register, a piping, flailing upper register, and a whining middle register, and when he couldn't

think of anything else to do, he growled. Above all, he
sounded cranky and querulous, but that was camouflage,
for he was the most plaintive and lyrical of players. He was
particularly affecting in a medium or slow-tempo blues.
He'd start in the chalumeau range with a delicate rush of
notes that were intensely multiplied into a single, unbroken
phrase that might last the entire chorus. Thus he'd begin
with a pattern of winged double-time staccato notes that,
moving steadily downward, were abruptly pierced by falsetto pumps. When he had nearly sunk out of hearing, he
reversed this pattern, keeping his myriad notes back to back,
and then swung into an easy uphill-downdale movement,
topping each rise with an oddly placed vibrato. By this time,
his first chorus was over, and one had the impression of having passed through a crowd of jostling, whispering people.
Russell then took what appeared to be his first breath, and,
momentarily breaking the tension he had established, opened
the next chorus with a languorous, questioning phrase made
up of three or four notes, at least one of them a spiny dissonance of the sort favored by Thelonious Monk. A closely
linked variation would follow, and Russell would fill out the
chorus by reaching behind him and producing an ironed
paraphrase of the chalumeau first chorus. In his final chorus,
he'd move snakily up toward the middle register with tissue-
paper notes and placid rests, taking on a legato I've-made-it
attack that allowed the listener to move back from the edge
of his seat.

Here is Russell in his apartment on King Street, in Greenwich Village, in the early sixties, when he was on the verge
of his greatest period. It wasn't a comeback he was about to
begin, though, for he'd never been where he was going.
Russell lived then on the third floor of a peeling brownstone.
He was standing in his door, a pepper-and-salt schnauzer
barking and dancing about behind him. "Shut up, Winkie,
for God's sake!" Russell said, and made a loose, whirlpool
gesture at the dog. A tall, close-packed, slightly bent man,
Russell had a wry, wandering face, dominated by a generous
nose. The general arrangement of his eyes and eyebrows was

mansard, and he had a brush mustache and a full chin. A heavy trellis of wrinkles held his features in place. His gray-black hair was combed absolutely flat. Russell smiled, without showing any teeth, and went down a short, bright hall, through a Pullman kitchen, and into a dark living room, brownish in color, with two day beds and two easy chairs, a bureau, a television, and several small tables. The corners of the room were stuffed with suitcases and fat manila envelopes. Under one table were two clarinet cases. The shades on the three windows were drawn, and only one lamp was lit. The room was suffocatingly hot. Russell, who was dressed in a tan, short-sleeved sports shirt, navy-blue trousers, black socks, black square-toed shoes, and dark glasses, sat down in a huge red leather chair. "We've lived in this cave six years too long. Mary's no housekeeper, but she tries. Every time a new cleaning gadget comes out, she buys it and stuffs it in a closet with all the other ones. I bought an apartment three years ago in a development on Eighth Avenue in the Chelsea district, and we're moving in. It has a balcony and a living room and a bedroom and a full kitchen. We'll have to get a cleaning woman to keep it respectable." Russell laughed—a sighing sound that seemed to travel down his nose. "Mary got me up at seven this morning before she went to work, but I haven't had any breakfast, which is my own fault. I've been on the road four weeks—two at the Theatrical Café, in Cleveland, with George Wein, and two in Pittsburgh with Jimmy McPartland. I shouldn't have gone to Pittsburgh. I celebrated my birthday there, and I'm still paying for it, physically and mentally. And the music. I can't go near 'Muskrat Ramble' any more without freezing up. Last fall, I did a television show with McPartland and Eddie Condon and Bud Freeman and Gene Krupa and Joe Sullivan—all the Chicago boys. We made a record just before it. They sent me a copy the other day and I listened halfway through and turned it off and gave it to the super. Mary was here, and she said, 'Pee Wee, you sound like you did when I first knew you in 1942.' I'd gone back twenty years in three hours. There's no room left in that music. It tells *you* how to solo. You're as good as the company you keep. You go with fast musicians, housebroken musicians, and you improve."

Russell spoke in a low, nasal voice. Sometimes he stuttered, and sometimes whole sentences came out in a sluice-like manner, and trailed off into mumbles and down-the-nose laughs. His face was never still. When he was surprised, he opened his mouth slightly and popped his eyes, rolling them up to the right. When he was thoughtful, he glanced quickly about, tugged his nose, and cocked his head. When he was amused, everything turned down instead of up—the edges of his eyes, his eyebrows, and the corners of his mouth. Russell got up and walked with short, crabwise steps into the kitchen. "Talking dries me up," he said. "I'm going to have an ale."

There were four framed photographs on the walls. Two of them showed what was already unmistakably Russell, in a dress and long, curly hair. In one, he is sucking his thumb. In the other, an arm is draped about a cocker spaniel. The third showed him at about fifteen, in military uniform, standing beneath a tree, and in the fourth he was wearing a dinner jacket and a wing collar and holding an alto saxophone. Russell came back, a bottle of ale in one hand and a pink plastic cup in the other. "Isn't that something? A wing collar. I was sixteen, and my father bought me that saxophone for three hundred and seventy-five dollars." Russell filled his cup and put the bottle on the floor. "My father was a steward at the Planter's Hotel, in St. Louis, when I was born, and I was named after him—Charles Ellsworth. I was a late child and the only one. My mother was forty. She was a very intelligent person. She'd been a newspaperwoman in Chicago, and she used to read a lot. Being a late child, I was excess baggage. I was like a toy. My parents, who were pretty well off, would say, You want this or that, it's yours. But I never really knew them. Not that they were cold, but they just didn't divulge anything. Someone discovered a few years ago that my father had a lot of brothers. I never knew he had *any*. When I was little, we moved to Muskogee, where my father and a friend hit a couple of gas wells. I took up piano and drums and violin, roughly in that order. One day, after I'd played in a school recital, I put my violin in the back seat of our car and my mother got in and sat on it. That was the end of my violin career. 'Thank God that's over,' I said to myself. I tried the clarinet when I was about twelve or thirteen. I studied with Charlie Merrill, who was in the pit band in the only theatre in Muskogee. Oklahoma was a dry state and he sneaked corn liquor during the lessons. My first job was playing at a resort lake. I played for about twelve hours and made three dollars. Once in a while, my father'd take me into the Elks' Club, where I heard Yellow Nunez, the New Orleans clarinet player. He had a trombone and piano and drums with him, and he played the lead in the ensembles. On my next job, *I* played the lead, using the violin part. Of course, I'd already heard the Original Dixieland Jazz Band on records. I was anxious in school—anxious to finish it. I'd drive my father to work in his car and, instead of going on to school, pick up a friend and drive around all day. I wanted to study music at the University of Oklahoma, but my aunt—she was living with us—said I was bad and wicked and persuaded my parents to take me out of high school and send me to Western Military Academy, in Alton, Illinois. My aunt is still alive. Mary keeps in touch with her, but I won't speak to her. I majored in wigwams at the military school, and I lasted just a year. Charlie Smith, the jazz historian, wrote the school not long ago and they told him Thomas Hart Benton and I are their two most distinguished nongraduates." Russell laughed and poured out more ale.

"We moved back to St. Louis and I began working in Herbert Berger's hotel band. It was Berger who gave me my nickname. Then I went with a tent show to Moulton, Iowa. Berger had gone to Juárez, Mexico, and he sent me a telegram asking me to join him. That was around the time my father gave me the saxophone. I was a punk kid, but my parents—can you imagine?—said, Go ahead, good riddance. When I got to Juárez, Berger told me, to my surprise, I wouldn't be working with him but across the street with piano and drums in the Big Kid's Palace, which had a bar about a block long. There weren't any microphones and you had to blow. I must have used a board for a reed. Three days later there were union troubles and I got fired and joined Berger. This wasn't long after Pancho Villa, and all the Mexicans wore guns. There'd be shooting in the streets day and night, but nobody paid any attention. You'd just duck into a saloon and wait till it was over. The day Berger hired me, he gave me a ten-dollar advance. That was a lot of money and I went crazy on it. It was the custom in Juárez to hire a kind of cop at night for a dollar, and if you got in a scrape he'd clop the other guy with his billy. So I hired one and got drunk and we went to see a bulldog-badger fight, which is the most vicious thing you can imagine. I kept on drinking and finally told the cop to beat it, that I knew the way back to the hotel in El Paso, across the river. Or I thought I did, because I got lost and had an argument over a tab and the next thing I was in jail. What a place, Mister! A big room with bars all the way around and bars for a ceiling and a floor like a cesspool, and full of the worst cutthroats you ever saw. I was there three days on bread and water before Berger found me and paid ten dollars to get me out." Russell's voice trailed off. He squinted at the bottle, which was empty, and stood up. "I need some lunch."

The light outside was blinding, and Russell headed west on King Street, turned up Varick Street and into West Houston. He pointed at a small restaurant with a pine-panelled front, called the Lodge. "Mary and I eat here some-times evenings. The food's all right." He found a table in the back room, which was decorated with more panelling and a small pair of antlers. A waiter came up. "Where you been, Pee Wee? You look fifteen years younger." Russell mumbled a denial and something about his birthday and Pittsburgh and ordered a Scotch-on-the-rocks and ravioli. He sipped his drink for a while in silence, studying the tablecloth. Then he looked up and said, "For ten years I couldn't eat *any*thing. All during the forties. I'd be hungry and take a couple of bites of delicious steak, say, and have to put the fork down—finished. My food wouldn't go from my upper stomach to my lower stomach. I lived on brandy milkshakes and scrambled-egg sandwiches. And on whiskey. The doctors couldn't find a thing. No tumors, no ulcers. I got as thin as a lamppost and so weak I had to drink half a pint of whiskey in the morning before I could get out of bed. It began to affect my mind, and sometime in 1948 I left Mary and went to Chicago. Everything there is a blank, except what people have told me since. They say I did things that were unheard of, they were so wild. Early in 1950, I went on to San Francisco. By this time my stomach was bloated and I was so feeble I remember someone pushing me up Bush Street and me stopping to put my arms around each telegraph pole to rest. I guess I was dying. Some friends finally got me into the Franklin Hospital and they discovered I had pancreatitis and multiple cysts on my liver. The pancreatitis was why I couldn't eat for so many years. They operated, and I was in that hospital nine months. People gave benefits around the country to pay the bills. I was still crazy. I told them Mary was after me for money. Hell, she was back in New York, minding her own business. When they sent me back here, they put me in St. Clare's Hospital under an assumed name—McGrath, I think it was—so Mary couldn't find me. After they let me out, I stayed with Eddie Condon. Mary heard where I was and came over and we went out and sat in Washington Square park. Then she took me home. After three years."

Russell picked up a spoon and twiddled the ends of his long, beautifully tapered fingers on it, as if it were a clarinet. "You take each solo like it was the last one you were going to play in your life. What notes to hit, and when to hit them—that's the secret. You can *make* a particular phrase with just one note. Maybe at the end, maybe at the beginning. It's like a little pattern. What will lead in quietly and not be too emphatic. Sometimes I jump the right chord and use what seems wrong to the next guy but I *know* is right for me. I usually think about four bars ahead what I am going to play. Sometimes things go wrong, and I have to scramble. If I can make it to the bridge of the tune, I know everything will be all right. I suppose it's not that obnoxious the average musician would notice. When I play the blues, mood, frame of mind, enters into it. One day your choice of notes would be melancholy, a blue trend, a drift of blue notes. The next day your choice of notes would be more cheerful. Standard tunes are different. Some of them require a legato treatment, and others have sparks of rhythm you have to bring out. In lots of cases, your solo depends on who you're following. The guy played a great chorus, you say to yourself. How am I going to follow *that?* I applaud him inwardly, and it becomes a matter of silent pride. Not jealousy, mind you. A kind of competition. So I make myself a guinea pig—what the hell, I'll try something new. All this goes through your mind in a split second. You start and if it sounds good to you you keep it up and write a little tune of your own. I get in bad habits and I'm trying to break myself of a couple right now. A little triplet thing, for one. Fast tempos are good to display your technique, but that's all. You prove you know the chords, but you don't have the time to insert those new little chords you could at slower tempos. Or if you do, they go unnoticed. I haven't been able to play the way I want to until recently. Coming out of that illness has given me courage, a little moral courage in my playing. When I was sick, I lived night by night. It was bang! straight ahead with the whiskey. As a result, my playing was a series of desperations. Now I have a freedom. For the past five or so months, Marshall Brown, the trombonist, and I have been rehearsing a quartet in his studio—just Brown, on the bass cornet, which is like a valve trombone; me, a bass, and drums. We get together a couple of days a week and we *work*. I didn't realize what we had until I listened to the tapes we've made. We sound like seven or eight men. Something's always going. There's a lot of bottom in the group. And we can do anything we want—soft, crescendo, decrescendo, textures, voicings. What musical knowledge we have, we use it. A little while ago, an a. & r.

man from one of the New York jazz labels approached me and suggested a record date—on his terms. Instead, I took him to Brown's studio to hear the tapes. He was cool at first, but by the third number he looked different. I scared him with a stiff price, so we'll see what happens. A record with the quartet would feel just right. And no 'Muskrat Ramble' and no 'Royal Garden Blues.' "

Outside the Lodge, the sunlight seemed to accelerate Russell, and he got back to King Street quickly. He unlocked the door, and Winkie barked. "Cut that out, Winkie!" Russell shouted. "Mary'll be here soon and take you out." He removed his jacket, folded it carefully on one of the day beds, and sat down in the red chair with a grunt.

"I wish Mary was here. She knows more about me than I'll ever know. Well, after Juarez I went with Berger to the Coast and back to St. Louis, where I made my first record, in 1923 or 1924. 'Fuzzy Wuzzy Bird,' by Herbert Berger and his Coronado Hotel Orchestra. The bad notes in the reed passages are me. I also worked on the big riverboats— the J. S., the St. Paul—during the day and then stayed at night to listen to the good bands, the Negro bands like Fate Marable's and Charlie Creath's. Then Sonny Lee, the trombonist, asked me did I want to go to Houston and play in Peck Kelley's group. Peck Kelley's Bad Boys. At this time, spats and a derby were the vogue, and that's what I was wearing when I got there. Kelley looked at me in the station and didn't say a word. We got in a cab and I could feel him still looking at me, so I rolled down the window and threw the derby out. Kelley laughed and thanked me. He took me straight to Goggan's music store and sat down at a piano and started to play. He was marvellous, a kind of stride pianist, and I got panicky. About ten minutes later, a guy walked in, took a trombone off the wall, and started to play. It was Jack Teagarden. I went over to Peck when they finished and said, 'Peck, I'm in over my head. Let me work a week and make my fare home.' But I got over it and I was with Kelley several months." Russell went into the kitchen to get another bottle of ale. "Not long after I got back to St.

Louis, Sonny Lee brought Bix Beiderbecke around to my house, and bang! we hit it right off. We were never apart for a couple of years—day, night, good, bad, sick, well, broke, drunk. Then Bix left to join Jean Goldkette's band and Red Nichols sent for me to come to New York. That was 1927. I went straight to the old Manger Hotel and found a note in my box: Come to a speakeasy under the Roseland Ballroom. I went over and there was Red Nichols and Eddie Lang and Miff Mole and Vic Berton. I got panicky again. They told me there'd be a recording date at Brunswick the next morning at nine, and don't be late. I got there at eight-fifteen. The place was empty, except for a handyman. Mole arrived first. He said, 'You look peaked, kid,' and opened his trombone case and took out a quart. Everybody had quarts. We made 'Ida,' and it wasn't any trouble at all. In the late twenties and early thirties I worked in a lot of bands and made God knows how many records in New York. Cass Hagen, Bert Lown, Paul Specht, Ray Levy, the Scranton Sirens, Red Nichols. We lived uptown at night. We heard Elmer Snowden and Luis Russell and Ellington. Once I went to a ballroom where Fletcher Henderson was. Coleman Hawkins had a bad cold and I sat in for him one set. My God, those scores! They were written in six flats, eight flats, I don't know how many flats. I never saw anything like it. Buster Bailey was in the section next to me, and after a couple of numbers I told him, 'Man, I came up here to have a good time, not to work. I've had enough. Where's Hawkins?'

"I joined Louis Prima around 1935. We were at the Famous Door, on Fifty-second Street, and a couple of hoodlums loaded with knives cornered Prima and me and said they wanted protection money every week—fifty bucks from Prima and twenty-five from me. Well, I didn't want any of that. I'd played a couple of private parties for Lucky Luciano, so I called him. He sent Pretty Amberg over in a big car with a bodyguard as chauffeur. Prima sat in the back with Amberg and I sat in front with the bodyguard. Nobody said much, just 'Hello' and 'Goodbye,' and for a week they drove Prima and me from our hotels to a midday radio broadcast, back to our hotels, picked us up for work at night, and took us home after. We never saw the protection-money boys again. Red McKenzie, the singer, got me into Nick's in 1938, and I worked there and at Condon's place for most of the next ten years. I have a sorrow about that time. Those guys made a joke of me, a clown, and I let myself be treated that way because I was afraid. I didn't know where else to go, where to take refuge. I'm not sure how all of us feel about each other now, though we're 'Hello, Pee Wee,' 'Hello, Eddie,' and all that. Since my sickness, Mary's given me confidence, and so has George Wein. I've worked for him with a lot of fast musicians in Boston, in New York, at Newport, on the road, and in Europe last year. I'll head a kind of house band if he opens a club here. A quiet little group. But Nick's did one thing. That's where I first met Mary."

At that moment, a key turned in the lock, and Mary Russell walked quickly down the hall and into the living room. A trim, pretty, black-haired woman in her forties, she was wearing a green silk dress and black harlequin glasses.

"How's Winkie been?" she asked Russell, plumping herself down and taking off her shoes. "She's the kind of dog that's always barking except at burglars. Pee Wee, you forgot to say, Did you have a hard day at the office, dear? And where's my tea?"

Russell got up and shuffled into the kitchen.

"I work in the statistics and advertising part of Robert Hall clothes," she said. "I've got a quick mind for figures. I like the job and the place. It's full of respectable ladies. Pee Wee, did I get any mail?"

"Next to you, on the table. A letter," he said from the kitchen.

"It's from my brother Al," she said. "I always look for check in letters. My God, there *is* a check! Now why do you suppose he did that? And there's a P.S.: Please excuse the pencil. I like that. It makes me feel good."

"How much did he send you?" Russell asked, handing Mrs. Russell her tea.

"You're not going to get a cent," she said. "You know what I found the other day, Pee Wee? Old letters from you. Love letters. Every one says the same thing: I love you, I miss you. Just the dates are different." Mary Russell, who spoke in a quick, decisive way, laughed. "Pee Wee and I had an awful wedding. It was at City Hall. Danny Alvin, the drummer, stood up for us. He and Pee Wee wept. I didn't, but *they* did. After the ceremony, Danny tried to borrow money from me. Pee Wee didn't buy me any flowers and a friend lent us the wedding ring. Pee Wee has never given me a wedding ring. The one I'm wearing a nephew gave me a year ago. Just to make it proper, he said. That's not the way a woman wants to get married. Pee Wee, we ought to do it all over again. I have a rage in me to be proper. I don't play bridge and go to beauty parlors and I don't have women friends like other women. But one thing Pee Wee and I have that no one else has: we never stop talking when we're with each other. Pee Wee, you know why I love you? You're like Papa. Every time Mama got up to tidy something, he'd say, Clara, sit down, and she would. That's what you do. I loved my parents. They were Russian Jews from Odessa. Chaloff was their name. I was born on the lower East Side. I was a charity case and the doctor gave me my name, and signed the birth certificate—Dr. E. Condon. Isn't that weird? I was one of nine kids and six are left. I've got twenty nephews and nieces." Mary Russell paused and sipped her tea. Then she was off again.

"Pee Wee worships those inchbrows. Lucky Luciano was his dream man."

"He was an acquaintance," Russell snorted.

"I'll never know you completely, Pee Wee," Mrs. Russell said. She took another sip of tea, holding the cup with both hands. "Sometimes Pee Wee can't sleep. He sits in the kitchen and plays solitaire, and I go to bed in here and sing to him. Awful songs like 'Belgian Rose' and 'Carolina Mammy.' I have a terrible voice."

"Oh, God!" Russell muttered. "The worst thing is she knows *all* the lyrics."

"I not only sing, I write," she said, laughing. "I wrote a three-act play. My hero's name is Tiny Ballard. An Italian clarinet player. It has wonderful dialogue."

"Mary's no saloon girl, coming where I work," he said. "She outgrew that long ago. She reads about ten books a week. You could have been a writer, Mary."

"I don't know why I wrote about a clarinet player. I hate the clarinet. Pee Wee's playing embarrasses me. But I like trombones: Miff Mole and Brad Gowans. And I like Duke Ellington. Last New Year's Eve, Pee Wee and I were at a party and Duke kissed me at midnight."

"Where was I?" he asked.

"You had a clarinet stuck in your mouth," she said. "The story of your life, or part of your life. Once when Pee Wee had left me and was in Chicago, he came back to New York for a couple of days. He denies it. He doesn't remember it. He went to the night club where I was working as a hat-check girl and asked to see me. I said no. The boss's wife went out and took one look at him and came back and said, 'At least go out and talk to him. He's pathetic. Even his feet look sad.' "

Russell made an apologetic face. "That was twelve years ago, Mary. I have no claim to being an angel."

She sat up very straight. "Pee Wee, this room is hot. Let's go out and have dinner on my brother Al."

"I'll put on a tie," he said.

BACK FROM VALHALLA

six

Even during its most celebrated phase, between the years 1935 and 1945, the career of Jess Stacy had a suspended quality. It seemed recollected while it was happening. One reason was that Stacy spent most of these years as a big-band pianist with Benny Goodman and Bob Crosby and Horace Heidt, and his main job was to supply an endless flow of accompanying chords and fill-ins behind the sections and the soloists. (Stacy was cast even farther into the shadows of the Goodman band by the presence of a second and equally superb pianist, Teddy Wilson, who became the hero of the Goodman trios and quartets.) Another reason for Stacy's shadowiness had to do with his style. He *was* often audible within a band, but his marvellous background countermelodies had a way of—to use his word—"melting" into the whole. And the rare solos he was given didn't free him of the scrim he seemed trapped behind, for they had an elusive, hurrying quality. The sparkling bell chords drifted away like smoke, the quiet, flashing runs disappeared almost before they registered, and the silken tone verged on transparency. But in spite of himself, Stacy did take a famous solo. It came about accidentally, during Goodman's bellwether 1938 Carnegie Hall concert. The band was nearing the closing ensemble of its elephantine showpiece, "Sing, Sing, Sing," when, after a Goodman-Gene Krupa duet, there was a treading-water pause, and an astonished Stacy, suddenly given the nod by Goodman, took off. The solo lasted over two minutes, which was remarkable at a time when most solos were measured in seconds. One wonders how many people understood what they were hearing that night, for no one had ever played a piano solo like it. From the opening measures, it had an exalted, almost ecstatic quality, as if it were playing Stacy. It didn't, with its Debussy glints and ghosts, seem of its time and place. It was also revolutionary in that it was more of a cadenza than a series of improvised choruses. There were no divisions or seams, and it had a spiralling structure, an organic structure, in which each phrase evolved from its predecessor. Seesawing middle-register chords gave way to double-time runs, which gave way to dreaming rests, which gave way to singsong chords, which gave way to oblique runs. A climax would be reached only to recede before a still stronger one. Piling grace upon grace, the solo moved gradually but inexorably up the keyboard, at last ending in a superbly restrained cluster of tintinnabulous upper-register single notes. There was an instant of stunned silence before Krupa came thundering back, and those who realized that they had just heard something magnificent believed that what they had heard was already in that Valhalla where all great unrecorded jazz solos go. Stacy, it seemed, had pulled off his finest vanishing act. But Goodman has always worked in mysterious ways. Twelve years later, long after Stacy had left the scene to settle in California and piece out a living as a soloist in desolate piano bars, and long after his triumph at Carnegie Hall had come to seem a twist of the imagination, Goodman announced that his sister-in-law Rachel had discovered some old records in a closet of his recently vacated New York apartment. They were recordings of the 1938 concert. The concert, it turned out, had been relayed to a recording studio on West Forty-sixth Street. The recording was made at the behest of a well-to-do entrepreneur named Albert Marks, who presented one of the two copies to his wife, Helen Ward, a Goodman vocalist, and the other to Goodman, who put the records in the closet and forgot them. A two-L.P. set was released by Columbia, and hundreds of thousands of copies were sold. The records reveal that memory does not always exaggerate; Stacy's solo is even more remarkable now.

A man of consummate modesty, Stacy was evasive and belittling when he was asked about the solo. The night before, he had ended a fourteen-year retirement by playing in Carnegie Hall at the Newport Jazz Festival-New York, and now he was in a cab headed for the studios of Chiaroscuro Records, on Christopher Street, where he was to record his first solo album in fifteen years. He appeared as relaxed as he had the previous night, when, entering the hall for the first time since the Goodman concert, he sat down without ado, reeled off three near-perfect ballads, and received a roaring ovation. "Well, that 1938 solo was a funny thing," he said, in his soft Southern voice. "Benny generally hogged the solo space, and why he let me go on that way I still don't know. But I've thought about it, and there are two things that might explain it. I think he liked what I'd been doing behind him during his solo, and I think he was mad at Teddy Wilson and Gene Krupa and Lionel Hampton, because they had all told him they were leaving to form their own bands. When I started to play, I figured, Good Lord, what with all the circus-band trumpet playing we've heard tonight and all the Krupa banging, I might as well change the mood and come on real quiet. So I took the A-minor chord 'Sing, Sing, Sing' is built around and turned it this way and that. I'd been listening to Edward MacDowell and Debussy, and I think some of their things got in there, too. I didn't know what else to do, and I guess it worked out pretty well. It ended up, of course, that I left Goodman myself later that year in San Francisco and went with the Bob Crosby band.

"Benny wasn't easy to work for. He had this way of looking right at you and not seeing you. Once, at the Congress Hotel, in Chicago, I was fooling around with a little blues before a set started, and he came over and stood next to me and listened awhile, and then said, '*That's* the blues?' I hadn't been with him very long, and I was crushed. I joined him in 1935, just before the band hit it big. I was working in a group in Chicago led by Maury Stein, Jule Styne's brother, and I got a call one night from New York from somebody who said he was Benny Goodman. I thought it was a put-on, but it *was* Benny. He told me that John Hammond had heard me in a joint called the Subway Café and had recommended me and that he wanted to hire me. He said the band was about to leave for the West Coast and that he'd pay me sixty-five dollars a week." Stacy's eyes twinkled and he laughed. "And, you know, I worked him all the way up to a hundred and seventy before I left! Well, I was nothing in that band at first. I felt like a little outcast sitting there with people like Goodman and Gene Krupa and Bunny Berigan. But Benny had the Fletcher Henderson book, and I loved to listen to those arrangements. It's history that the band laid an egg all the way across the country. We played some tacky ballroom in Michigan and thirty people—most of them musicians—turned up, and when we did the Elitch Gardens, in Denver, everybody was across town listening to Kay Kyser. Goodman couldn't see very well at night, so I'd drive him home after work, and he began saying he was going to quit this nonsense and go back into radio in New York. I said, 'Benny, get over the mountains first and see what happens.' I didn't tell him 'I told you so,' but when we got to Sweet's Ballroom, in Oakland, they were standing in lines a block long, and when we got down to the Palomar Ballroom, in Los Angeles, everybody went crazy. And on our way back it was that way in Chicago, at the Congress Hotel, and in New York, at the Pennsylvania Hotel and the Paramount Theatre. The big star after Benny, of course, was Krupa. I mean, you can't ask all drummers to keep good time, but he was our salesman, our showman, and he worked hard. You could wring water right out of his sleeves when he finished a set."

Hank O'Neal, the owner of Chiaroscuro Records, greeted Stacy at the studio and asked him if he'd like a drink. "No, thanks," he said, "but I'll take a Coke. I don't know what it is, but when I take liquor these days it goes right to my fingertips. So I try and stay away from it, just like cigarettes, which I gave up in 1951. I guess I just got tired of burning holes in pianos and dropping ashes all over myself. Let me just sample that piano." Stacy took off his jacket, which was royal blue, and hung it on the back of a chair. The rest of his ensemble lit up the studio—bright-red pants, a red-and-white checked shirt, and blue sneakers. He has taken on a front porch, but he looks much the way he did when he was a fixture around New York in the mid-forties. His handsome, aquiline Irish face is compact and smooth, and his hair is still dark and combed flat. His ready smile is shy and pursed, and his eyebrows, which shoot up a lot, are imperious. Stacy sat down, worked his way through several choruses of the blues, and got up. He played twin arpeggios in the air with his fingers, then kneaded each hand. "That piano's loose as a goose. I like 'em to fight back a little. And the upper registers sound a little flat. But I don't suppose it matters. I've got the check Hank O'Neal sent me for the session right in my pocket, and if the session don't work out I'll just hand it right back to him." O'Neal reappeared, with Stacy's Coca-Cola, and told him a tuner was overdue and to make himself comfortable meanwhile. Just then the tuner walked into the studio, nodded at O'Neal, and went to work on the piano.

Stacy sat down on a sofa and sipped his Coke. "I surprised myself last night, because I wasn't a bit nervous when I went on that stage. The only problem was the air-conditioning backstage: it turned your hands to ice. Teddy Wilson was back there, and we talked about the Goodman concert—how it was so crowded in the hall they'd seated people right on the stage, making it so your arms were practically pinned to your sides when you played. Last night was easy compared to what I had to do to get ready for it. It was like training for a fight. I'd let myself go something terrible when Marie St. Louis, from the Newport Festival office, called to ask if I'd like to come East and play in the Festival. Fact, when I got to the phone from out in the back yard, where I was watering, I was puffing like a buffalo. I was really out of kilter. But I told her yes, I'd do it, because I figured it might be my last picture show. Then, after I'd signed the contract, I got so nervous I started throwing up. I'm a natural worrier, and I began asking my wife, Pat, What if no one comes to the concert? And I told her if they didn't to please clap long enough so that I could get seated at the piano. The only playing I'd done since I quit, in 1960, was some Bach preludes, which I struggled through. So I started practicing, doing double thirds and double sixths and scales and octaves. Right away, to my chagrin, I found my back was weak, and I couldn't sit at the keyboard more than twenty minutes at a time. I began doing sit-ups, going for two at first and finally getting up to thirty. And Pat and I took four- and five-mile walks every day, and I went on a diet. Pretty soon I was practicing three and four hours a day, and it all began to come back to me.

"I hadn't been sorry at all to leave the music business. After the Bob Crosby band broke up, in 1942, I rejoined Goodman, at the New Yorker Hotel, and stayed with him about a year. It really makes me laugh now, because he fired Jimmy *Rowles* to hire me. After that came a low point in my life. I joined Horace Heidt when Frankie Carle left him to form his own band. He paid me three hundred a week and tried to make a showman out of me, which was ridiculous. I married Lee Wiley in 1943, and that lasted two and a half years. She had million-dollar tastes and I didn't have any money. She got me to form a big band and she wanted equal billing, and it was a disaster, what with the bum wartime bookings and so many good musicians being in the service. So in the late forties I went to California to live and started playing in piano bars. It was all new to me. I'd always been a band pianist, and I hardly knew any tunes. I did have five or six years that were all right. The people in the bars would ask for 'On Moonlight Bay' or 'Clair de Lune,' which I always thought of as 'Clear the Room.' But they'd pretty much leave me alone, and sometimes they'd even clap or some guy would lay a tip on me. But around 1955 TV began keeping the nicer people home, and I came to feel those piano bars were snake pits. I had to walk around the block six or seven times every night to get up enough courage to go in. While I was playing, somebody would put a nickel in the jukebox or some fellow would ask me if I'd play real quiet so he could watch the fights on the bar TV. Or else they'd all get drunk and sing along. My last job was in a snake pit in La Crescenta on Friday and Saturday nights, and I stayed friendly as long as I could, but it was so bad I finally got the message and jumped ship. I took a job in the mail room at Max Factor. It was a lowly job, and I guess you'd call it beneath my station. I walked ten miles a day delivering mail, but at least I enjoyed the first vacations with pay I'd ever had. I worked there six years, and when I hit sixty-five they retired me."

The piano ready, Stacy warmed up with "How Long Has This Been Going On," and then made an excellent take of it. His style has long been said to be a direct offshoot of Earl Hines', but the resemblances—the little tremolo-vibratos at the end of key phrases, the easy tenth chords in the left hand, and the busy, packed right-hand chords—are more than balanced by Stacy's originality. His playing muses. Each number has a quiet, firm inner voice that never varies, no matter what the tempo. It suggests many things: a maiden aunt summoning up her childhood, moonlight blowing through green trees, a lemon slice sliding over hot tea. But this lyrical Stacy is deceptive, for every now and then—in a singing, two-handed tremolo, in a deftly placed blue note, in a complex, intense run—a deep keening suddenly appears. Then cheerful octave chords and short arpeggios brightly surface, and the solo sails quickly back into the sunlight. Stacy allowed his melancholy strain to appear briefly in two long, ruminative takes of "Gee, Baby Ain't I Good to You" and in an otherwise sturdy, straightforward "Lover Man." Then he shook his fingers out and declared he needed a rest. He sat down on the sofa and took a sip of Coke.

"When I play, it's mostly coming off the top of my head. Nothing is contrived or ahead of time. I don't know what I'm doing and I can't explain it to anybody. But I wish I could, because I'd give it to them for nothing. It's a kind of cybernetics. I can hear what I'm going to do a couple of bars ahead, and when I get near the end of those bars a couple more open up. I often think of my playing as a crap game— sometimes I get real lucky. I can't remember lyrics, but I think of the melody all the time and execute around it. Maybe the guy who wrote the tune would hate me for say- ing it, but in my mind I think I'm improving the melody. I don't look for every note to be a pearl. Sometimes they turn out to be meatballs. Which was mostly what I played until I finally made it to Chicago, in 1925. I'd been born an only child in nineteen-and-four in Bird Point, a train layover in southeast Missouri, where we lived in a boxcar. It was right on the Mississippi—was, because it's since been washed away. My dad, Fred Stacy, was from De Soto, Illinois, which is close to Little Egypt. He was a railroad engineer. He took the first high-speed express train from Centralia, Illinois, to New Orleans, in 1898. It had a speedometer in the observation car, and I believe it registered as high as eighty-five miles an hour. Five years before that, when he was carrying gold from Centralia to the Chicago World's Fair, his train was robbed. The gold was in the baggage car, right behind the coal tender, and the robbers unhooked the rest of the train and told my dad to drive what was left of it to a crossroads where a truck was waiting. One of the robbers had a pistol trained on my dad, and suddenly, while they were highballing along, my dad turned and cold-cocked him. The robber fell out of the cab and lost both legs. The railroad gave my dad a medal and some shares of stock, which must have been et, because I never saw any of them. When he was in his fifties, his eyesight began to fail, and after he couldn't drive a locomotive anymore he spent most of his time hunting. He had a big heart and was carefree and he never worried, which was the exact opposite of my mother. She was born Vada Alexander, in Union City, Tennessee, and all her folks fought on the Confederate side in the Civil War. My mother was a seamstress, and she supported us when my dad's eyes went bad. We were poor as Job's turkeys. I helped out by being a Western Union boy and sweeping out the town drugstore in the mornings and jerking sodas in the afternoons. If you made fifty cents a day, it was darn good money. By then, we'd moved to Malden—about seventy-five miles from Bird Point.

"Neither of my parents was musical, so the first music I heard was played by an old music teacher, from across the street, who knew things like 'Memphis Blues' and 'In the Blue Ridge Mountains of Virginia.' When I was twelve, my mother took in an orphan girl—actually, her mother had died and her father had run off—named Jeannette McCombs.

She had a piano, which was moved in, and she took lessons. I'd listen to her practicing and then sit down and play what I'd heard by ear. When my mother caught me doing that, she said I should have lessons. The teacher was Florina Morris, and she'd get you in and out pretty fast and give you a piece of pie along the way to keep you from playing too much. In 1918, we moved to Cape Girardeau, Missouri, which is right on the Mississippi. It had a population of about ten thousand souls, and every one of 'em was as square as a bear. But it was where I first heard the music I wanted to play. Word had come from Cairo, about fifty miles downriver, that there was a fantastic band on the Streckfus boat the S.S. Capitol. It was led by Fate Marable, and I heard it when the boat stopped in Cape Girardeau for a moonlight excursion. That band had Louis Armstrong and Johnny Dodds and Baby Dodds, and they played big hits like 'Whispering' as well as the Dixieland numbers. Marable was a tremendous band pianist, and I marvelled at the way he held everything together. I took lessons in Cape Girardeau from Professor Clyde Brandt, and he had me playing Beethoven sonatas and Mozart and Bach partitas, and I think it was then I realized that Bach was the first swing pianist. I'm sorry now I didn't practice more, but all I wanted was to play in a dance band and get the hell out of Cape Girardeau. I'd played at country clubs and at fraternity dances in a school group called the Agony Four, and after I graduated from high school, in June of 1920, I got my first chance. The steamer Majestic stopped in town, and the band on board, which was led by a fiddle player named Berry, needed a piano player, because theirs had drowned up in Alton. I was with that group a month and a half, and then I joined Tony Catalano on the Capitol. He was a New Orleans trumpet player, and we had to play a lot of Dixieland or else they would have pulled the boat over in the bulrushes and thrown us off. We travelled from Paducah, Kentucky, to Red Wing, Minnesota, and part of my job was to play the calliope, for which I got five dollars extra a week. It was up on the top deck, and it had one hundred and fifty pounds of steam pressure and a piano keyboard of two octaves. The keys were made of copper, and you had to practically stand on 'em to make 'em move. They got so hot I had to keep my fingers taped, and I had to wear a raincoat and a hat, so that the steam and cinders didn't make me unpresentable when I went back downstairs to join the band. I'd play the calliope to announce all-day excursions or moonlight excursions. It could be heard thirty miles away, and we called it the Whooper.

"When we got to Davenport, Iowa, Bix Beiderbecke came aboard and sat in with Catalano. He'd already made his first records, with the Wolverines, and so we knew who he was. But the first thing he did was sit down at the piano and play 'Baby Blue Eyes' and 'Clarinet Marmalade,' and I couldn't believe it. He played what I'd been hearing in my head but couldn't do yet. When he took up his cornet, there was no effort; his cheeks never even puffed out. And his fingering was just as unorthodox as it was on the piano. He was a shy person, and I genuinely believe he didn't know how good he was. I was a jitterbug over Bix. Later, in Chicago, I'd see him walk into the Sunset Café when Louis was playing there, and Louis would turn almost white. But I think they were scared of each other. I left Catalano in Davenport, in August of 1924, and joined Joe Kayser, who had a territory band. In those days, every town of three hundred people had its own dance hall, so we played all over Wisconsin and Iowa and Illinois. The band made it to Chicago, and we were at the Arcadia ballroom for six months, and then we had a summer job in Duluth before the band broke up and I found myself back in Chicago, stranded and on my own. It was the beginning of a ten-year scuffle. I worked for every imaginable kind of group. I was with Floyd Town, who had Muggsy Spanier and Frank Teschemacher, and I remember Benny Goodman coming in when he was still a kid and standing behind a pillar to listen to Tesch, who was *the* clarinet player then. I worked for Earl Burtnett, who had fiddles and a harp and needed an Eddy Duchin piano player instead of me. I was in Art Kassel's band, and I worked in the Canton Tea Garden with Louis Panico, who didn't tell me how to play. Most of the time, I was in Chicago, but one summer I played on the Million Dollar Pier, in Atlantic City, with Al Katz and His Kittens. We wore funny hats and all that, and we had a radio wire, and when we went on the air Katz would say, 'Are you ready, kittens?' And we'd shout 'Meow!' and he'd say 'All right. Let's go.' Joe Venuti and Eddie Lang were at the Silver Slipper, and I'd bought all their records in Chicago. In those days, you got in trouble if they found booze on you, but pot was still legal—in fact, it was better for you than most of that rotgut bathtub gin—and when Eddie Lang found I'd brought two Prince Albert tins of it with me he stayed so close it got stuffy.

"I lived on the North Side of Chicago, on Wilson Avenue, which was a bad neighborhood even then. When the Depression hit, people like Eddie Condon and Gene Krupa and Dave Tough went on to New York, but I'd gotten married to my first wife and had a kid, and it was all I could do to keep my family alive where I was. There was no choice but to work for the gangsters. They didn't pay much, but they didn't bother us, either. We'd play forty-five-minute sets, starting at ten and ending at six in the morning. If you played the North Side, you worked for Bugs Moran, and if you worked on the South Side, it was for Al Capone. At one point I told Bud Freeman, who was still in Chicago, that it might be better to get into the delicatessen business or something, but he said all our musician friends would come and eat on the cuff and put the store out of business. The best days in Chicago were the early ones, when Louis Armstrong and Earl Hines were in a band at the Sunset Café led by Carroll Dickerson. I'd go there with people like Muggsy Spanier, and we'd stay until five or six in the morning, even though it would take us hours to get home. I was sitting there one night digging Hines, who had an influence on me, when Jelly Roll Morton, who was making his Hot Pepper records, tapped me on the shoulder and looked over at Hines and said, 'That boy can't play piano.' Cab Calloway used to go around and sing at the tables, and we'd chase him away when he tried to drink our gin."

Stacy sat down at the piano, and within an hour he had made good takes of "Riverboat Shuffle," "Memphis in June," "I Would Do Anything for You," "Doll Face," and a blues for Eddie Condon. He finished the session with two of his own tunes—"Lookout Mountain Squirrels" and "Miss Peck Accepts." The latter is a medium-tempo blues and the former a complex, up-tempo number built around a tricky ascending-descending figure. Stacy made three takes before he felt he had it right. Then he put on his jacket and told O'Neal he would see him the next day for a session with a Bud Freeman trio. He found a cab on Christopher Street and headed uptown to his hotel. "Those last two numbers were inspired by my present wife, who was Miss Peck, and by all the squirrels we have on our little place, which is on Lookout Mountain Avenue, up in the Hollywood Hills. Pat and I married in 1950, even though I'd told her I was just a band pianist and that I had a miserable past. I couldn't ask for a better wife. She was a botany major, and she's eighteen years younger than I am. When we got married, we bought the five-room house we have now. We own it, and the taxes are less than seven hundred a year. It's eleven hundred feet above sea level, and it's on a lot that's a hundred and twenty-five feet deep. We have seven holly bushes, one plum tree, two peach trees, two apricots, and three apples. And we have grapefruit and lemons and limes. When we get up there, it's quiet, it's like the wilderness, even though you're only five minutes from Sunset Boulevard. There are deer running around, and all those squirrels the song is about, and sometimes you can hear the gophers munching on the irises in the front yard. And coyotes bay at night. There's a big forest right behind us, and because of the fire danger I keep it very wet back there. My job is to water and cut the grass and do the weeding, and I also do the housework and the vacuuming, since Pat has a part-time job in a small business-management company. We're stay-at-homes and lazy, and we've learned to live on practically nothing. I may even give lessons on how to do it."

Stacy appeared once more during the Festival, in an Eddie Condon memorial concert, and right after that he flew back to the Coast. A month later, a letter arrived: "A few evenings ago, Pat and I took a walk a way up the mountain, and all of a sudden this big police dog appeared and bit me in the rear—right through my pants and all. Well, I'm scared of dogs anyway, and I began worrying about rabies and such. I had a tetanus shot and we found out that the dog was O.K. But I think that that dog was trying to tell me something, trying to say, 'You may be a big shot when you're in New York, making records and playing in Carnegie Hall, and all that, but around here you're nothing.' "

THE MUSIC IS MORE IMPORTANT

"Please don't call it a vibraphone," Red Norvo said. "I play the vibra*harp*, a name coined by the Deagan Company, which invented the instrument in 1927 and still supplies me with mine. Of course, I started on the xylophone and marimba in the mid-twenties, and up until then they were vaudeville instruments, clown instruments. They differ from one another chiefly in range, like tenor and alto saxophones. The xylophone is higher than the marimba, but both have piano-like keyboards, with three registers. The bars, or what would be the keys of a piano, are made of rosewood. The vibraharp has the same keyboard, but it is lower in range than the marimba. It's an electronic instrument, and its bars are made of aluminum. It's electronic because the resonator tubes that hang down underneath the bars, like an upside-down organ, have little paddle-shaped fans in them called pulsators that are driven by a small electric motor. When they're in motion, they enable the performer to get that rolling, mushing-out vibrato you hear from most vibes players. Vibraharps also have loud, or damper, pedals, similar to the piano's, which lift the bars off felt pads, and when you use the damper pedal *and* the pulsators you get that *uh-uh-uh-uh-uh* sound. On the vibraharp—pardon my saying it—you can cheat by using the pulsators and the damper pedal. It's been done and is done. I've never used a motor, but what I do have now is an amplifier, which Jack Deagan designed for me six years ago. It helps acoustically in bad rooms. Before, if you had just one microphone and you set it near the center of the keyboard, the upper and lower registers would be cold. Deagan put little crystal mikes in each resonator tube, but at first I couldn't get even amplification, and once when I flew into Las Vegas for a gig they left the instrument out in hundred-and-twenty-degree heat at the airport and all the mikes melted. The mallets you use affect the sound of the instrument. I have hard-rubber ones for the xylophone, and on the marimba rubber ones with a twine cover, which I use on vibraharp, too. Dixie Rollini, Adrian's widow, still wraps them for me. She doesn't do it for anyone else now. It's a nice gesture and I appreciate it. I also use slap mallets, which I invented in 1928. They're rectangular and flattish and the size of a big kitchen spoon, and they're made of cork covered with felt and buckskin, and they cause a dead, tramping effect. The vibraharp is a peculiar instrument because it tends to take on the characteristics of the people who play it. Sometimes the instrument becomes the personality. And it's peculiar because vibraharpists are a pretty warm fraternity. Guitarists are also like that. Certain people choose certain instruments, and vibraharpists in general are gentle, quiet people. Trumpet players and drummers, on the other hand, can be pretty argumentative. But the main thing is to play the *right* instrument. So many musicians go through their lives on the wrong instrument. You hear guitarists who should be tenor players and pianists who should be trumpeters and drummers who should maybe be out of music altogether."

Norvo was sitting in his living room in Santa Monica. The room is big and blue and white, with a fireplace at one end and a Pennsylvania Dutch dining table, surrounded by Windsor chairs, at the other. A sofa and several more chairs, one of them a handsome eighteenth-century corner chair, ring the fireplace, and over the mantel is a forthright painting of Norvo playing his vibraharp. An apothecary's chest is against one wall, and near it, in a bay window, stands a beautiful marimba. The dining area is weighed down by a pine cupboard filled with Staffordshire china and a Shaker dry sink filled with spongeware. Opposite the marimba, a pair of open glass doors lead out into a small patio. It was a stunning smogless, ninety-degree southern-California day, and the sun itself seemed to be in the room.

Norvo poured himself a cup of coffee from a small espresso pot. "Ralph Watkins, who used to run the Embers in New York, gave me this pot. You can't buy them here, or at least I've never been able to find one. You have to go to New York or San Francisco, and it's the same with the coffee. I used to drink it straight all day, but now I water it down some." He jumped up and opened a couple of windows behind the marimba. "It's hot in here, and I don't see why I have to keep all the windows shut. This is Santa-Ana-wind weather. The wind blows straight from the desert and across the mountains to the ocean. I was up early last Sunday and we went up to the Angeles National Forest to do a little varmint hunting. There were a lot of deer hunters down in the gullies and we were up on the high rocks, and so were the deer. We could see the brush fires starting and the wind was blowing like hell. It's usually very cold up there, but when we got out of the car it was *hot*, in the nineties. It was a shock. I hunt every chance I get. In Vegas you can practically lean out and touch the mountains from downtown, which makes hunting there a cinch."

In profile, Norvo, who is medium-sized, is S-shaped. He holds his head forward and his shoulders are bent from more than forty years of stooping over his instruments. He has a comfortable front porch and his legs bow out behind, like a retired hurdler's. Head on, he suggests a mischievous Scottish saint. His blue eyes laugh, and they are set off by V-shaped laugh lines. His nose is generous but subtly beaked, and he has a beard. The beard is orange-red, and so is his receding hair, which is long and thick in back. When he laughs, his eyes nearly close, and his teeth, in the surrounding foliage, shine like the sun in a fall maple. His voice is even and rich, and it anchors him. He was dressed in a green-and-white checked sports shirt—worn outside of olive pants—and leather sandals.

A short, pretty woman with dark hair in a feather cut and a Rubens figure came into the room. It was Norvo's wife, Eve. She was dressed in a nurse's white uniform, with white stockings and shoes, and she had a wide, dimpled smile and serene eyes. She stood in front of Norvo with her hands crossed and said, "Can I get you some more coffee?" He said no. "Where are you playing tonight, Red?"

Norvo consulted a pad. "In a motel in Huntington Beach called the Sheraton Beach Inn. We start around nine and I don't know where it is, so I better leave at seven. That'll give me time for getting lost and setting up."

Norvo waited until she had left; then he got up and waved his arms around and laughed. "Eve took the job she has at St. John's Hospital, which is near here, a couple of years ago, when I was playing a long gig in Las Vegas. I was home one weekend and she said she was getting tired of sitting around, so I said, 'Go out and get a gig.' Well, she did, but when the job in Vegas was over I told her she might as well quit. 'Quit? What do you mean, quit?' She got real insulted. When she got her first paycheck she came home real cool and laid twenty dollars on me, she was that proud. I laughed and told her, 'Some big spender.'

"Eve and I were married in 1946, a year before we moved out here from New York. She's always called me Red, but my first wife, Mildred Bailey, called me Kenneth, and so did John Hammond and my mother. They were the only people who always called me Kenneth. Norvo isn't my real name. I was born Kenneth Norville, in Beardstown, Illinois, in three thirty-one oh-eight. My daughter, Portia, who lives with us, is twenty-two, and she even has a little towhead kid. I got the name Norvo from Paul Ash, in vaudeville. He could never remember my name when he announced me. It would come out Norvin or Norvox or Norvick, and one night it was Norvo. *Variety* picked it up and it stuck, so I kept it. Norville is Scottish, and my family came from around Roseville, which is a little town near Galesburg. I had two brothers and a sister—Howard, Glen, and Portia. They're all gone. My father was a railroader, a dispatcher for the C. B. & Q.—the Chicago, Burlington & Quincy. He worked for the railroad all his life, and we moved around a lot before I arrived. I believe Portia was born in Hillsdale and Howard in Macomb and Glen in East Alton. My mother was eighty when she died out here, and we buried her in Roseville. My father was tall and dark and bald. He was stern but quiet-tempered. He liked to say things like 'It takes you all your life to learn to live, and when you have, you don't have time left to live.' He didn't drink, but he'd smoke a cigar and he was religious. He died a thirty-second-degree Mason. He built the new Masonic Temple in Beardstown and they gave him the door knocker from the old one. I still have it around the house. He played piano—you know, mainly chords—and he'd sing in a big voice. He died before

I was twenty. My mother was blond, always very thin and very proud. And she was astute about people—she never missed. Her name was Estelle, and we all called her Stell. She was always very strong on getting us out of small-town life. Of my parents, she had the edge where humor was concerned. Beardstown had a population of about seven thousand, and we lived on the edge of town. My brother Glen had a pony, Prince, and when he went away to college he kind of passed it down to me, but I never felt it was mine, so once when he was home on vacation I said, 'You should *give* me that pony. I don't feel it's mine.' 'All right,' he said. 'Jump off this porch and onto that pony and open up and get around the block in a minute flat and I'll give it to you.' My mother was in the back of the house, and she looked out the window and saw me streaking by and she came running out and yelled, 'The pony's running away with Kenneth, the pony's running away with Kenneth,' and when I came tearing around the corner of the house she could see—she'd known horses all her life—that I was in control, and we all laughed. I used to go into town on Prince to get groceries, and they'd load me up with a bag under each arm and I'd ride home using just my knees. Prince would stop right by the front door when I had groceries, but if I didn't have any he'd lickety-split it right into his stall and I'd grab an iron bar over the door and let him go and drop to the ground. Every Saturday we rode out into the country, and in the fall I got up real early and went up in the hills to get walnuts and pecans. We were on the Illinois River, and I got to know all the riverboats. The Capitol tied up at Beardstown around six o'clock in the warm weather and everyone piled on and she cruised until eleven. She always had a dance band, and one whole floor, one whole deck, would be a ballroom. There were all-day excursions that started at eight in the morning. Some stores gave out tickets like supermarkets give out trading stamps and the boat would go to a picnic ground and come back around six. Showboats came, too, twice a summer. They were like floating theatres, and they gave all the old clichés—'The Drunkard' or a minstrel show or 'Little

Eva.' I remember one night excursion I heard Bix Beiderbecke and Frank Trumbauer. I couldn't have been more
than ten or eleven. I was fascinated with Trumbauer. I spent
the whole evening sitting and watching. I was thrilled, it
sounded so good. And of course it was on the riverboats that
I first heard Louis Armstrong."

Norvo's son Kevin, who's around sixteen or seventeen,
sauntered in. He was dressed in a T-shirt and blue jeans, and
he is a miniature Red Norvo. He has an undeveloped S-figure,
red hair, pale skin, and freckles. "I've got an orthodontist's
appointment at four," he said.

"O.K.," Norvo replied. "But will you pick up my shirts at
the cleaners'? I don't have any to wear tonight. The ticket's
out on the harvest table by the front door. I'll feed you
when you get back."

"Money?" Kevin asked.

"Money! I gave you some money the other day."

Kevin smiled and backed out of the room.

"Isn't he something? The other night some people were
here and he told them I was the oldest beatnik in California.
Where was I? Oh, the river. Every spring the river rose, and
sometimes the levees held and sometimes they didn't. The
water rose as high inside houses as that apothecary's chest,
and I can remember fishing off our front porch. Once it
rained and rained, and the principal of our school called us
into assembly one morning and said, 'Grab your stuff and
get home as fast as you can. The levee's broken.' The water
was above my knees when I got home. I put Prince on the
front porch and got his feed bag and straw and bedded him
down. The cellar flooded and the heat and lights went out.
It was cold. That lasted a couple of days, and my father decided to send my mother and my sister and me down to
Rolla, Missouri, where my brother was in college at the Missouri School of Mines. We got through very slowly on the
train, and I guess we stayed down there six weeks or so, and
that's where it all began. When I was six or seven, I'd taken
piano lessons and I'd had a dozen before my teacher dis-

covered I couldn't read a note of music. I was doing it all by ear. One of my brothers or my sister would play what I was supposed to practice and I'd learn it by ear. My teacher rapped my hands with a ruler when she found out—she didn't mean anything by it—and I got frightened and never went back. But in Rolla I heard a man named Wentworth playing marimba in the pit of the theatre. I got fascinated and watched him every night. I was about fourteen. Then it turned out that Wentworth was in the same fraternity as my brother, and he told me I could go over to his room any time and fool around with the marimba he had there. I did, and when I got back to Beardstown it started eating on me and I thought about that marimba and thought about it. A friend of my father's who played wonderful blues piano got me a Deagan catalogue and I saw what I wanted. So I sold Prince for a hundred dollars and worked all summer on a pickup gang in the railroad yards, loading ties and jacking up the cars so that the wheels could be repaired or ground. The reason I sold my pony and went to work was that my father told me, 'You want this marimba bad enough, you get it.' I guess he was tired of paying for lessons and instruments when nothing came of it—like when one of my brothers came home from college, where he had taken up football, and put his violin away for good because it was considered sissy for a football player to play violin. My father was right. It was the best thing in the world for me because it made me really serious about it. When I'd saved enough I bought a table-model xylophone for a hundred and thirty-seven dollars and fifty cents. I never took any lessons. I taught myself to read as I went along and I learned harmony later, when I was on the road."

Norvo went out to the kitchen and got a 7-Up. "I haven't had any beer in the house since 1952, when I gave up drinking. And I gave up smoking six years ago. Once when I came home from a gig in Vegas I was smoked out and I just decided that's that. What I did was fast for a whole week. All I took was a little grapefruit juice and hot water or a little grapefruit, and I was so busy thinking about how hungry I was that I forgot all about the smoking. When I started eating again, the desire was gone.

"The training the marimba and xylophone gave me taught me about evenness of tone. The notes die very quickly on wooden bars and you have to hit each one just right to get the time value you want. If you need a legato passage you really have to *play* legato and not depend on the damper pedal or pulsators, and staccato or fast things have to be clean and hard. If I want a vibrato effect, I add a little roll or tremolo to the end of the phrase, which has to be perfect and is one of the hardest things to do on the instrument. I can never play anything the same twice. Years ago, when I worked in vaudeville, I used to think I had to play things people could latch onto, things they would associate with me. So I worked out about a dozen figures, and every time I tried one it came out differently. Improvisation is like somebody running. Your reactions are fast and you're listening all the time. One ear's on what you're playing and the other's on what's being played behind you. You develop so you listen at a distance, you listen about twelve feet around you. I use the bass line—the melodic flow the bassist is getting—and I improvise against that. The bass line compensates for the way you are going to roll. Improvising is never dull. Each night is like a new happening to you. Tempos, moods, atmosphere, they vary all the time. One night you might play 'I Surrender, Dear' real legato and another night you might find yourself doubling and even tripling the tempo. I work with the construction of a tune, too. I consider its harmonies and linear design and its bridge. What is characteristic notewise in the tune you're working on can be the key to what you do."

Norvo yawned and shook his head. "Nap time. I'm up early every morning, but I need a couple of hours in the afternoon to get me through the evening. And I have no idea what this Huntington Beach gig will be like." He got up and went into the kitchen, a spacious, bright room with a gas stove, a wall oven, and a charcoal grill he had encased in brick. "At one point we had so much Colonial furniture and stuff I had to rent a garage near here to keep the overflow in. I started collecting when I was with Mildred, and it has become a kind of madness with me. I drop into junk shops and antique shops wherever I am in the country, and I've picked up a lot of things out here. People from the East bring beautiful furniture and china out with them, and then they die and their kids don't want anything *old* in their houses, so they sell it." Norvo had passed through the kitchen into a formal dining room. "Those candlesticks and goblets on the shelves in front of the window are Sandwich glass. That one's a sapphire blue and that's vaseline and that's canary. Those are green and purple, and we call the milky color clam broth, and that blue is cobalt. Most of the lamps in the house are also Sandwich glass. I generally convert them myself. The corner cupboard is cherry and it's from Ohio. The china inside is Eve's. It's Canton, and the old clipper-ship captains brought it over as a kind of ballast and then sold it when they got here. The other corner cupboard is Connecticut, and you can see how much more delicate it is than the Ohio one. The dining chairs are Queen Anne side chairs with block-and-turn legs and Spanish feet. You wouldn't believe it, but I got them from a *museum*. Museums get overstocked, and I picked them up that way." Norvo went into a big front hall. "The grandfather clock in the corner is extremely rare. It's from Lebanon, Pennsylvania, and is by a clockmaker named Miety. The wood is maple, and the horizontal stripes in it gave somebody the bright idea of calling it tiger maple. The harvest table is tiger maple, too. That's a tilt-top candlestand, and the graceful little feet are snake feet, and the sofa by the clock is—oh, hell, what is it?—O.K., a camelback Chippendale. And that's a Queen Anne wing chair across from it." Norvo went through the front room into the bedroom, which was filled with a canopy bed and two highboys—one with a delicate fluted top and one with a heavy, sedate bonnet top. "This is my little room in here," Norvo said. "Eve never touches it, and as a result it's filthy. I keep my Bennington ware in this cabinet. It was made about a hundred years ago and I've got everything—a footwarmer, which I found covered with dirt in a junk shop in New York, and mugs, pitchers, coachman jugs, picture frames, doorknobs. You name it, I've got it. I'm told it's much sought after now. And I keep my gun collection in this closet." It was a walk-in closet. Part of one wall was hung with rifles, and a long row of pistols, each in a leather case, were lined up on a shelf. Big glass jars held bullets of every size and shape, and on a small workbench were two pistols in repair. "Maybe I love guns the most. There's nothing more beautiful than a beautiful gun used in the right way."

Norvo is the father of his instrument, and, like most originators, he is a visionary. In 1933, he made a startling avant-garde recording on xylophone that had Benny Goodman on bass clarinet, Dick McDonough on guitar, and Artie Bernstein on bass. One side was Bix Beiderbecke's "In a Mist," and the other was Norvo's "Dance of the Octopus." Both numbers are full of odd harmonies and notes and arhythmic collective passages that suggest free jazz. A couple of years later, he formed a small band that tidily mirrored a big band, using arrangements and riffs and the like. It was, as Norvo has pointed out, the first non-Dixieland small band. His professional liaison with Mildred Bailey marked the first time a jazz vocalist had a first-rate jazz band built around her. In 1945, he headed a brilliant, groundbreaking recording date that brought together bebop (Dizzy Gillespie, Charlie Parker) and swing (Teddy Wilson, Flip Phillips, Slam Stewart, Specs Powell), and not long after that he played with Benny Goodman and Wilson and Stewart in Billy Rose's famous revue, "The Seven Lively Arts." Then he joined Woody Herman, becoming the first vibraharpist to play full time with a big jazz band, and he made small-band Herman recordings that adventurously echoed his own band of a decade before. He assembled a trio in the late forties, with Tal Farlow on guitar and Charlie Mingus on bass, that remains one of the most celebrated in jazz. It lasted nearly a

decade, with varying personnel, and in the late fifties Norvo
went into the recording studios again, to make four timeless
sides for Victor with Harry Edison on trumpet, Ben Webster on tenor saxophone, and Jimmy Rowles on piano. Since
then he has had a steadily changing succession of small
groups, each challenging and original, each light on its feet
and light on the ear.

Norvo's style owes very little to anyone else. There are
suggestions in his minute tremolos and in his admixture of
sudden runs and lagging single notes of Earl Hines, whom
he listened to in the late twenties, and his compactness and
fleetness sometimes recall Teddy Wilson. He is always improvising. In the first chorus of a number, he will lead the ensemble with a refined, airy version of the melody, generally
played somewhat behind the beat. He seems to pick out the
best notes, suspending them briefly before the listener like a
jeweller holding good stones up to the light. When he goes
into his solo, everything doubles in intensity. He picks out
single notes in the upper register with just his right mallet, occasionally jarring them with contrapuntal left-hand notes, in-
serts an abrupt, two-handed ascending rush that is topped by
octave chords, returns to right-hand single notes (the last of
them played flatfooted, with the mallet held on the bar after
the note is struck to deaden the sound), plays a two-handed
run that covers all three registers in both directions, and finishes his first chorus with a legato statement of the melody.
Norvo's flow of notes is startling; a pianist has the equivalent
of ten mallets, but he has four at the most. Each note is crys-
talline, polished, cherished. His rhythms shift constantly, and
his choice of notes and harmonies is daring and questing. His
solos are extrovert. They are full of good cheer, and when
he plays a slow blues the emotion transmitted is clean and
gentle and free of self-pity. A first-rate Norvo solo is like a
piece of Eve Norvo's Canton china; its color and weight
and glaze and design are in fluid balance.

Fred Seligo, a professional photographer and an admirer of
Norvo, was seated in a dark circular room on the main floor

of the motel in Huntington Beach where Norvo was to play. The floor was carpeted and the walls were carved wood. There were hanging plants, and a circular dance floor, set in a well, was surrounded by tables and a trellis wall. Seligo looked around him. "Early phony Polynesian," he said. "And I'll bet that bar in there is called the Lanai Lounge. I guess Red plays at a lot of places like this all over the West—motels and hotels and the lounges in the casinos at Vegas. Red told me once that the owner of a place in Vegas where he had a gig called him into his office one afternoon and said he had to shave his beard off. In half an hour, Red and the band were packed and headed back to the Coast. Not only that. Nobody listens to you in those places. The whole scene is sad when you think of it, but it doesn't seem to bother him. And I think he plays better now than he ever has." Norvo had set up about fifteen feet from the outside of the trellis in the entrance of what Seligo called "the piano bar." He had bass and drums with him, and he went into "Blue Moon," in cha-cha time.

"Blue Moon" was followed by a brisk "Sunday" and a brilliant "I Surrender, Dear," which started at a slow tempo, slipped into double time, with Norvo dodging back and forth between the original tempo and the new one, and ended in a triple time closed by an abrupt, free-fall return to the first speed. "Undecided" came next, and the set ended with a fast blues. Norvo talked to his musicians for a minute and then sat down at the table and ordered a coffee.

"Boy, what a set! Nothing went right. I couldn't hear the piano and the drums sounded like they were underwater, and the piano and drums couldn't hear me. And the lighting is crazy. Whenever I lift the bars with the loud pedal, the light catches the aluminum and it makes me feel seasick, a little dizzy. It depresses me, but I don't let it get to me. My musicians are all down in the mouth, so I just told them, 'All right, the set was bum, but it's *over,* and there's nothing you can do about it now. You're all good musicians, professionals, and you *know* what the trouble is, so you can fix it in the next set.' If you're a leader, you can't show your feel-

ings about depression and the like. You can't excuse yourself
that way, any more than you can let drunks and such get to
you. If they do, it's your fault.

"It's just an excuse to spout off, to insult them. It deterio-
rates you. The main thing is that jazz should be fun. After
all, the *music* is more important than any of us musicians.
I'm beginning to think it's not that way anymore, which is
too bad. We've come into an age of geniuses, of big musicians swaggering down the sidewalk, and nobody has any
fun anymore. I've never done anything musically unless I
liked to do it. Of course, experience is the most important
factor in being a musician. Gradually, through the years,
you build a higher and higher level of consistency, and no
matter how bad the conditions are—in an impersonal place
like this you almost always feel like you're in left field—you
never drop below that level. But if things *do* go wrong, you
just accept it. You might not like what you are doing, but
you accept it, and I've found at my time of life that that's
the hardest thing of all. Like with my hearing, which I've
had trouble with since I was a kid and had mastoids and the
doctor lanced my ears. Then I got a fungus condition in
Florida in the thirties, and that took a long time to clear up.
Then early this year, in Palm Springs, there were times
when I couldn't hear the piano, and one night I discovered
that the E-flat I thought I was hearing in my head was
coming in my ear a D. It scared me. I came home and my
whole left ear—my right one has only had sixty-per-cent
hearing since I was a kid—collapsed. It was frightening. I
got so I couldn't hear a dial tone, and I watched TV with
the sound off. I stopped playing, and in June I was operated
on, and when I was back in my hospital room my hearing
was perfect. Since then it has been off and on. Sometimes I
have trouble hearing the top and bottom of the keyboard,
but the bones in the ear have begun to vibrate again, and
that's a good sign. So now I just try to stop second-guessing
myself when I play, to stop being so damned critical and just
move straight ahead."

The next set began with "Our Love Is Here to Stay." The

drummer had tightened his drumheads and he sounded crisp
and clear, and the lid of the piano had been propped open.
Norvo himself seemed to open up, and his solos took on an
urgency that were missing in the first set. Even his motions
became more exuberant. He stooped over his vibraharp like
a chef sniffing sauces. His head was jutted forward, chin up,
and it swivelled from side to side, giving the impression that
he was searching the audience for an expected friend. At the
same time, he rocked on his feet, his cocked, outrigger elbows seemingly keeping him upright. Occasionally he looked
down at his hands, following closely a complex run as if he
were an entomologist tracking an ant, but then the head
came up again, the beard pointing and the eyes scanning and
scanning. A bossa nova and a slow ballad followed, and then
Norvo picked up his slap mallets and played a funny stop-
time chorus. In the next number, he sat down beside his vibraharp and played bongo drums, laughing and rocking
back and forth. The group caught his cheer, and the final
number, "Perdido," with Norvo back in the pilot's seat, was
a beauty.

The Norvos' house, which is on Alta Avenue in Santa Monica, is gray and hugged by shrubs and—because it is clapboard—it is an oddity in southern California. The street is
wide and pleasant. Towering palms and short magnolia trees
line it, and the lawns are manicured. The ocean is only a
block or two away. A light fog was ballooning up the street
as Eve Norvo pulled up in front of the house the next morning. "I don't see Red's car," she said, taking off her glasses.
"I guess he must have gone out for a few minutes. I'm a
transplanted Easterner, too. I guess I don't miss the seasons
anymore. If we want snow we can go up in the mountains,
and of course we have the ocean. Sometimes I walk over and
take a path that runs for three miles beside it. It's never the
same. One day it will be peaceful and blue and the next it
will be black and angry. And as Red says, New York used
to have an atmosphere it doesn't have anymore. He used to
feel that if he left town and just went to Chicago that he

was camping out. And everyone in New York goes like a locomotive. Here the pace is sensible. I was born in Great Barrington, Massachusetts, and I grew up in Lee, which isn't far from there. My father was a tailor and my mother worked with him. Six months before I graduated from high school they moved to New York, and I stayed in Lee with friends until I was finished. I met Red backstage at the Paramount, where he was with Benny Goodman. Five days later he called me—he already knew my brother, Shorty Rogers, the trumpet player—and asked me to have dinner with him. I had been married before, and I have a son, Mark. I think Red's greatest asset is his humility. He is a humble, kind, generous man, and—oh, there he is."

Norvo was standing in the front door of the house.

"I thought you were out," she said.

"They took the car to put new plugs in it."

Eve Norvo went into the kitchen to make some espresso.

"We're getting straightened around down there at the motel. We moved the vibes a little forward and opened the piano up all the way and we began to hear each other by the last set. A couple of guys came in late, and one of them asked me if I was the same Red Norvo who played the Commodore Hotel in New York with Mildred Bailey in 1938, and I said I was, and the guy with him told me, 'He jackknifed so fast to get in here when he saw the sign "Red Norvo" out on the road that the car nearly turned over.' Tonight they're coming back with their wives and families. The same thing happened to me a while ago at the Rainbow Grill. People came up and said, 'Do you remember me? You played a dance in Pottstown, Pennsylvania, in 1936, and that was the night I met my wife.' Well, you can't remember those things, but it gives you pleasure that other people do. The thirties were a bad time for a lot of people, but Mildred and I—we were married in 1930—made it pretty well. I spent the last part of the twenties in vaudeville. I tried college twice—once at the University of Illinois and once at the University of Detroit. But it never took, and by Thanksgiving both times I was back on the road with the Collegians or the Flaming Youth Revue in some vaudeville troupe. I sang and played piano or xylophone, and I worked out a routine where I traded breaks with myself, playing xylophone and dancing. But I was never really happy in vaudeville. I had a Victrola I took everywhere, and I drove everybody backstage crazy playing jazz records on it. Then I worked my way up to being a single, and finally to leading house bands in Milwaukee and Kansas City and Detroit and Minneapolis, and when I went up to Chicago in 1929 I got a staff job with N.B.C., and we played radio broadcasts with Paul Whiteman and backed Mildred, who was with him then. I was already playing vibraharp and even a little timpani. I had my first band in New York with Charlie Barnet, and after that was the summer known as the Maine Panic. We got a gig to play Bar Harbor, and I got together Chris Griffin on trumpet and Eddie Sauter, who were both with Goodman later, and Toots Camaratta, and I think we had Herbie Haymer on sax and Pete Peterson on bass and Dave Barbour on guitar. I was the director of the band, and I'd got arrangements by Fletcher Henderson and Teddy Hill, but the people up there were used to Meyer Davis. They'd never heard wild music like ours, and we didn't get paid because no one came back to hear us, and the only way we kept alive was with little gigs around Maine. We came back from one of them in a pickup truck, and when we got home we looked in the back and all the instruments were gone. We'd bounced them out, so the next day we retraced the road and we'd find a saxophone in a ditch and a trumpet in a cornfield and a snare drum in the bushes. We survived on apple pies made from stolen apples, flounders, and clambakes on the beach, with butter bummed from a farmer. Finally it got so bad, though, that Mildred had to come up and get me. But it was the most enjoyable panic of my life. Not long after, I put together my first real group. It had trumpet and tenor and clarinet and bass and guitar and xylophone. No drums and no piano. We opened at the Famous Door, on Fifty-second Street. I had the group a couple of years and we worked the Hickory House and Jack Dempsey's, on

Broadway, and the Commodore, where I enlarged into a thirteen-piece group. Mildred joined us at the Blackhawk, in Chicago, in 1936. We were there all winter and came to be known as Mr. and Mrs. Swing, compliments of George Simon, the jazz writer. I had the group until 1940, but I had to give it up when Mildred developed diabetes and had to quit travelling."

Eve Norvo brought in the espresso and poured Norvo a mugful. "I got the idea for my trio, which I put together in 1949, after I'd moved out here. I figured a group with just vibes and guitar and bass could go into almost any place on the Coast, which would mean I could spend more time at home. Naturally, what happened was that our first booking was into Philly. We were playing opposite Slim Gaillard, who was swinging hard and making a lot of noise, and I felt naked. I wanted to know, what do you *do* behind a guitar solo with a vibraharp? Use two mallets, four mallets? What? It was awful. But by the last couple of days it began to unfold for me a little. Then we went to New York, and one night I stopped in to eat at Billy Reed's Little Club, where they had this sissy group. The guitarist, who I didn't know, played sixteen bars of something that spun my head. Mundell Lowe was on guitar with me, and he wanted to stay in New York, but he said he knew a guitarist who would be just right and I told him I'd heard one who would be just right, too. I insisted Mundell hear my man and Mundell insisted I hear his man, and you know what happened—they turned out to be the same guy, Tal Farlow. I took the trio to Hawaii, and when we got back to the Haig, here in Los Angeles, my bass player wanted to leave, and one night Jimmy Rowles came in and asked me if I remembered the bass player I had used when we backed Billie Holiday in Frisco a while back. I said I did—Charlie Mingus. We called all around Frisco and no one knew where he was, and finally we found him right down here—carrying mail. He wasn't playing at all and he was big. I'd watch him sit down and eat a quart of ice cream and I'd say, 'Hey, what are you doing?,' and he'd say, 'Man, I can eat *three* of these at one sitting.' But he went down in weight with us, and by the time we opened at the Embers he was fine. He could play those jet tempos that most drummers can't touch and he was a beautiful soloist. We stayed at the Embers a year or so, and Mingus was with us a couple of years."

Eve Norvo appeared with her daughter, Portia, who was carrying her son, Christopher. Norvo kissed Portia, who in figure and coloring is another chip off the old block, and took Christopher and held him at arm's length. "Well, how is it today?" he asked Christopher. "Have they been feeding you right?" Christopher blinked and looked at Norvo's beard. "You're sort of pensive this morning." Norvo put Christopher on his feet by the coffee table.

Eve Norvo and Portia sat down, and Christopher sidled over to his mother.

"He's a swinger, when he has a mind for it," Norvo said. He picked up a pair of bongo drums and put them between his knees and began an easy rock-and-roll beat. Christopher smiled and edged his way around the coffee table, stopped, looked at Norvo and then up at the painting over the fireplace. He pointed at it and pointed at his grandfather. Then he giggled, sat down abruptly, and got up again. Norvo continued playing. "Come on, what's the matter with you? Don't you want to swing this morning?" Suddenly Christopher let go of the coffee table and started a tentative dance. He swung from side to side, arms crooked, and Norvo laughed. "Now we're going, now we're going." Christopher danced some more, lost his balance, and tipped over, and his mother picked him up. Both women laughed, then Eve Norvo got up. "We have to go out and do some shopping, and then I have to get ready for work, so I'll see you later. How did it go last night? How long did it take to get there?"

"It was a drag for a while, but it picked up. It's an hour or so down there, but I didn't have any trouble finding it. It looks like at least a two-week gig."

The women left with Christopher, and Norvo settled back in his chair, holding his coffee cup on his stomach.

"My years with Mildred are a hard thing for me to put together now. They were wonderful years in my life, but it's been so long ago it's almost like I read it all in a book. When I met her in Chicago, in 1929, she gassed me as a singer. I really dug her, and we started having a bite together now and then. The first thing we were going together, and after we were married and came to New York with Whiteman we lived in an apartment in Jackson Heights and then we bought a house in Forest Hills, on Pilgrim Circle. It was a great house. It was open in back all the way to Queens Boulevard, and when it snowed—there was a little hill down to the garage—we'd get snowed in. There wasn't much jazz in New York then, outside of a few theatres and the Savoy and some Harlem clubs, so we had a lot of musicians and music in the house. The Benny Goodman trio came into being there. One night Teddy Wilson and Benny were there and they started jamming. Carl Bellinger was on drums. He was at Yale at the time, and on weekends he flew down from New Haven to Roosevelt Field in a little Waco he had and sat in on drums, which he left out on our sun porch. Teddy and Benny hit it off, and they brought in Gene Krupa, and that was that. Bessie Smith and her husband came to the house, too. Bessie was crazy about Mildred. She and Mildred used to laugh at each other and do this routine. They were both big women, and when they saw each other one of them would say, 'Look, I've got this brand-new dress, but it's got too *big* for me, so why don't *you* take it?' and they'd both break up. And Fats Waller came out. We loved to go to his place, too, and eat. His wife and mother-in-law did the cooking. Fats was always a boisterous man. It was no put-on. And Jess Stacy came out, and Hugues Panassié and Spike Hughes and Lee Wiley and Bunny Berigan and Alec Wilder. Red Nichols lived right across the street. Sometimes, in those days, people came up to me and said, 'When did you start playing vibes? You had the Five Pennies, didn't you?' That would get me and I'd introduce myself as Red Nichols, and Red told me that the same thing happened to him, and he'd introduce himself as Red Norvo. Mildred was a great natural cook, and she loved to eat. After she knew about her diabetes and was supposed to be on a diet, she'd say, 'Now I've ate the diet, so bring on the food.' She was an amazing person—very warm, very talented. She had a childlike singing voice, a microphone voice, but what singer hasn't? I think her diction got me almost more than anything. It was perfect. When she sang 'More Than You Know' I understood the words for the first time. She made you feel that she was not singing a song because she wanted you to hear how she could sing but to make you hear and value that song. And she had an emotional thing with audiences. I heard it once at the old Blue Angel when there was an ugly hoopla crowd, a messy crowd, and Ellis Larkins, her pianist, played the intro and she started, and before two bars were over—silence. That crowd was down. Mildred loved to laugh and she was very inventive in language. She nicknamed Whiteman Pops. People's opinions of her were very different. They used to say she was temperamental. Sometimes when people don't do or think exactly what they're told they're called temperamental. Either that or they're called geniuses. Mildred got the temperamental bit. She was just astute. She *knew* what was right and she stayed by that knowledge. The first time she heard Billie Holiday, who was just a kid, she said, 'She has it.' Then later she spotted another kid, Frank Sinatra, the same way. She had imaginative ears. We had some pretty strong brawls. Some of them were funny when you look back on it. Once, in the thirties, Benny Goodman and I went fishing out on Long Island, and every time we stopped at what looked like a good place Benny said, 'Come on, Red. I know a better place further on.' Pretty soon we were out near Montauk. We stayed a couple of days—Montauk was a sleeper jump then—and when I got home I could tell that Mildred was hacked. Things were cool, but I didn't say anything, and a night or two after, when we were sitting in front of the fire—I was on a love seat on one side and she was on one on the other side—Mildred suddenly got up and took this brand-new hat she had bought me at Cavanaugh's and threw it in the fire.

I got up and threw a white fox stole of hers in the fire, and she got a Burberry I'd got in Canada and threw *that* in. By this time she was screaming at me and I was yelling at her, so finally I picked up a cushion from one of the love seats and in it went. The fire was really burning. In fact, it was licking right out the front and up the mantel, and that was the end of the fight because we had to call the Fire Department to come and put it out."

Norvo laughed, and went over to a window. The fog was thicker and the light in the room was gray. "But we were compatible most of the time. I don't know what happened eventually. It developed into a thing where there were no children. She wanted children very badly, and it got to the point where we were talking about adopting a child. We lived on Thirty-first Street by then, and I looked around me and it was a madhouse—the maid running around, dachshunds running around, the telephone ringing—and I thought, This is no place to bring kids up in. But it was a slow thing. The car skids a little before it stops, the carburetor skips a little before it quits. I'd move out and we would go back together and I'd move out again. It lasted twelve years before we were divorced. But I always had cordial relations with Mildred. After Eve and I were married, we would take the kids up to Mildred's farm, in Stormville, New York. She loved the children and she gave each of them a dappled dachshund. We still have one of the descendants out in the patio. Mildred died on December 12, 1951. I was at the Embers with the trio, and when I arrived for work I got a message to call home immediately. Mildred had wanted me to do something for her in New York, and I had talked to her earlier that evening on the phone. She was in the hospital in Poughkeepsie for a checkup—she had had pneumonia the year before—and when I reached Eve she told me that the hospital had called and that Mildred had died peacefully in her sleep. It was her heart. She was just forty-four."

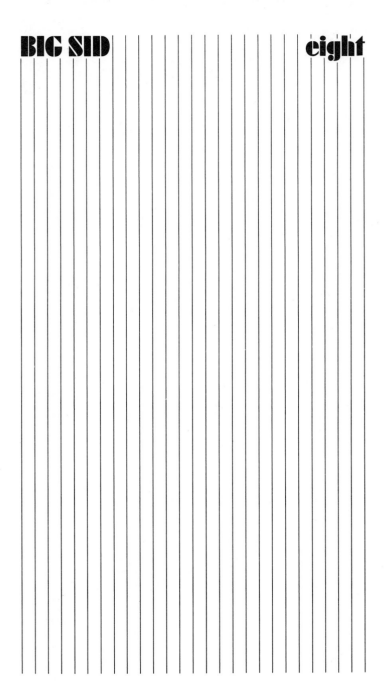

BIG SID

eight

idney Catlett, the magisterial drummer who died in 1951, has yet to be matched. He has outstripped two batches of pursuers—the drummers of his own generation or persuasion and the modernist drummers. The first group includes Jo Jones, Buddy Rich, Louis Bellson, Shelly Manne, and Joe Morello, and the second includes Kenny Clarke, Max Roach, Elvin Jones, Tony Williams, and Milford Graves. And he has remained the Master despite those periods since his death when almost none of his recordings were available in any form—when, in truth, he was in oblivion.

Here are the bones of Catlett's life: He was born January 17, 1910, in Evansville, Indiana, and was raised on the South Side of Chicago. There he attended Tilden Technical High School. Between 1929 and 1944, he worked for Sammy Stewart, Elmer Snowden, Benny Carter, Rex Stewart, the Jeter-Pillars band, Fletcher Henderson, Don Redman, Louis Armstrong, Benny Goodman, and Teddy Wilson. He led his own groups from 1944 to 1947, and then joined the Louis Armstrong All Stars, which included Barney Bigard, Jack Teagarden, Earl Hines, and Arvell Shaw. A heart attack in 1949 forced him to leave the All Stars. During the last two years of his life, he shuttled back and forth between Chicago, where he was the house drummer at Jazz Ltd., and New York, where he might turn up at Central Plaza or Jimmy Ryan's. He died backstage at the Civic Opera House in Chicago, of a heart attack, on Easter Sunday. He had gone there not to play but to visit with his friends, who were legion, and some of whose voices will be heard here. The first is the singer Helen Humes:

> There was a whole bunch of us standing around backstage at the Opera House, where a concert was going on. Sid had come óver to say hello from Jazz Ltd. He was standing behind me and had his arms clasped around my waist, and he was telling one of his stories. It came near time for me to be onstage, so I said, "Sid, let me go put some powder on. I'll see you after." I walked away, and right off I heard this funny sound: a kind of *whummpp*. I turned around and there was Sid lying on the floor, and that was all there was to it. He died right away.

ARVELL SHAW (bass): He had his first heart attack at Billy Berg's club, in Los Angeles, in 1949. He complained of pains in his chest one night after work. He left the All Stars at the Blue Note, in Chicago, not too long after, and Red Saunders took over until Cozy Cole arrived.

JOHN SIMMONS (bass): It's a wonder he lasted as long as he did. After his first heart attack, Joe Glaser sent him to the mountains for a rest, but he didn't stay long enough. But way before that I'd say to him, "Sid, one of these days you're going to crumble up in small pieces." The reason was that he never went to bed. After work, he'd go to after-hours places, and when he'd finished playing in them he'd go out and play the numbers all day.

JOHNNY WILLIAMS (bass): He'd go home after work and take a shower and change his clothes. Then maybe he'd stop in at the Apollo and sit around backstage and gab and play cards. Then it was over to an after-hours place on the Hill, where they served whiskey in coffee cups. Then he'd go home again in the morning and take a shower and change his clothes and go back out and be on the streets all day, until it was time to shower and change again and go to work.

SIMMONS: He'd get home an hour and a half before work and sleep some. By the last set at work that night, his eyes would be at half-mast, but later he'd pep up and start the same old routine again.

SHAW: He loved life. He loved to play cards. He loved to gamble. He loved women. He liked to be around the guys. He didn't like to waste his time sleeping.

JOHN HAMMOND: I don't know how many hundreds of dollars he was in to me over the years. I never knew anyone so crazy about gambling.

RUBY BRAFF (cornet): He was not a well person in the last couple of years of his life, and it showed. If you asked him how he was, he'd say, "What do you care?"

GLADYS CATLETT (his widow): He had rheumatic fever as a child and that gave him an enlarged heart. And he had dropsy at the end, too. He didn't rest enough after his attack. He wasn't supposed to be going up and down stairs and climbing all those hills around a Hundred and Fifty-sixth Street, where we lived. And he had no business being out there in Chicago working.

Catlett was nobly constructed. He was six feet three or four inches tall, and everything was in proportion: the massive shoulders, the long arms and giant, tapering fingers, the cannon-ball fists, the barn-door chest and the tidy waist, his big feet, and the columnar neck. His head was equally imposing. He had high, flaring cheekbones, large, wide-set eyes, and a full, governing nose. His forehead was high, and he wore his hair flat, as was the custom. Majestic expressions flowed across his face when he played. He would stare into the middle distance and look huge and mournful, or he would send out heavy, admiring glances to the pretty women in the room. Big men are often more graceful than small men, and Catlett was no exception. He could swim, play football and basketball, and dance beautifully. But he never learned to drive a car.

SIMMONS: He was a good athlete. His mother didn't want him to play football, but he did, and one day he came home wearing his football uniform. When she opened the door and saw him standing there in all those shoulder pads and such, she said, "What have they done to my son?" Oh, my, he'd laugh so hard when he told that story. He was a great storyteller and a great comedian. When we were in Louis Armstrong's big band, Louis and Sid would sit up on the bus or train and tell each other jokes, from town to town, all night. Louis would type some of them up, and I think he even had a little collection called "The Big Sid Joke Anthology." Louis always typed up jokes that way, and instead of writing people letters he'd mail them a joke. Anyway, Sid could have become a comedian or a dancer or a singer. He was a good singer, and he even wrote songs, which were good, too. He was a marvellous dancer. He learned by watching and listening to dancers like Teddy Hale and Baby Laurence. He'd back them up, and then play exactly what they had danced on his drums.

GLADYS CATLETT: His parents were very unselfish, loving people. He was an only child, and they thought there was no one good enough on the earth for him. His father chauffeured and his mother was a good cook, who worked for wealthy people. I believe his Aunt Minnie worked for those same people. It was through them that he took some drum lessons from an old German teacher. Sidney was the only colored student he had. His mother wanted him to be a lawyer, but the teacher told her, "You let this boy play the drums and he'll be the greatest drummer in the world."

MILT HINTON (bass): I knew Sid at the Wendell Phillips High School, at Thirty-ninth and Calumet. He went to Tilden, but it seems he must have hung out a lot with us. You hear about the Austin High School in Chicago, but not much about Wendell Phillips. Ray Nance went there, and Nat Cole and Lionel Hampton and Hayes Alvis and Razz Mitchell and myself. The bandmaster was Major N. Clark Smith. He was a Negro, and he was a stickler for dignity and discipline who wasn't above throwing a drumstick at your head and knocking you down if you didn't behave. Zutty Singleton was *the* drummer in Chicago, and Sid learned from him, pestering Zutty to let him sit in. Sid also learned from Jimmy Bertrand, who was with Erskine Tate at the Vendome Theatre. Bertrand could read music. He could play the xylophone, and he had a solo he played on tuned tympani. And there was a drummer around Chicago named Jimmy McHendricks. He was dark and short and had a lisp, but he had flash, throwing his sticks in the air and carrying on like that. Hampton and Sid would watch him all the time.

EARL HINES: Sid left Chicago for New York in 1930, in Sammy Stewart's band. It was a hotel-type orchestra, a hicky-dicky group. Stewart only hired light-complected guys, so he took Sid but he wouldn't have anything to do with Louis Armstrong and myself.

TOMMY BENFORD (drums): I believe he picked up a lot around New York when he first came from Chicago. He listened to Kaiser Marshall and George Stafford and Walter Johnson and old man Brooks, who played at the Lincoln Theatre. And he learned a little from me, too.

HAMMOND: I'd grown up thinking Gene Krupa was a great drummer. I had heard him on the McKenzie-Condon records in 1928, and I heard him in the pit band at Gershwin's "Girl Crazy." He was always George Gershwin's favorite drummer. In 1931, I was at Yale and playing violin in a string quartet, and every chance I got I went up to Small's Paradise, in Harlem. Elmer Snowden had the band, and in it were Sid and Roy Eldridge, who both had just come in from the Midwest, and Dickie Wells and Don Kirkpatrick and a sax section of Wayman Carver and Otto Hardwick and Al Sears. I would go night after night with Artie Bernstein, the cellist in my quartet, and what did I hear? This huge, powerful drummer, this huge, powerful ensemble musician who made that whole band go, and I realized: *here* was a great drummer."

DICKIE WELLS (trombone): When you came into Snowden's band, Sid asked you what you wanted him to play behind you. If you told him brushes, he'd play brushes. If you told him sticks, he'd play sticks. If you told him the Chinese cymbal, he'd play the Chinese cymbal. And he'd do whatever it was until you told him to change it. He was a dear, a beautiful person, the prettiest person in the world.

ROY ELDRIDGE (trumpet): Sid was a big cat, a fun-loving cat, and very nice. I can't recall any time he'd get so upset he'd want to go to war. What was so amazing about him, for all his size, was he was so smooth. He was smooth as greased lightning. Me and him and Chu Berry would hang out together in New York. We'd make sessions after work, and sometimes we didn't get home until two or three in the afternoon. That was where you did your practicing, at those sessions. We all drank in those days, but Sid was always clean on the job.

HINES: He was a great soloist and a great accompanist. He never overshadowed whoever was performing around him. He had a feeling for embellishment, for what you were doing in your solo, that made it seem like he knew what you were going to play before you did yourself.

BOB WILBER (clarinet): Hearing Sidney de Paris and Catlett together was something. DeParis had a unique rhythmic sense. He'd place his notes anywhere but where you expected him to, and Sid would go right along with him, anticipating his weird placements with accents and playing this complex hide-and-seek with him.

BRAFF: He arranged his drums so tightly around him they looked like little balls hanging off him. Watching him take a solo was a thrill. He hypnotized you. His sticks went so fast they were blurred. But they also looked like they were moving in slow motion. Each solo had a beautiful sense of composition. Most drummers can't even count, but if he took a twelve-bar solo he played exactly twelve bars and if he took a thirty-two-bar solo he played exactly thirty-two bars. And each solo sang its own song.

Catlett's accompanying had an unfailing freshness and authority. He made everything that went on in front of him sound new. "Why, man, I never heard you play *that* before," he seemed to say to each instrumentalist. His wire brushes achieved graceful, padding effect at slower tempos and a hurrying, relentlessly pushing effect at faster tempos. When he switched to drumsticks in mid-performance, as he often did, it was dramatic and lifting. His library of accompanying techniques was endless. He used different cymbals behind different instruments—a heavy ride cymbal behind a trumpet; the high hat, its cymbals half closed, behind a trombone; a Chinese cymbal, with its sizzling sound, behind a clarinet. All the while, his left hand worked out an extraordinary series of accents on the snare drum. They

never fell where you expected them to, and they were pro-
duced in a variety of ways. He would hit the snare directly,
or hit the snarehead and the rim (a rim shot), or rest one
stick on the snarehead and hit it with the other, or tick the
snare rim. His bass-drum accents were loose and booting,
and were scattered ingeniously through these punctuations.
Catlett was supremely subtle. He implied more than he
stated in his background work, yet he controlled every performance. He told Ruby Braff he could swing seventeen
men with a single wire brush and a telephone book to play
it on, and he was right. He reined in the obstreperous,
pushed the laggardly, and celebrated the inspired. His taste
was faultless, his time was perfect (most drummers, no
matter how proficient, play a split second behind the beat,
but Catlett was *purposely* a split second ahead), and the sound
he got on his drums was handsome, careful, and rich.

Most drum solos exist for themselves, but Catlett's heightened the mood and texture around him, and they were free
of clichés. His solos on alternate takes of his recordings are
invariably different, and so were the solos he played during
a night's work and from night to night. They were rhythmically irresistible. There is a section of his long and empyrean
solo in "Steak Face" on the Decca "Satchmo at Symphony
Hall" album in which he plays a repeated figure with a loose,
and then increasingly complex, arrangement of rim shots,
and it is astonishing. It makes you want to dance and jig and
shake. Its timing and taste and impetus are such that the
passage stands at the very heart of rhythm. One of his sim-
pler solos might start with unbroken, surging, snare-drum
rolls, whose volume rose and fell sharply, and whose wave-
like patterns became more and more intense before suddenly
exploding into rim shots. Then a stunning silence—followed
by lightning shots delivered all around his set, by another
silence and several choked-cymbal beats, and the solo was
over. His solos grew more complex at faster tempos. They
also had an urgent, buttonholing quality. He'd start with a
fusillade of rim shots, sink into a sashaying figure that strode
back and forth between his tomtoms, go back to his snare

for more crackling rim shots, this time unbelievably laced with double-time strokes, drop into a silence, wade heavily and joyously through his cymbals, start roaring around his set, and finish with a sequence of funny and limber half-time bass-drum beats. His solos had an uncluttered order and logic, a natural progression of textures and rhythms and timing that made them seem predesigned. One was transfixed by the easy motion of his arms, the postlike rigidity of his great body, and the soaring of his huge hands, which reduced his drumsticks to pencils. He was also a sensational show drummer. He'd spin a stick in the air, light a cigarette, and catch the stick. Or he'd bounce his sticks off the floor and catch them. Or he'd get up and dance around the set. But it wasn't disruptive clowning; it was cheerful and enhancing and breathtaking.

HINES: I loved Sid very much. He was a very jovial fellow. In fact, the only harm he ever did in his life was to himself. He never knew how to say no, and he never raised an arm in anger. I saw him stand up and cry in front of Louis. Louis would say things once in a while to Sid that weren't tasty, that weren't nice, and Sid would bite his lip and cry. Yet Sid was always Louis's favorite drummer.

ZOOT SIMS (tenor saxophone): Sid was beautiful and easy to work with, but he didn't care for ethnic crossups. One night in New York, Sid said, Let's go uptown. He flagged an empty cab and the cab went right by but stopped a block away at a light. Sid ran up the street and—you know how big he was—pulled the driver out of the cab and held him in the air and dropped him back in his seat, and we got in and went uptown.

TEDDY WILSON (piano): He was a great big nonviolent man, and yet he was very emotional. His feelings were easily hurt. And he could shed a tear when that happened. He was also quick to laugh, and in between shows at Café Society Uptown he'd entertain us backstage for forty-five minutes at a time with his jokes.

He also entertained everybody out front. One night, he filled in, at Teddy Wilson's behest, for a member of the floor show who was late. He started on his cymbals with his wire brushes, a whispering of breezes, and ended ten minutes later with his sticks, having reached a density and momentum that were volcanic.

BARNEY BIGARD (clarinet): He was like a big baby, real gentle, real fine. There's nothing bad anyone could say about Sid.

SHAW: When I first joined the Louis Armstrong All Stars, I was real green. Sid took me under his wing. He taught me about show business, about how to be on the road, about the music. He said the drums and bass should be a single pulse, and he taught me how to produce my part of the pulse. He'd say to me, "If you're not going to do the best you can when you go onstage, why go on at all?"

HARVEY PHILLIPS (tuba): The drummer in the Ringling Brothers' Circus band was Red Floyd. He had a lined, pruny face, and looked like Old Man Time. I think he had played in New Orleans. He had a crippled left arm, but he was an extraordinary musician. He played all the mallet instruments, and he did a beautiful snare-drum roll with one hand by holding two sticks parallel in that hand like extra fingers and seesawing them so fast they became a blur. When we played New York, Sidney Catlett would spend all afternoon at the Garden watching Red, and then ask him to autograph a pair of his sticks.

BRAFF: He took me everywhere with him when I first came to New York from Boston. He'd arrive at a job and tell the manager, "I brought the other person."
"What other person?"
"Ruby Braff."
"I didn't hire him."
"If you hired me, you hired him."
And I'd be hired.

SIMMONS: Sid loved children. They called him Uncle Sid, and he always gave them silver dollars from the roll he carried with him.

Three scenes from a life spent travelling:

SHAW: He and Earl Hines were deathly afraid of flying, and when the All Stars went to the Nice Jazz Festival, in 1948, he and Hines walked from New York to Paris on that plane. Up and down, up and down. Every bump, Sid's eyes would get as big as pizzas. He was a nervous wreck when we landed.

BRAFF: I'd drive him around in the Chevy coupe I had, and he always sat in the front seat. In fact, he was a famous front-seat driver, and I don't know how many front seats he ruined, pushing his knees into the dashboard and leaning back in the seat until it nearly broke. When he got into my coupe to come to New York, the right side of the car went down until it about touched ground. I thought Sid had broken the springs. So I said, "Sid, get out a minute, and let's see if the car comes back up again." Well, it did, so he got in again and off we went, the right side down low and the back of the car piled with suitcases full of his clothes, which he had so many of it was unbelievable.

WILLIAMS: When we'd cross the country on the train in the early forties with Louis Armstrong's big band, Sid and I would go back to that little platform outside the observation car. We'd sit there and get all smutty, get sand in our noses and mouths, and we'd listen to the humming of the wheels on the tracks, to the different rhythms the train made when it went over a crossing, to the changes in the rhythms when the train slowed or speeded up. Sidney would tap out the rhythms with his hands on the railing around the platform, and later I'd hear those rhythms in one of his solos.

Catlett's adaptability was endless. Some of the musicians he recorded with between the end of 1943 and the end of 1945 were Eddie Condon, Lester Young, Louis Armstrong, Art

Tatum, Albert Ammons, Ben Webster, Billie Holiday, Harry the Hipster Gibson, Earl Hines, Teddy Wilson, Sidney De Paris, James P. Johnson, Charlie Parker, Dizzy Gillespie, Sidney Bechet, Don Byas, and Duke Ellington.

Musicians revered Catlett, but his name never got before the public in the way that Gene Krupa's and Buddy Rich's did. The closest he came to celebrity was during the short, disastrous time he spent with Benny Goodman in 1941. Catlett was with Goodman three or four months, and then Goodman fired him. The episode has long been a puzzle, but now it grows clearer:

HAMMOND: The rhythm section that Benny put together in 1941 terrified him, and he had no control over it. Charlie Christian was on guitar, John Simmons on bass, Mel Powell on piano, and Big Sid on drums. When I heard that Sid had nearly caused a riot with his solo during Benny's concert at Soldier Field in Chicago, I thought, Oh Jesus. Sidney's cooked.

SIMMONS: We played a concert at Soldier Field, and Sid took a solo in "Don't Be That Way." Well, he started playing and then he threw a stick in the air—and dropped it. On purpose, of course. He got up and walked around in front of his drums and picked up the stick and sat down and started playing again. Then he threw the stick in the air and dropped it again—and so forth. They were rolling in the aisles, and when he finally stopped horsing around and got down to business, that place nearly blew up. I remember watching Benny's face. It wasn't a cheerful sight. Benny didn't like anyone taking away the spotlight.

When we got back to New York, we had a little layoff, and the night Sid reported for work at the hotel where Benny was, he found another drummer sitting up on the bandstand in his place. Benny gave Sid two weeks' notice and told him to report every night at nine until his time was up—just in case he needed him.

HINES: He loved to play just for the sake of playing, and he loved to play the way he wanted to play. Which is one of the reasons he and Benny Goodman couldn't get on. In the old days in Chicago, when all the young musicians would come in to where Louis and Zutty and myself were playing they'd ask to sit in, and of course we'd say yes. But Benny wanted to *be* asked, and Louis would never do it. So there Benny'd stay, standing over behind a pillar."

Big Sid used to go over to Jimmy Ryan's on Monday nights around 1949 or 1950 and sit in. Tommy Benford remembers: "I have a pair of Sid's drumsticks, and this is why. I was at Ryan's with Jimmy Archey's band, and one Monday, after Sid had sat in, he left his sticks behind on the stand. I called to him as he was leaving, 'Sid, you left your sticks,' and he said, 'That's all right, man. I'll be back next week.' But he hasn't been back yet."

SUPER-DRUMMER nine

Buddy Rich is the last thriving member of the septet of great swing drummers who came forward in the thirties. The others were Chick Webb, Sid Catlett, Dave Tough, Jo Jones, Gene Krupa, and Cozy Cole. Webb, Tough, Krupa, and Catlett are dead and both Cole's and Jones' work had begun to thicken, but in their prime these men had an empyrean quality. They generally sat behind and slightly above the band, encircled by the pleasing geometry of their cymbals and drums. In the proper light, they were super-Pans peering through gold-and-silver foliage. They were the engines that drove the band, and when they soloed—as they did more and more in the late thirties—they became hypnotists as well. The very sounds of their drums were abstractions of all good sounds. Rimshots were puck shots and the crack of an axe on wood; their cymbals breathed and blew and splashed; their wire brushes suggested slippers on polished floors or hail on metal; their sticks on snare drums and tomtoms had the majesty of storm clouds. Best of all, they toyed with rhythm, suppressing its rigidity and celebrating its surprises.

Webb, who led his own band throughout the thirties, was the daddy of the group. He first learned how to heft a big band, supporting it with *hooshing* high-hat cymbals and marble-like rolls. Catlett superimposed on Webb's girders the down-home press rolls and snare-drum figures of Zutty Singleton and Baby Dodds, adding a matchless delicacy and sense of taste. Jo Jones, with his wind-in-the-firs cymbals, slocking rimshots, and sidestepping bass-drum work, aerated the old Basie band, and he became, like Catlett, one of the founders of present-day drumming. Dave Tough was a marvel. He poured his cymbals into ensembles and onto soloists, seemingly matching their thoughts with his accents and all the while keeping Greenwich-meridian time. Rich, a bit younger than these men, learned from each of them. He supplied an urgency and speed that suggested the million explosions that course through a gasoline engine. He never backed up a band; he catapulted it.

Rich was staying at the Warwick Hotel, and when he walked out of the elevator on his way to a benefit performance at Rikers Island, he shot out, spraying the lobby with early-morning glances. He was dressed in a hip-length, single-button, black-and-white checked sports coat, pipestem black trousers, black Italian shoes, and a blue shirt open at the neck, and he had a black duffel coat over one arm. He is short and lithe and slightly stooped, and he has monkish pepper-and-salt hair. His somewhat battered nose connects his two most striking features—a generous mouth and Buddha eyes, which are kept at a steady, alert squint. The bags under his eyes suggest Duke Ellington's seignorial pouches, and deep lines run down from the sides of his nose. He looks like a middle-aged man with a boy peering out from inside. He smiled, showing big, very white teeth. "Man, I was up I don't know how late last night at Sol Gubin the drummer's house out in Jersey," he said. "His wife is a magnificent Italian cook and I couldn't eat enough. We were still at it at two in the morning. It was beautiful."

A black man with a brush mustache approached Rich and they shook hands. "Hey, Carl," Rich said. "This is Carl Warwick, or Bama, as we used to call him. He played trumpet in my band in 1946. He's with the city now and he set up this Rikers Island thing. He came in the club the other night and spread out all these papers on the table and began this spiel about the prison and the boys and this and that and I said, 'Hell, Carl, you want me to come out and play for you say so and I'll come out and play. It's as simple as that.' "

Warwick laughed. "O.K., Buddy. We've got a car and a driver outside."

"What kind of cats you got out there, Carl?" Rich asked after they had gotten in.

"Mostly short-term misdemeanors. Anything from a month to three years. Petty thievery and some addicts. If you steal anything worth over ninety-nine dollars, that's a felony. So very few of these cats ever take over ninety-nine dollars' worth. They know the value of *every*thing. We've got about five thousand inmates. Most of them are repeaters. I had a guy who was back an hour after he got out. He was supposed to report to the Parole Board that day and didn't and they picked him up. And a lot of cats come back when it gets cold, when that old malnutrition and Jack Frost set in."

"If one of them gets hit three times, is he finished?" Rich asked.

"Not with misdemeanors—just felonies. You can get nine thousand misdemeanors but only three felonies. Rikers Island is like a big Y.M.C.A. The only rough place is processing, where they try to get the idea across that you're in a prison. We have a pretty good prison band now, but we're short on drummers."

"Don't look at me, Carl. I'm happy in my work." Rich laughed. "You know, I've never been in jail—I mean as a non-visitor. The C.I.A. and the F.B.I. investigated me before I made a State Department tour. Clean. 'The man doesn't even spit on the sidewalk,' the report said."

Rich shook his head in presumed self-admiration and looked out the window. The car was on the Queensboro Bridge, and the river below was furrowed with sunlight.

"My new band is a straight-ahead band. I've never compromised and I'm not about to start now. People come up to me and say, 'How come you don't smile when you're up there playing?' I say, 'Did you come to see my teeth or to hear me play?' I'm no Charlie Glamour. If you like my playing, never mind *me*. When I was thinking of organizing this band, a man who was interested in backing it came to my house in Las Vegas. He told me, 'You have to forget what you are and who you have been. It's not that important—that you're a great drummer and all. Start fresh and be commercial and you'll be safe and make some bread.' I told him to get the hell out of my house. I'm the same with the guys in the band. I tell them, 'Your life's your own when you're off the stand. But every night I *own* you for five hours.' I ask no more than I give myself. I kill myself every night, and I expect them to wipe themselves out, too. And everybody's got to be clean. If a new guy comes on the band, he's got to match the personality of the band. No cliques. No headaches. Everybody jells, everybody gets along. If a guy plays consistently well for a couple of weeks, I'll lay ten more on him a week. If a guy cops out on me, I'll buy him a first-class one-way ticket to wherever he wants to go. The great thing about the guys in the band is that they think like me. It makes me feel good. There's a certain resentment when you have to tell people what they have to do. If musicians are unhappy, they won't play well. If they are playing beneath them, they won't play well. I want them to play with *their* emotion. I ask them, 'Who do you want for this arrangement? Who'd sound right?' And we all decide. I'm rejuvenated about what's been going on with my band. I look forward to going to work every night. And I look forward to tomorrow. A lot of draggy things happened in the so-called good old days. Sorry about the Civil War and all that, but *I* don't remember the Civil War."

At the gate to Rikers Island, Rich signed the register and was given an identification badge. The car passed through a flat, treeless expanse, broken here and there by wire fences and low buildings, and stopped in front of one of the buildings. Rich was greeted inside by a portly, rumpled, cigar-smoking black man—Warden James Thomas. Thomas ushered Rich into his office. The walls were covered with enormous paintings done by the inmates. Rich, frail and birdlike in the surroundings, stared at a dark painting of the head of Jesus crowned with thorns. Then he smiled. "That's amazing. You know who that is? Sammy. Sammy Davis. Look at the nose and the mouth and the chin. Even the eyes. All Sammy's."

The warden, puffing on his cigar, sat down behind his desk. "We get a lot of the stars out here to entertain the inmates," he said. "Dizzy Gillespie was here not long ago, and so was Carmen McRae. The hall only holds fifteen hundred men, so there is a lot of jockeying for seats. But we try and rotate the men."

Warwick poked his head into the office and said the band had just arrived. Thomas led the way through two steel doors and into a long corridor. He pointed out a dining room, a corridor hung with more paintings, and a cell block.

"You might want to see where the inmates sleep," he said. "We're overcrowded. This block was designed for three hundred men and there are nearly five hundred in here." There were several tiers of small, dark cells. Each cell had a double bunk, a toilet, and a basin. Rich shook his head. "Can you *believe* people *live* here!" he said in a low voice. "Animals have a better deal in the zoo." Clumps of flat-eyed prisoners stood against the walls in the corridor. Rich, walking quickly, his hands clasped under the tail of his duffel coat, looked at them and nodded. One man raised his hand in a half salute and started to smile. Rich said, "Hello. How are things?" Rich entered a gymnasiumlike hall packed with men. A ten-piece prison band, set up below the stage, was pumping unevenly through a Charlie Parker blues. Recognition flickered across the faces of the musicians as Rich went by, and he ducked his head and smiled. He took the steps at stage right two at a time. His band, in tan uniforms, was putting up its music stands in front of a backdrop of Park Avenue on a wet winter night. The words "Welcome Buddy Rich" were pasted across the middle of it. Rich's limousine-size set of drums was already in place, and he sat down behind them. There were two crash cymbals, and between them, at a lower level, a tiny sock cymbal and a giant ride cymbal. His snare drum, a high-hat, and a small tomtom formed a semicircle in front of him, and to his right were two bigger tomtoms. His bass drum was large and old-fashioned. He tunked each drum with a stick, moved his high-hat closer, and looked down at the assembled band. "All set? O.K. Number Thirty-five." The musicians riffled through their music.

All true professionals can step in an instant from the world into their work. A veil of concentration immediately dropped over Rich, and he bent forward and began a soft roll on his snare drum. A half smile masked his face and he kept his head turned to his left. He brought the roll to a quick crescendo, dropped into a pattern of rimshots and heavy bass-drum beats, and shouted, "One, two, three, four!" The band roared into a medium-tempo blues. Rich

sat back and looked out at the audience. A broad-toned lyrical tenor saxophonist soloed. Midway, Rich shouted
"Hmmmmyeh!" and tossed off a fill-in that shot from his
snare to his big tomtoms and ended on the bass drum. He
underlined the close of the last ensemble chorus with generous cymbal splashes. Then his pianist jumped up, lifted his
right hand, and, at a nod from Rich, brought it down, and
the piece finished with a resounding thump. The applause
was scattered. Rich, ignoring the audience, called out another number and gave the downbeat. It was a fast blues.
The applause was again scattered, and scattered after Duke
Ellington's "In a Mellotone." A good part of the audience,
which appeared to be in its late teens and early twenties,
didn't know who Buddy Rich was, and Rich suspected it,
for the next arrangement was a rock number called "Up
Tight." The audience began to tap its feet and sway back
and forth. The tenor soloed, and rhythmic handclapping
began. The number ended and the audience whistled. Rich
smiled and called to his pianist, who started "Green Dolphin
Street" at a medium tempo. Rich picked up his wire brushes.
The pianist played the first chorus, and for the next two he
and Rich exchanged eight- and four-bar breaks. Rich's
breaks were delicate and funny and elusive. In one, he
worked out a soft tap-dancer's pattern on the snare, paused,
struck his bass drum twice, then rattled his brushes over the
tops of his cymbals. In another, he slipped into double time,
racing from his small tomtom to his snare to his big tomtoms
in sudden stops and starts. Each break was met by pleased
guffaws, and after the last one, in which he whisked lazily
between his cymbals and the rim of his snare, the audience
shouted and laughed.

He mopped himself with a towel, picked up his sticks,
and began a fast swelling-and-subsiding series of rolls, his
bass drum in sonorous half time underneath. He machine-
gunned his high-hat, moved back to the snare and into a
thousand-mile-an-hour tempo, and shouted, "Yeh go-oh!"
The band burst into "Clap Hands! Here Comes Charlie!"—
one of Chick Webb's great display pieces. There were alto,

tenor, and trumpet solos. The band fell silent, and Rich, crouched over his snare drum, his teeth clenched, his elbows flat against his sides, fashioned a steady, whispering series of snare-drum figures. He slowly multiplied the beats, letting his volume build, all the while keeping a beat on the bass drum. The snare-drum figures were flattened into a roll, which presently became stately sea swells. Mouths fell open in the audience and the wings of the stage filled with onlookers. Rich began dropping in rimshots, at irregular intervals, that energized the creamy thunder of the rolling. He abandoned his snare and began flying around his entire set, flicking one crash cymbal again and again. Back to his snare drum and a flurry of rimshots backed by a succession of jammed bass-drum beats—elephants moving in quickstep. The bass drum fell silent and Rich's left hand chattered by itself on the snare while his right hand floated lackadaisically between his crash cymbals and his tomtoms. His volume began to sink, and he loosed ticking, dancing figures on his snare rims, abruptly crashed into a complex roll, and settled on the upper half of his snare, his sticks moving so fast that they astonishingly formed two sets of triangles, their apexes joined. The audience shouted, Rich waded around in his cymbals, the band came sailing in, and the number ended. Warden Thomas appeared, shushing the audience. "We thank Mr. Rich, we thank him with all our hearts. And I would like to tell you that Mr. Rich has told me that he is donating—yes, donating—the very set of drums he has just played on to Rikers Island."

Rich draped a towel around his neck and tucked it into his soaking shirt. "I didn't know I'd get this wet," he said, "or else I would have brought a change of clothes. Whooeee! I'm dripping, man, dripping. Where's my coat? I've got to get back to New York. What time is it?" Warwick said it was three-thirty, and pumped Rich's hands. Rich ran down the stairs into the auditorium. The house band was playing again and the hall was beginning to empty. A guard grabbed one of Rich's hands and shook it. He looked to be about Rich's age. "That was fantastic, Mr. Rich. I came in to see you at the club the other night with the wife. If I'd knew you'd be out here today, I wouldn't have spent all that money. Wonderful, Mr. Rich."

In the car, Rich shivered a little, pulled his duffel coat around him, and leaned into the corner of his seat. He looked tired. "That was weird, wasn't it? I thought for a while we wouldn't get those cats moving. They were sort of lifeless, but what do you expect? The whole penal system is rank. It hangs me up—people in jail. Can you imagine *two* guys living in one of those cells? There must be some better way. I know a lot of hoods. Maybe I dig more of them than I do straight cats. They're what they are and if you're what you are with them—beautiful. Everything's straight. And when someone pulls a Brink-type job and no one is hurt, that's brilliant, that's groovy. Four stars. He beat you with his brain. He's a swinger. But of course crime is a drag and so's prison, and so what are you going to do?

"I had a beautiful family and I guess that's one of the things that keeps you straight. I was born in Brooklyn. My father and mother were a vaudeville team—Wilson and Rich. My mother was from Brooklyn. She was a singer and a heavy-made woman and very pretty. She died much too young, about fifteen years ago. My father was a soft-shoe dancer and a blackface comedian, which embarrasses me now, but it was accepted then. He was from Albany. He's a little shorter than I am and he lives in Miami. He was a liberal father, a good father, a good man. He was strong and nice-looking and had a great sense of humor. When you stepped out of line you got a shot in the mouth and that straightened you out. He came to see me at the Sands in Vegas a little while ago and he got upset when I wouldn't let him stay up for the four-o'clock show. My mother and father called me Pal and my two sisters—they're older—called me Broth. I have a kid brother who's in television. Until twenty years ago we lived in a great big house near Sheepshead Bay. There was fun going on constantly. It was the kind of house that when I worked at the Astor with Dorsey in the early forties and came home at two o'clock in the morning everybody would be up and we'd all sit down in the kitchen and have French toast and they'd say, 'All right, what happened tonight? How did it go? Who came in?' Everything's still groovy. No jealousy. I stayed with my sister in L.A. a little while ago and it was a ball. One sister is a fair dancer and one is a fair singer and my brother played tenor for a while. I started as a dancer and a singer and a drummer. By the time I was two I was a permanent part of my parents' act. They'd bring me onstage dressed in a sailor suit or a Buster Brown collar and I'd play 'Stars and Stripes Forever' on a drum. I had long, curly hair. When I was seven I travelled around the world. My part of the act gradually became more powerful and my parents gradually stepped aside. My father travelled with me, and sometimes we took a tutor. I only made it through the sixth grade because we were always on the road. I taught myself mainly to read and write. By the time I was fifteen—that would have been in 1932 or so—I was making a thousand dollars a week. I was the second-highest-paid kid star, after Jackie Coogan.

"I started getting interested in real drumming, jazz drumming, in my early teens. I heard the Casa Loma band at the Colonnades Room at the Essex House and Tony Briglia was on drums. He had the greatest roll I've ever heard. Smooth as milk. I began to study drummers and I listened to O'Neil Spencer for his brushes and to Leo Watson, who was a scat singer *and* a terrific drummer, and to Lee Young, Lester's brother, and to Chick Webb. Webb was startling. He was a tiny man with a hunchback and this big face and big, stiff shoulders. He sat way up on a kind of throne and used a twenty-eight-inch bass drum which had special pedals for his feet, and he had those old gooseneck cymbal holders. Every beat was like a bell. And I loved to listen to Davey Tough. He tuned his drumheads so loose they flapped. And he hated soloing. But he had that touch. Gene Krupa appealed to me for his showmanship. It overshadowed his playing. And I watched Sid Catlett. He was the best cymbal player I've ever heard. I listened to everybody and decided

I wanted to be my own self. I don't think I sound like anyone but myself.

"Around 1937, I started hanging out in a place in Brooklyn called the Crystal Club. It had a small group with Henry
Adler on drums and Joe Springer on piano and George Berg
on tenor. Henry would invite me to sit in, and Artie Shapiro, the bassist, would sit in, too. Shapiro was with Joe
Marsala's group at the Hickory House and he asked me to
one of the Sunday-afternoon jam sessions they used to have
there. Everybody in New York fell in. I went three Sundays
in a row and never got to play. On the fourth Sunday, at
about five-forty-five—the session ended at six—Marsala sum-
moned me. I played 'Jazz Me Blues,' or something like that,
and then Marsala said, 'Let's play something up.' In those
days, I lived up. I started out at a tempo like this—taptaptap-
taptaptap—on a thing called 'Jim-Jam Stomp.' People were
beginning to leave, but they turned around and started coming back in just as if a Hollywood director had given instructions in the finale of some crummy Grade B movie.
The number broke the place up, and Marsala invited me
back to play that night. I called my dad and he said he
guessed it would be O.K. I played two sets and Marsala
asked me to join the band. My dad was a dyed-in-the-wool
vaudevillian, and when I told him he said, 'What are you
going to *be*, Pal? A *musician?*' I said, 'Just give me a chance.'
I joined the union and went to work for sixty-six dollars a
week, which I took home to Dad. He gave me an allowance
of ten bucks a week. Marsala told me just to play with
woodblocks and a sizzle cymbal and no high-hat and a lot of
ricky-tick stuff on the rims. But gradually I brought in other
equipment and we moved over to a four-four beat. I didn't
know any musicians and I discovered pretty quickly that
you have to build up protection, an immunity to feelings.
It was Dickie Wells, who was a club owner and a big man
in Harlem, who gave me the confidence. One morning the
Three Peppers, the intermission group at the Hickory
House, took me up to Wells' place for a breakfast dance. A
group named the Scotsmen were playing there, and they

wore kilts. They had Teddy Bunn on guitar and Leo Watson on vocals and drums. They later became the Spirits of Rhythm. I'd never been to Harlem and I was worried because I knew they really played up there. The Peppers introduced me to Wells and he told me, 'I want you to *play* and if you don't it'll be your you know what.' He wasn't very encouraging. Well, I played and it was a very exciting thing for me. I came off the stand and Wells hugged me and said, 'You're my hundred-year man.' Beautiful. From that time on it was straight ahead. For some reason, I've always had a great thing going with colored cats. No conflict —just with white cats.

"I stayed with Marsala a little over a year and then I joined Bunny Berigan. His records don't show the enthusiasm of the band. It was a fun-loving band, with music second. I was on the band six months. We had two one-week location jobs and the rest of the time it was one-nighters. Bunny was one of the great drinkers of our time. We were doing a one-nighter in York, Pennsylvania, and when the curtains opened Berigan came out playing his theme, 'I Can't Get Started.' He walked right off the front of the stage and into the audience and lay there laughing—with a broken foot. But he had the foot set and came back and finished the night. I went with Artie Shaw next. I made my first movie with the Shaw band—'Dancing Co-Ed.' It had Lana Turner and Lee Bowman. And we also did the Old Gold radio show. Bob Benchley was the master of ceremonies. I got to know him very well. He liked me. I used to laugh at the subtle things. He struck me as being a beautiful man. My stay with Shaw ended at the Pennsylvania Hotel here. One night he got fed up and walked off the bandstand and went to Mexico and didn't come back. A conflict grew up as to who would take over the band, so I left and joined Tommy Dorsey. That was in 1939, and I was on the band for most of the next six years. Dorsey was the greatest melodic trombonist in the business, but he was a drag to work for. We never really got along. He was another heavyweight in the juice department. Leaders like to have you play their way, but I knew what I wanted to do and did it. He always resented my talking back to him, but he respected what I played and knew it was good for the band. When I left, he hired Alvin Stoller. Stoller and I hung out together, and I guess Stoller had acquired some of my personality, because he gave T.D. such a rough time that Dorsey finally told him, 'There are three rotten bums in the world—Buddy Rich, you, and Hitler—and I have to have two of them in my band.' "

Rich laughed and rubbed a hand over his face.

"I formed my own big band in 1946. Frank Sinatra backed it with two certified checks, each for twenty-five thousand dollars. I knew what I wanted in music, but it was the beginning of the decline of big bands. People advised me to cut the band down. I had nine brass, five reeds, and four rhythm. But I couldn't see it. I'm a very stubborn guy. I maintained there were enough rooms around the country to supply work. In two years I was flat broke. We'd gone from twenty-five hundred a night to seven hundred. It became a panic band. But it went down swinging and it went down in one piece.

"I worked on and off in the fifties for Norman Granz' Jazz at the Philharmonic with cats like Bird and Sweets and Pres and Oscar Peterson, and most times it was musically satisfying. I organized a small band in 1952 and had it about a year, but I missed that big-band thing. You don't shout with a small band. I got a call from Harry James, but that got to be a bore after a while. I was never really satisfied after having my own band. The perfect big band was always in my mind. Then, in 1959, I learned the hard way that I had to slow down."

The car pulled up in front of the hotel. In his room, Rich took off the towel, which was still draped around his neck, and his shirt and sports jacket, then put on a bathrobe. He ordered coffee and drummed on a table with his fingers. Then he sat back and put an unlighted cigarette in his mouth.

"I had another small group at the time and we were playing in a bar in New Orleans. I was getting into a solo when my left hand began to go numb. I tried to get the feeling back in my fingers and then I had difficulty breathing. I didn't know what was happening. I had never thought about a heart attack in my life. I played a short solo and then I told John Bunch, who was with me then, that I wasn't feeling so well, and I walked back to the Roosevelt Hotel. I couldn't seem to get air in my lungs. I walked into the lobby and the desk was way down at the end. It looked about a mile away. When I got there, the night clerk said, 'Mr. Rich, somebody better go upstairs with you.' A bellboy came up. I drew a hot tub and sat in it until daylight. Well, I ended up in an oxygen tent. I was there ten days, and then I was in the hospital here for several months. The opinion was that I would never play drums again, and I was told to go home to Miami and stay there for a year. After a month, I'd had it. When you're not doing anything, everything is amplified. I called Joe Glaser and told him I wanted to go back to work, but he wouldn't have any part of it. I'd made several records as a singer, so I took a job here in the Living Room. I was successful enough, but the audiences kept saying 'When will he play? When will he play?' and that forced me back into playing. A couple of things happened since then—once on the thirteenth tee at the Paradise Valley in Vegas. I was playing with B.—Billy Eckstine—and he was driving and I started to wheeze and grabbed my chest. He started running up and down the fairway yelling and shouting like a bunch of Keystone Cops. Then I keeled over. When they got me back to the clubhouse, all B. said was 'You'll do anything to win a hole.' Beautiful."

The coffee arrived.

"Who knows why? I was told it was twenty years of anxiety, temperament, and unhappiness. And I used to have terrible eating habits—three pounds of spaghetti at four in the morning after work and then go to bed. Put all those things together, and it tears you apart. Well, I'm not a drinking man and I'm strong by nature, with good recuperative powers. I use my mental capacity to fight bad things off. I never wanted any part of sympathy. I had only one arm for a while. It was about fifteen years ago and we'd just gotten off the bus in Dayton, Ohio. I never could sleep when we arrived anywhere and so I went and played some handball and I tripped and broke my left arm in three places. It was put in a cast and I had a sling made to match my band uniform, and I played with my right hand and used my foot as a left hand. Solos, too. I never missed a day for the three months the cast stayed on."

Rich refilled his cup and lit a cigarette.

"Of course I'm never supposed to get excited because I have the worst temper in the world. When I lose it, oh baby. Whatever happens to be around—an axe, shoes, a bottle—I'll use it. One night a singer who was splitting the bill with us barged into my dressing room and started cursing me up and down and asking me who do I think I am and telling me what a stuck-up son of a bitch I am. Well, it happens this girl bugs me. She's got star eyes about herself. So I just sat there and smiled and looked at her. Joe Morgen, the press agent and an old, old friend, was with me. She started swinging at my head. I can't stand anybody putting their hands on me. I covered my head, and Morgen, who's a little guy, pinned her arms behind her back and said 'Why don't you behave like a lady?' and hustled her out of the dressing room. When the door was shut the top blew off. My mind was red. I picked up a chair and smashed it to pieces against the wall. The only thing that kept me from killing her on the spot was the thought in the back of my head: You do this, idiot, and there goes the band and everything else. It was the only thing that saved the broad. I was a pretty rough guy in the old days, and I made some enemies. Matter of fact, I've had three or four threatening calls since I've been here. One time this voice says, 'O.K., Rich, we're going to break your wrists,' and another time a different one—or maybe the same voice disguised—says, 'You come out of the hotel tonight and we'll break both your legs.' In the old days I would have made a few calls to Brooklyn and gone out and found the bastard. I can't tell you how many beefs I got into in the Marines, which I enlisted in in 1942. I was 3-A—the sole support of my family—but I was affected by the war propaganda. I became a judo instructor and a combat rifleman, but they never sent me overseas. I was the only Jew in my platoon, and I wasn't used to hearing stuff about the Jews don't know how to fight, the Jews don't do anything but make money, the Jews started the war, and so forth. After the first dozen beefs, I didn't hear any more talk like that."

Rich looked at his watch. It was six-thirty. "Hey, time to get dressed. I like to get to the club around eight-thirty. I'll grab a bite at Mercurio's, which is just around the corner, and then walk over."

Ten minutes later, Rich came out of his bathroom. He looked brand-new. He had on a double-breasted navy silk-and-mohair suit with a hip-length jacket, a blue-and-white striped shirt with a high collar, and a blue tie. He picked up a gray tweed overcoat and slapped all his pockets.

The elevator was empty except for a tall heavyset man with a crew cut. Rich stared at him, leaned over, started to say something, and stopped. In the lobby, he said, "You know who *that* was? That was Johnny Unitas, man."

The headwaiter at Mercurio's greeted Rich effusively. Rich ordered a vodka gimlet, veal piccata, and a large side dish of spaghetti with meat sauce.

"Maybe my technique is greased elbows, and maybe it's because the Man Upstairs talked to my hands and said 'Be fast' and they were. I've never had a lesson in my life and I never practice. I stay away from drums during my daytime adventures. You won't find a pair of sticks or a practice pad or anything connected with drumming in my house or my hotel room. That way each night is an expectation, a new experience for me. All these guys get from practicing is tired wrists. If you have something to play, you hear it in your heart and mind, and then you go and try it out in front of an audience. I read a little drum music, but an arranger can't write for a drummer. Only the drummer knows where the fills and the accents go. When we get a new arrangement, I don't play it. I sit out front and listen. Then I play it

once and that's it. I don't see anything in my mind when I
solo. I'm trying not to play clichés. I tell myself, 'Make sure
you don't play anything you played last night.' Playing a
drum solo is like telling a story. It has a beginning, a middle,
and a bitch of a punch line. I try and play a drum solo constructed along a line. What comes out is what I feel. I'm telling you about my wife, my daughter, what nice people I
was with before I got on the stand. When Johnny Carson
comes in I try and play in that light, funny way he has.
When Basie comes in, I play with love. Some nights people
tell me I've played vicious, and they're right. Maybe I've
been thinking about thirty years of one-nighters or maybe
about what a drag it was in the Marines. But the next night
I'll come to where I'm playing and say, 'Sorry, little drums,
I'll be tender tonight.' Drums can be as musical as Heifetz.
You don't pick up sticks as if they were hammers. It's a matter of using your hands to apply pressure. You *apply* the
power, the beauty. When I think that I can't play the way
I want to play, I'll hang up my sticks. That'll be it. There'd
be nothing more horrible than to hear some guy say, 'Poor
Buddy Rich, he doesn't have it anymore.' "

Rich took a forkful of spaghetti.

"I'm told I'm not humble, but who is? I remember being
interviewed by a college kid once, and he said 'Mr. Rich,
who is the greatest drummer in the world?' and I said 'I am.'
He laughed and said, 'No, really, Mr. Rich, who do you
consider the greatest drummer alive?' I said 'Me. It's a fact.'
He couldn't get over it. But why go through that humble
bit? Look at Ted Williams—straight ahead, no tipping of
his cap when he belted one out of the park. He knew the
name of the game: Do your job. That's all I do. I play my
drums."

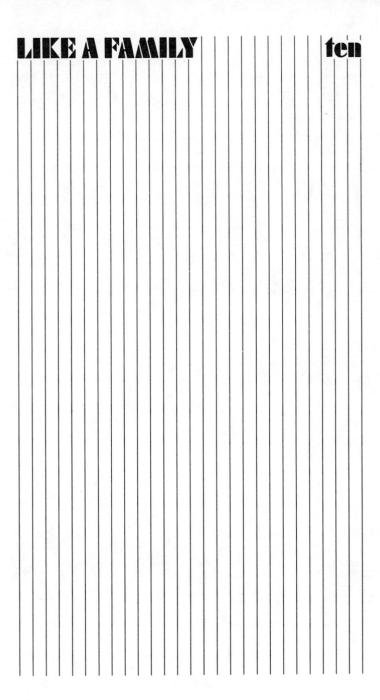

LIKE A FAMILY

A little bored and a little tired, the Modern Jazz Quartet, which was made up of John Lewis on piano, Milt Jackson on vibraharp, Percy Heath on bass, and Connie Kay on drums, finally broke up in 1974. It had much in common with the Duke Ellington band. Both groups were shepherded by gifted pianist-composers, who used their ensembles both as canvases and as test pilots for their compositions. Each group had a unique collective sound, which had as much to do with the ultimate effect of what it played as the composition itself. Both groups refused to compromise (Ellington occasionally faltered, while the M.J.Q. was, if anything, too highfalutin), and both elevated the course of jazz and of Western music itself. And both remained astonishingly constant: Harry Carney was with Ellington from 1927 until his death in 1974, and the M.J.Q. had just two personnel changes in its twenty years of existence. But the Modern Jazz Quartet accomplished things that even the Ellington band didn't. It invented a semi-improvised collective approach that defied the banality of the endless solo and the rigidity of conventional arrangements. It developed the heart-to-heart and head-to-head musical interplay and sensitivity of a great string quartet. And it perfected a subtlety that misled the unknowing into regarding it as a cocktail group and the knowing into scoffing at it as staid and stuffy.

The Quartet, because of its instrumentation and its constant interweaving, had a tintinnabulous texture. It shimmered, it rang and hummed, it sounded like loose change. As in any first-rate mechanism, its parts were as notable as their sum. Lewis's style is single-noted and highly rhythmic. His simple, seemingly repetitive phrases are generally played just behind the beat, where much of the secret of jazz lies. He is an intensely emotional pianist—in a transcendental way—and he succeeds, where most pianists fail, in transmitting his emotion. Jackson was a consummate foil. He is profuse, ornate, affecting, and original. His solos, inspired by Charlie Parker and Dizzy Gillespie, are open at both ends; that is, they seem to have started long before we hear them and to go on long after they have actually stopped. Whereas Lewis has a dry, belling tone, Jackson reverberated and rolled, continually threatening to spill over onto the rest of the group. Heath moved between, through, and under Lewis and Jackson, supporting them with a beautiful tone and an easy exactness. Kay is much the same. He is precise yet driving, and he gets a resilient, perfectly tuned tone on his drums and cymbals that both embellished and strengthened the total sound.

Onstage, the M.J.Q. often resembled, with its solemn, dark-suited mien, the rostrum at a morticians' convention. But this was only a mask; close-ups revealed life and variety. Heath is tall and thin and patrician. He has a high, receding forehead and a pharaoh's nose. Kay is even taller, with a full, monolithic face that conceals sharp, lively eyes. Jackson is a gnome. He is short and bird-boned, and is dominated by a slightly askew owl face. Lewis looks like a Teddy bear, and when he moves he runs, even from room to room. But he has the handsome, untroubled, intelligent eyes that professors of philosophy should have. Even the voices of the Quartet jostled one another. Lewis speaks softly, allowing his constant smile to carry half the weight of his words. Heath's near-shouting is rounded by continual laughter. Jackson's speech is quiet and slurred and almost subliminal, while Kay sounds like his bass drum.

If the Modern Jazz Quartet had ever recorded an autobiographical work, it might have sounded like this:

I. MASTERS OF THE MUSIC

Lewis

The original Quartet was made up of Milt and Ray Brown and Kenny Clarke and myself, and we decided to try and become a group after a record date early in the fifties for Dizzy Gillespie's recording label. There were things wrong in the music around us that we all agreed on, and some of them were long, long solos and that formula on a tune of everybody playing the melody in the first chorus, followed by a string of solos, and then the melody again. We didn't work together steadily until 1954. We lost Ray Brown before we really got started, because he married Ella Fitzgerald and we couldn't afford him anyway. Then I went back to school—the Manhattan School of Music—and after I'd graduated Milt didn't know whether he wanted to be just a member of a group or the leader, so while he was deciding I took a job with Ella as her accompanist, during which time the Quartet, or a quartet, with Percy Heath and Horace Silver on piano and Clarke and Milt worked the first Newport Jazz Festival. We made our first record in 1952 and had our first gig late that year, at the old Chantilly, on West Fourth Street. Kenny Clarke left us in 1955. He was sick and we talked about it and he said he knew he'd be better off on his own just then, so he left and Connie Kay came in. Kenny is still one of my favorite drummers. He's profound. You can listen to him all by himself, without anything else. And I think he plays even better now in Europe than he did then.

Kay

I joined the Quartet in February of 1955. Lester Young, who I'd been with, was out of town with Jazz at the Philharmonic, and I was thinking of taking a job with Sonny Stitt, the alto player, until Lester got back, but Monte Kay, the Quartet's manager, called me one morning and said the Quartet had a concert that night in Washington, D.C., and then a two-week gig at Storyville, in Boston, and would I like to go along? I met John at Penn Station and he filled me in on difficult pieces like "Django" going down on the train. I knew Milt real well and I'd met Percy and John. I understood it was a two-week gig, but when it was over nobody said anything and nobody has yet and that was seventeen years ago.

Jackson

The quartet has been like a marriage. It's become a way of life. You get to know each other's habits and mannerisms. At all times, each one knows what the other is going to do. John and I are more active than Percy and Connie musically. In fact, John is more than active, he's reckless the way he runs from place to place. He's been hit a couple of times by cars. He's got to be more careful of himself. John is always coming up with new ideas, and that keeps it from getting monotonous. Of course, there are times when I like to straighten out and just swing, get away from that controlled thing and play that old-time music. I generally take a group out in the summer—maybe Jimmy Heath, Percy's brother, and Cedar Walton and Bob Cranshaw and Mickey Roker. I took a band out several years ago and there was quite a lot of work, but things are slow now, so I've given up on it. I make records on my own, and I've thought of setting up a studio and teaching, just as a means of coming off the road. But as long as the Quartet is going the way it is, I don't have the time. So when I'm not working, I'm home playing pool and learning to swim.

Heath

I guess I took over the job of handling the Quartet's money because I handled the contract for our first gig at the Chantilly. I'm supposed to give out the checks every week, just as Connie is supposed to make hotel reservations and take care of transportation, but we have an attorney and a road manager and a booker and a travel agency now, and they take care of most of those details. But we used to do it all, and I suppose you have to go through that discipline at first. We probably make as much money as any jazz group. Our payroll is about seventeen hundred dollars a week. Twenty-five thousand dollars a year goes into just moving us around. In Europe, they generally pay your travel, and some festi-

vals do here, but most of it is on us. And we spend a good
deal of our pocket money on the road just to live right. We
consider that we're of such calibre and station that we
should stay in the best places and eat the best food. Some
years the Quartet has a little money left over, and one year
we invested it in a new ski resort in New York State, which
was fine until they foreclosed the lift. I understand the en-
terprise is a great success now. But we've kept aside enough
to start a pension plan and we have our own publishing company, but none of us could live on that. Milt and John probably make twice as much as I do. John has his movie scores
and royalties, and Milt has royalties and recordings and the
separate gigs he takes every summer. But I have no com-
plaints. June, my wife, hasn't had to work since 1949, when
we first moved to New York and lived on Sugar Hill, where
we had some fish-and-chip days. But the whole thing with
the Quartet is that we have made some money, but we have
never conformed. We have built up a lot of prestige, and
been paid for doing it.

Lewis

I got out of the Army in 1945, and when I went back to the
University of New Mexico they told me I might as well go
to music school. I'd met John Hammond through David
Sarvis, who taught in the drama department at the university, so I went to New York and entered the Manhattan
School of Music, and John helped me financially and every
other way. Before I'd left home, in Albuquerque, I'd heard
radio broadcasts from Billy Berg's, in Los Angeles, where
Charlie Parker and Dizzy Gillespie were playing with Ray
Brown and Milt Jackson, and it was unbelievable. When I
got to New York, I played one-nighters while I was waiting
out my union card. I worked on Fifty-second Street with
Allen Eager and Eddie Davis and with a band that Hot Lips
Page and Walter Page had. Joe Keyes, a most remarkable
trumpet player, was in it. In the meantime, Kenny Clarke

had come back from the service and through him Dizzy hired me as a pianist for my summer-school recess, and then he asked me to come and play with the band. I had to make a decision about the school and Dizzy. I decided I'd learn more from Dizzy, so I joined him in September, 1946. Kenny was in the band, and Ray Brown and James Moody. We went on ninety one-nighters in a row, and it was a very emotional tour—always a lot of fun and a lot of crying. Ray Brown left and we lost two drummers and the pianos were always half a tone out of tune and the audiences weren't too great because they didn't know how to dance to that music. It was really a concert band, which we found out when we went to Europe, in 1948, where we left everybody's mouth hanging open. Dizzy was marvellous to work under. He was never late, and that was when I learned not to be late. You have to get that over with.

I was disgusted with my playing at the time and I told Dizzy he better get someone else. But he talked me into staying. He always looked after me. Once, when I got sick on the road, he brought me all the way back to New York to the hospital. He's not as funny as he used to be, and I guess there's a good reason: It's a very strange country we live in now. I finally left Dizzy because I wanted to go back to Paris. If you ever go to Paris, you'd leave anything because of it. It's the jewel of jewels. I stayed there for five months, then came back to join Miles Davis' little band, with Gerry Mulligan and Eddie Bert and Max Roach. It was exciting, something new. Then Miles got me a job with Illinois Jacquet, who had his brother Russell and J. J. Johnson and Joe Newman and Jo Jones. I was with the band about eight months and I never saw so much money. Jacquet was making suitcases of money. We had to play "Flying Home" about four times a night, but I always found something in it. Norman Granz wanted me to come with his Jazz at the Philharmonic, but I decided I wanted to go back to the Manhattan School of Music. I got all the way to the airport on the way to meet Granz before I turned around and came back. Norman is a hard man to say no to and we weren't the greatest of friends for five or six years. But I got my Bachelor of Music, and in 1953 my Master of Music.

Kay

Sid Catlett was my man, my idol. The first time I heard him I was working after school and on Saturdays in a Chinese art gallery in the Fifties, and one day I passed Café Society Uptown, which was between Lexington and Park on Fifty-eighth Street and is now the Fine Arts Theatre, and the door was open and music was coming out. I stepped in and Teddy Wilson's band, with Big Sid, was rehearsing, and when I heard Sid that was it. I got to meet him a while later, when he was working on Fifty-second Street at the Downbeat Club. He was out on the street after work trying to get a cab to go home and I offered him a ride in a little raggedy 1935 Studebaker I had. "O.K., Bub," he said, which is what he called everybody. I drove him to One Hundred and Fifty-sixth and Amsterdam, where he lived, and after that I'd drive him all over and he'd always tell me to stop by any time—ground floor, right at the back. One night we drove around to a lot of clubs. We went into Nick's and he sat in, we went somewhere else and he sat in with a bebop band, and then he sat in with a swing group. He could play with anybody or anything. He was a happy-go-lucky person. Nothing bothered him. I think the secret of his playing was in his attitude toward things. He wasn't fazed even when he took a job at Billy Rose's Diamond Horseshoe. These show-girls would each bring a part of his drums onto the stage, singing something about him while they did, and then leave him up there all alone, where—bam!—he was supposed to play an unaccompanied solo absolutely cold, the lights on him and on his tuxedo, which was covered with sequins. He taught me little things. He'd stop by where I was working and tell me my left hand was too inactive or my beat on the ride cymbal was too loud, and he'd show me things at his house. But I learned the most from him in his attitude—

his quiet, beautiful way toward things, whether it was the world situation or just people.

Lewis

I was less influenced by piano players than by other instrumentalists, like Lester Young and Coleman Hawkins and Ben Webster, and trumpet players like Roy Eldridge and Harry Edison. I was formed more from hearing horn players. I learned some things from Earl Hines, not too many, and some of Count Basie's things, and of course one of the greatest pianists was Art Tatum. I'm happy it happened that way. I didn't get trapped into mechanical things, piano things.

When I take a solo, I try not to look at my fingers. It distracts me from the music-making. And after I learn a piece, I stop thinking about the rules—the bars and the harmony and the chords. I think about other things, even other music. If you break through those mere rules, destroy them, that's good, and it can become quite a marvellous experience. It's not just sadness or joy, it's something beyond that, perhaps exhilaration, but that's rare. Several years ago, at Monterey, I played with Illinois Jacquet and Ray Brown and Ray Nance, and that was exhilarating. When you start to play, an idea comes along, and that dictates where you have to go. Sometimes things go wrong, and many times you find a nice way of getting out of a phrase that is better than the original way you were going. But you have to be a musician first and an instrumentalist second. It's more important to be a master of the music than a master of an instrument, which can take you over.

Kay

I don't like to take drum solos at all. Drums are a flat instrument, and besides Catlett is gone and there's only one Buddy

Rich. I know how I feel when other drummers solo. It seems like you've heard them all before. There just aren't that many original people around. But when I do solo I think of the tune I'm playing. I try to fit what I'm playing into the composition rather than do just twelve bars of rudiments. The melody goes through your mind and you go along with it, fitting yourself to it. Also, my solos are always short, which I learned from Lester Young. He never took more than two or three choruses and neither did Charlie Parker, but they always managed to say all they had to say.

Jackson

When I solo I come down from the melodic line and the chords that are being played, or anything else, like a phrase the drummer might play, which can turn what you're doing into something lyrical. And I keep the melody in mind. I always remember the melody and then I have something to fall back on when I get lost, and with the human element I do get lost, but I've always been able to find my way back. Of course, your troubles and pleasures will come out in your music. But you do the best you can to entertain. Jazz is an art, but it's in the form of an entertaining art. I'm most relaxed in the blues or in ballads, which are my criterion. I get the most results from myself then and I reach the audience quicker. My blues come from church music and my ballads from the fact I'm really a frustrated singer. Lionel Hampton was the only influence I've had technically on the instrument. I heard him one night at the Michigan State Fair, in 1941, when he had Dexter Gordon and Howard McGhee, and that night really got to me. In style and ideas, I adapted myself to Charlie Parker and Dizzy. I can get around the mechanical feeling of my instrument by making glisses and grace notes, so that it sounds more like a horn. I still use a prewar Deagan vibraharp, and every two or three years the Deagan people take it apart and put it together again for me.

Lewis

When I'm working behind Milt, I try and be out of the way and at the same time supply something that might even improve on what he's playing. And I try to supply patterns that are strong rhythmically. It's easy to underestimate rhythm-making. I can never guess what Jackson is going to do next. I'm supporting him but I'm also moving along parallel to him. I learned to play collectively in Dizzy's band. I was trying to find a way to function, to add something, since most of the time I could play anything and no one would hear me anyway, and one night it happened up in Boston behind Dizzy when he played "I Can't Get Started." My discovery was related, too, to the way Kenny Clarke played drums in Dizzy's band. He complemented everything that was going on.

Kay

My drums are black pearl, but the fittings and stands are brass, which looks like gold. They're Sonor drums and are made in Aue, Germany, by people named Link. They're the oldest percussion-makers in Europe. We had a German bandboy who had worked for Stan Kenton and once he brought me a Sonor snare drum to try, and when we were in Europe next he took me down to Aue to meet Horst Link. He didn't speak English, but I got across a few things I didn't like—the response of the snare and such—and they worked it out. The snare they made me is wider and deeper than most people use, and I have calfskin heads instead of plastic. Plastic is fine when you have to play out-of-doors or in a lot of dampness. My floor tomtom is fourteen by sixteen inches and my side tomtom is eight by eleven and the bass drum is fourteen by twenty. I use a timpani head on the beater side of the bass drum, which gives more ring, and I use a big soft full beater ball, like a marching band's. There's a rod coming up from the top side of the bass drum, and on

it are a little cymbal and a triangle and chimes. I designed
the rod and I call it a sound tree. I've tried to get it patented,
but have been told I can't. I also have two timpani drums
that Link makes for me. They're smaller than usual and they
don't have any pedals. I used to have two small Syrian drums
mounted on top of the bass drum, but I don't use them anymore. We no longer play the pieces that called for them, and
anyway they were hard to tune and had goatskin heads,
which were difficult to get. I have six cymbals, including the
two high-hat cymbals, and they're A. Zildjians. I picked
them out at the factory in North Quincy, Mass., and it took
hours and hours. Eventually, I got absolutely tone-deaf. I've
had them ten years and I don't think I'll ever change them.
Link also makes my drumsticks, which I designed. They're
very light and thin and are made of white ash finished with a
black lacquer. Even though they look fragile they have the
same strength and tone as heavier sticks and they don't chip
or break as easily.

Lewis

Ideas for compositions pop into my head all the time and I
write them down in a notebook. The things you hear and
see go back in the brain and eventually something comes
out—melodic fragments or an opening for a piece or ideas of
how something I've already written could be improved. The
music I've heard inspires me, but it works negatively. The
music I've heard suggests music I've never heard. It points
to something that doesn't exist, that might be a little better,
and I try to supply that. A piece can take a few hours or a
couple of days to write. My writing and my playing are
connected. I can take ideas I have written or maybe not
written down yet—ideas just floating around back there. I
can take those ideas or written things and expand on them
each time I improvise, so in that way the pieces I write are
never finished, never complete. The reverse—taking an idea
or a phrase from a solo of mine and letting it inspire a new

composition—is trying to happen to me for the first time, and I don't know whether to let it happen or not. In fact, there's something from a solo of mine on our new record that keeps running through my head. It's terrible, like a mosquito you can't get rid of.

The group dictates what I write. I think in dramatic terms. Anyone playing the solo part in a concerto is dramatic, and it's the same thing with our little tiny group. In a piece like "Three Little Feelings," the star characters are Percy and Milt and Connie. They are given things to do that focus on them. I have written a lot of pieces based on the commedia dell'arte. I find the idea of the commedia attractive. They had to do the same things as jazz musicians. They never wrote things down. They developed pieces based on the prominent characters or events of the town they were working—things which would attract their audience. So they *created* their jobs, just as jazz musicians do. And, of course, I love the blues. Blues pieces are easier to write. You have a little form to fill out. I try to find blues in all non-blues—just in the way a group of notes goes together in a particular short phrase. I keep feeling those elements in non-blues music—the music in southern Yugoslavia, in Hungary, the music in North Africa and the Middle East, and in flamencan music. I don't believe in too much form. Music should have surprise in it, and too much fugue or any formula like that takes away the pleasure, which is what bothers me about what Gunther Schuller was trying to do with his Third Stream. I'm not interested in that. But I am interested in the classical *orchestra*—particularly the stringed instruments, which still have to be brought successfully into jazz.

II. BEGINNINGS

Heath

I was born April 30, 1923, in Wilmington, North Carolina, but when I was eight months old we moved to Philadelphia.

I have an older sister, Betty, and two younger brothers—
Jimmy, the tenor player, and Albert, the drummer. Pop was
an automobile mechanic. He was a wild little guy, a great
guy, and sharp and handsome. He played clarinet with the
Elks. It was part of a weekly cycle. On Mondays he'd pawn
the clarinet and get twenty dollars and pay his bills, and on
Saturday, when he got paid, he'd get the clarinet out of
pawn and play with the Elks on Sunday, and on Monday,
back to the pawnshop. I said to him once, "Pop, if you just
keep the clarinet out of pawn one week you'll be all right
and you won't have to pay that dollar interest." But it was
his thing, his habit, and he never kicked it. He had Bessie
Smith records, and every once in a while he'd pull out his
clarinet and do Ted Lewis or his own Silas Green routine—
Silas Green from New Orleans. In the early thirties, he
rented space in a garage and had his own shop, and up until
then we had money. Then the Depression ran the small busi-
nesses out, and he took a W.P.A. job for a couple of years,
and went back to being a mechanic for somebody else. My
mother was a hairdresser. She was a choir singer, and her
mother before her, in the Baptist church, where I spent a
lot of time when I was growing up. Those old sisters screaming and falling out in church, you felt something going
through you when you watched them. We had a family
quartet. My grandmother sang alto and my mother soprano.
I used to sing on a sepia kiddie hour on the radio, and the
kids who made it on the show got special passes to the Lincoln Theatre, where we would get to go backstage and
shake hands with Fats Waller and Louis Armstrong and
Duke Ellington.

I went to school in Philly until the last two years of high
school. There was an all-colored school across the street
from my grade school and the Italian and Jewish kids in our
block had to walk three blocks to their school, which we all
thought was a joke. From junior high on it was integrated,
but six years of separation and the damage was done. Being
thrown suddenly together couldn't undo it. I played a little
violin in junior high and I had the second chair in the first-

violin section at graduation. But it was rough getting home through the streets—you know, a little skinny black guy named Percy carrying a violin. I chopped and hauled wood after school, and hauled coal and ice in the summer. I'd bring home four or five dollars a week, which was all right in those days. My father's mother had a grocery store in Wilmington, and we used to go there for the summers, and so I stayed down there and finished up high school. I came back to Philly when I was seventeen, and went to work with my father and the two of us enrolled in a night school that specialized in mechanics. This lasted a year or so, and when I saw I wasn't getting anywhere at the shop—I'd be upstairs really involved in a carburetor job when they'd call up, "Hey, Percy, come on down and wash this car or do this grease job"—I said, "O.K., Pop, maybe I'm a dummy, but I'm going someplace else." I went to work for the railroad and ended up handling big equipment, moving engines around the yard, and I earned a boiler-washer's rating. I started going out with girls and I had a car. I was making a lot of overtime and I'd get these fat paychecks—eighty dollars and more every two weeks, which beat the twenty bucks I was making with Pop. Then after a year or so I got a bright idea—volunteer for the Air Force and get into aircraft-mechanics school. I took the physical. Underweight. They told me to come back in thirty days. I went home and slept late and ate bananas and went back. Still underweight. My number came up and I was drafted and I realized why I was underweight: They didn't have any colored aircraft-mechanics school.

I made a great score in the mechanical part of the aptitude tests the Army gives you, and one day I was asked, "Do you want to be a pilot or a navigator or a bombardier?" I was amazed. I remembered reading about some guy standing up in Congress when this program was announced and saying, "This is all very well and they've come a long way, but they aren't ready for *flying* yet." I was sent to Keesler Field, in Biloxi, Mississippi, where we lived in tents in a low area way over on the wrong side of the base, separate and unequal.

The closest we got to an airplane was at Saturday parades when somebody would look up and say, "Hey, there goes a B-24." Then we were shipped to the Tuskegee Army Air Force Base, at Tuskegee, Alabama. I graduated in January, 1945. Seven hundred of us started out and twenty-eight graduated. I was a lieutenant and had my wings and my boots and everything but a forty-five, which is the last thing they issue before you go overseas. I never got my forty-five. The European war ended and I got out and there I was with all that training and no place to use it. There were umpteen million white pilots with multiple-engine ratings coming back and I was a Negro with a single-engine rating. So I had to find something captivating to me. Having become an officer and a gentleman, I naturally didn't want to go back to all that dirt and grime. I'd heard a record with Coleman Hawkins and Sid Catlett and John Simmons, the bass player, and decided that's for me. I decided to go back to music. I went to the Granoff School of Music in Philly and studied harmony and I took lessons on the bass from a little old guy named Quintelli. I learned the C scale and how to read stock parts and I joined the union. I'd already worked in non-union places in some really funky neighborhoods in Philly. Then my brother Jimmy came home from Nat Towles' band. He'd heard Charlie Parker for the first time, and Johnny Hodges and Cleanhead Vinson just weren't it anymore. So we had continuous practice sessions at home. My mother was a great woman to put up with it. We even wrote out Parker's "Billie's Bounce" for Pop to play on clarinet. He made it sound just like a march. So we learned bop and had gigs. I worked with a Nat Cole-type trio for five or six months and then became part of the house rhythm section at the Philly Down Beat Club, along with Red Garland and Charlie Rice. Everybody played with us—Coleman Hawkins and Eddie Davis and Howard McGhee. I worked in a rhythm-and-blues band led by Joe Morris and joined McGhee in 1947, and I was with Fats Navarro and J. J. Johnson and Bud Powell and Art Blakey and Miles Davis after that, and in 1950 I went with Dizzy.

Kay

My parents lived in New York, but my mother's brother lived in Tuckahoe, and I was born there on the twenty-seventh of April, 1927. I was the only child. My parents are West Indians who came from an island named Montserrat. Their name is Kirnon and I was born Conrad Henry Kirnon. Originally the name was Kiernan, which was the name of one of my great-great-great-grandfathers, who was Irish. My father had a tailor shop in New York, and when that didn't do too good he got a job as an elevator operator, which he did until he retired. My mother had odd jobs doing housework and down in the garment center. She was musically inclined. She played piano and organ in church and she sang a little. She taught me how to play piano. She insisted I learn, but I didn't like it. My father played a little guitar. My mother used to let me stay up and listen to Cab Calloway broadcasts and I'd take the wooden bars out of coat hangers and shape them into drumsticks and play on the hassock. And a friend of mine had an uncle who kept a snare drum under his bed and we'd sneak it out and play it. So I always loved drums. I had my first gig right around the corner from where we lived in the Bronx, at a place called the Red Rose. All the guys were young and the only seasoned professional was the piano player, Jimmy Evans. He'd grown up in Monk's neighborhood, in the West Sixties, along with Elmo Hope and Tiger Haynes. The drummer at the Red Rose got sick and they had heard me practicing out of the window and asked me if I wanted to go to work. My parents said yes, and I stayed there weekends on and off for a couple of years. After the Red Rose, I was at Minton's, in Harlem, in a trio with Sir Charles Thompson and Miles Davis. We'd play one set and generally that was it. The rest of the evening it would be people sitting in—Charlie Parker and Dizzy Gillespie, Milt Jackson, Georgie Auld, Red Rodney. I remember when Ray Brown first came there. Freddie Webster came in all the time and he showed Miles how to

get those big oooh sounds, those big tones Miles uses now. I
was with Cat Anderson's band after that and then I toured
the South with a rock-and-roll group led by Frank Floor-
show Cully. I wanted to see what it was like down there.
Cully was a tenor player and he was just like his nickname.
He'd jump up and down when he played and stick the saxophone between his legs and do splits. Randy Weston, the
pianist, was in that band, and it wasn't a bad band. The bass
player hit all the wrong notes, but he had a hell of a beat.
You just closed your ears and felt the beat. We travelled in
a seven-passenger Chrysler, and we went as far as Lubbock,
Texas, and both coasts of Florida and Mobile, Alabama. I
wasn't too surprised because I'd heard how things were
down there, but it was still a revelation. We worked at a big
roadhouse for several weeks that used to feature people like
Blue Barron and Horace Heidt—we were the first colored
band that had ever played the place—and during intermission
we were supposed to go back in the kitchen and stay there.
But you'd be offered drinks by customers and you didn't
know whether to accept and stay out front or get on back.
In those days it didn't pay to be a pioneer. We'd pull up at
a restaurant and be told to go around to the kitchen and
there you'd find a regular booth with a Formica-top table
and all, which was fine with me because they always piled
your plate up. At orange-juice stands you'd have to drink
your juice off to one side, and if we stopped at a grocery
store they'd sell us cold cuts and canned stuff, but we had to
eat it in the car. Once we ate in a restaurant owned by a
colored cat and I told him if we get together, organize and
the like, maybe we can *do* something about all this crap.
Well, he wanted to fight *me*. He had two restaurants, he
said, and everything was *all* right.

By this time I could get a job with anyone. My main asset
was I could keep good time. I had made a whole lot of rock-
and-roll records for Atlantic Records. I was with Lester
Young off and on for five or six years. Lester and I were like
buddies. When I joined him, I already knew him, but he
didn't know *I* was joining him. I met him down in Penn Sta-

tion and asked him what he was doing, and he said, "I'm waiting for the drummer, Lady Kay," which is what he always
called me. "Well, I'm the drummer," I said. "What! You're
the drummer?," and he fell out. He was a sweetheart to me.
He was very shy. He didn't love crowds or to be around
strangers, and he didn't like to eat. All that alcohol. He'd
leave home for work with a fifth of Scotch every night and
everybody in the band would work on it to keep Lester from
getting too drunk. It was terrible I drank so much Johnny
Walker. Later, the doctor told him to switch to cognac—a *little* cognac—so it was a whole bottle of cognac every night.
He had a funny, codelike way of talking, with nicknames and
strange names for everything. Everybody was Lady So-
and-So, a chorus was one long and two choruses two longs,
and he had nicknames for all the different songs. A lot of the
jive talk you hear now on TV I first heard from Lester, and
when he and Basie and Old Man Jo Jones got together they
all talked it. He wasn't a forceful person, but he'd get fed up.
One time he had a trumpet player who took the same solo
on a certain tune every night, and when he'd start Lester
would look at me and say, "Damn, Lady Kay, there he goes
again," and we'd sing the whole solo note for note right
along with the trumpet player. Lester didn't feel he was getting the recognition he deserved and finally he got to the
point where he didn't care whether he lived or died. I used
to ask him why he didn't play his clarinet once in a while,
and he'd always say, "Lady Kay, I'm saving that for my old
age."

Jackson

There were six boys in my family and I was the second. I
was born in Detroit on January 1, 1923. My mother was
from Georgia and my father from Winston-Salem. She had
a very religious background—the Church of God in Christ,
which we call the Sanctified Church. She was a housewife

and she worked in a defense plant during the war. My father was quiet but very lively, always on the go. I guess that's why I stayed so small—always moving so much. Also, it's a trait of Capricorn. My father was a factory worker with Ford and Chevrolet, and he played three or four instruments—piano, guitar, and so forth. I started on guitar when I was seven, and I was completely self-taught. I didn't study anything until I took piano lessons at eleven from a Mr. Holloway. I took them two years. I've lost track of him completely, which I regret. I like to check those things out. By the time I got to high school I was playing five instruments—drums in the marching band, timpani and violin in the symphony, guitar and xylophone in the dance band—and I sang in the glee club and choir. But I was concentrating on drums. Then the music teacher asked me if I wanted to take lessons on the vibraharp, as something else to do. I'd finished the drum course and was even helping other kids on drums, so I tried vibraharp and got hung up on it immediately. I gave up the drums altogether and concentrated on vibes. By 1939 I had two things going. I travelled all over on weekends with a local gospel quartet, the Evangelist Singers. We broadcast every Sunday over CKLW from Windsor. I got into it through my playing in church. If they needed vibes, I made that; if it called for drums, I made that; if it called for guitar, I made that; if it called for piano, I made that. The other thing was I started playing vibes with Clarence Ringo and the George E. Lee band. Sugar Chile Robinson was in the first group I played with. I had met Dizzy Gillespie in 1942 and through him I had an opportunity to join Earl Hines' big band, which he was with. At least there were about to be negotiations to join the band, but I got drafted and ended up in Special Services in the Air Force. I never went overseas and I got out in 1944, and went back to Detroit, where I organized a little group called the Four Sharps. It had guitar, bass, piano, and me, and we were sponsored by the Cotton Club. Detroit was full of musicians—Howard McGhee, Al McKibbon, the Jones brothers, a good alto named Burnie Peacock, and Lucky Thompson. Yusef Lateef and I went through high school together and Billy Mitchell and I grew up together.

The Four Sharps stayed alive a year, and then Dizzy came through and sat in one night and persuaded me to go to New York, so I went, in October of 1945. He had Ray Brown and Max Roach and Charlie Rouse. We worked the Brown Derby on Connecticut Avenue in Washington, went back to New York, and out to Billy Berg's, in Los Angeles. We had Stan Levey on drums, Al Haig on piano, Ray Brown, Charlie Parker, Lucky Thompson, Diz, and me. We took the train. Man, four and a half days. We left on a Tuesday and got there Saturday. I guess we stayed out there six or eight weeks. Slim Gaillard had the other group at Berg's, and they wound up as the stars. People went for the new jive language he sang, and anyway Slim is a very entertaining man. And Frankie Laine would come in every night for his two numbers. The audiences couldn't understand what *we* were doing, but it didn't bother me. I'd just turn my back on them and listen to Charlie. That was all I wanted to hear. When we got back to New York, Dizzy organized his big band, and that's where I first met John Lewis. Klook— Kenny Clarke—was responsible for bringing John in. I stayed with Dizzy until 1947 and then worked with Howard McGhee and Jimmy Heath and Percy, and in 1949 and 1950 I was with Woody Herman, and then I went back to Dizzy.

John and Ray Brown and Klook and myself had actually played as a group as early as 1947. We'd play and let the rest of the band rest. I guess it was Dizzy's idea. I stayed with Dizzy until 1952, when we tried to get the Quartet going. Ray Brown left, so we hired Percy Heath. John suggested the name of the group.

Lewis

I was born in La Grange, Illinois, a suburb of Chicago, on May 3, 1920, but by July I was sitting in Albuquerque, where my grandmother and great-grandmother lived. They'd come from Santa Fe and my mother from Las Vegas, New Mexico, which was there long before that other one. My people came down from the Cherokees—the Virginia Cherokees. I don't know much about my father, Aaron Lewis, except that he came from Chicago and was an interior decorator and played good fiddle and piano. He and my mother were divorced not long after I was born, and my mother died of peritonitis when I was four. I remember that. So I was raised by my grandmother, who is still alive and comes to see us once a year, and by my great-grandmother, who died in 1953. Except for my mother, they were strong women. My great-grandmother knew Pat Garrett, who shot Billy the Kid, and I think she even knew Billy. And she knew Geronimo, the Apache chief, who was a remarkable man, a very clever, intelligent man. My grandmother was a caterer and my grandfather had a moving-and-storage company. I never knew him. He accidentally shot himself in the foot duckhunting and developed tetanus. And my great-great-grandfather had owned the Exchange Hotel in Santa Fe. I had a good childhood. Albuquerque was a town of just twenty-five thousand souls in those days and everything was so special—the Spanish culture and the air and the cleanness. We lived right in the middle of town and there were very few Negroes. It was the people of Spanish extraction, or Spanish and Indian extraction, who had the hard times, not the Negroes. I went to the public schools and the atmosphere was very competitive. Once you got on the honor roll, you had to *stay* on it.

Everybody played something in my family, so I started on the piano at five or six. It was drudgery, and I tried to revolt on the grounds the lessons cost so much, but failed. I took lessons forever. When I was ten or so I was in a little band. We were Boy Scouts winning music-achievement badges. Our first gig was in a real night club. We played from nine to twelve and were paid a dollar apiece and all we could eat, and someone came along to watch over us. There were local bands around and a lot of Southwest bands came through town. Eddie Carson had one of the local groups and I had cousins who played in it. Sticks McVea, who was a fantastic drummer, would bring his band in from Denver. Freddie Webster was in it, and he had a wonderful piano player named John Reger. John Hammond wanted Reger to play with Benny Goodman, but Reger's wife wouldn't let him go East. I'd take Reger's place some nights. And the Bostonians would come through, with Jay McShann on piano and Howard McGhee on trumpet. Lester Young sometimes played in town. He knew my whole family. He was a very gifted, talented genius-type person. He was like a poet. Everything came out as poetry when he talked. By the time I was fourteen or fifteen, I was working in dance halls and night clubs. I had to learn Spanish music to play the fiestas. When I went to the University of New Mexico, I became the leader of a dance band there, and Eddie Tompkins, the trumpet player who had been with Jimmy Lunceford, would sit in. I took arts and sciences for two years, then became fascinated with anthropology. I devoured everything on the subject, and kept my music going at the same time. Then, six months before graduation, I was drafted. It's the only thing I've ever had against the Japanese people. I was in the Army four years, in Special Services, and the best thing about it was that I met Kenny Clarke in France in 1943 or 1944. At the time, there was a surplus of pianists and drummers, so Kenny and I took up trombone. It was all right. In fact, I can still play it.

III. ROOM TO LIVE IN

Jackson

I built my house in Scarsdale several years ago. My wife, Sandra, and I moved up there with our daughter, who's seven, from Hollis, Long Island, where we'd lived for nine years. It's been beautiful. No hostility. The people around us have some money and they're not concerned with whether you're a Negro. We have all kinds—Jews, Italians, Negroes—and they just aren't concerned with it. I've handled the race thing fairly well. I've been pretty outspoken. I don't know whether it helps or hurts, but it gives me a clear outline on life and myself. The first thing a man has to do is take stock of himself. You have all these people who go to school and study and still don't know themselves or what they want in life. I never had that trouble. From the age of seven I knew I would play music. There was never any doubt in my mind. I've always had my feet on the ground, had a good idea of where I was going. Like in high school, I wanted to learn something about my ancestry. I wanted to know where my forefathers came from and what they did. I was regarded as a troublemaker, asking questions like that. And in 1943, during the Detroit race riots, I wanted to organize and go back to Detroit from the Army instead of going to Europe and fighting somebody else.

Heath

We live in a big old white 1902 house in Springfield Gardens, in south Queens. It's near Farmers Boulevard, where the farmers used to take their stuff up to market. I bet we live on the only block in the city limits that has just four houses on it—ours, an old Colonial house whose owner, a lady, was born in our house, and two others. There aren't even any sidewalks out front and we have fruit trees in the back yard. The neighborhood was a model integrated one when we moved there in 1958, but it's changed. The white families have begun moving out and the area has become one of families where both parents work and the kids have keys to their houses to let themselves in, which is where the trouble starts. We never go out when I'm home. I seldom go in to New York anymore, unless it's to rehearsals or if we have a gig there. It's too much to go and see all these cats standing around, half of them without gigs.

Lewis

We take a two-month vacation in the summer. It's based mostly on Percy. He has the older children and he wants to be with them when they are out of school. And Connie, who lives with his wife near Lincoln Center, has two boys, and he likes to be with them. We work steadily the rest of the year, and it has to be that way, with the vacations. The group is a coöperative and always has been. We have a corporation, the Modern Jazz Society. I'm president, Milt is vice-president, Percy is treasurer, and Connie is the secretary. We pay ourselves a weekly salary, and we don't have any such thing as a leader, in the old-time concept of a leader. I serve as artistic director and musical director. Occasionally I *have* to make the group do something, and later they generally see it's what we should have done. Sometimes I cut things so fine trying to make everyone happy it frightens me. We've gotten along well or we wouldn't still be together. We're smart enough and clever enough to give each other room to live in, to have respect for each other's personalities. It's not a perfect marriage by any means; it's normal travelling by sea, with stormy periods and all. The time we see of each other outside of our work is reduced even more than it was. We see enough of each other when we're out on the road, where we always have separate rooms. Milt gets up early and I do, too. Percy and Connie don't. Some of us, Connie in particular, like to watch TV and some don't. We have a fine for lateness. It's fifty dollars for the first five minutes and fifty dollars for each fifteen minutes thereafter, unless there's a sufficient excuse, which traffic and such isn't. You just start early enough. If anyone were to be late, it would probably be Percy or Connie. Milt and I generally come early.

I bring in the music and the arrangements and the group starts learning. Every now and then I put something in a piece that they can't play, so there isn't any dullness. They are fair readers. It takes us a long time to learn things, but they're much faster than they used to be. It generally takes us three hours to learn a piece, which is the length of a standard rehearsal. The whole thing on my part is to anticipate this or that musical difficulty, which means spending more time writing and thinking. We have over three hundred numbers in our repertory, and it grows and changes all the time. Sometimes I change certain passages in numbers, and tempos automatically tend to get faster through the years. And the group grows steadily and understands the music better, and that contributes to change. When we haven't played a number for a long time, we have to sit down and start all over with it. Gradually each piece comes to sound as if it is improvised all the way through. Some actually are and some are almost all written. The length of a piece is pretty much dictated by where it is in the concert program, and the program is figured out, balanced out, from the first number to the last, so that it has a design and structure. So the program as a whole comes first, the pieces next, and the solos last. We don't have any prearranged signals, aside from somebody just looking up from his instrument, for letting each other know when one of us is finishing a solo. Jackson almost always takes the same number of choruses and I just seem to know when he is finishing, and it's the same with him when I solo. We abhor long solos. If good things don't happen in the first chorus of any solo, it's generally not going to happen at all.

Heath

The group didn't take its first vacation until ten years ago. I guess I pushed hardest for it. My wife and I have three boys—Percy, twenty, Jason, fifteen, and Stuart, eleven—and this business of working all year for ten years, it was *nothing*. It was ten years of double existence. If I'm out there on the road worrying about what's going on here, I might as well not be there. So I had to tell June, "Whatever comes up is on you, Snooky," and she's handled it ever since—every-

thing, all the cuts and bruises and sicknesses that come along
with kids. When I first brought up the vacation idea, it was
"Oh, my . . . Hmm . . . Well, I don't know, the Quar*tet*
comes first." Damn! Anyway, we took our first vacation
out on Fire Island, and it was not the vacation we had hoped
for. I lugged all this electrical gear out there—hi-fi, tape recorder, toaster—and trundled it down the boardwalk to our
house, the people I passed nodding their heads and mum-
bling about what a great generator we must have, and of
course we got there and no electricity. Then I discovered
David Amram and some other cats were staying nearby, so
I ended up jamming every night. On top of that, fishing—
particularly surfcasting—is my thing, but nothing happened.
I don't think a fish passed that beach all summer. So the next
year we went out to Montauk and we've rented a house
there ever since. I have a camper, and for traction in the sand
I let the air out of the tires about halfway and we drive
down the beach and fish and never see anybody for miles.
There's a great group of people doing surf-fishing. They're
from all walks. Sometimes I go to the Rockaways just south
of where I live and once at dawn I was fishing and I noticed
this figure way down the beach. We moved toward each
other slowly and finally I thought, He looks familiar, and
when we got near enough to see each other there was Ed
Shaughnessy, the drummer on the "Tonight Show." We fell
out—two jazz musicians meeting up at dawn on an empty
beach. I don't see how people *don't* fish. To get that close
to the fish in Montauk and not get involved—I don't see how
people do it. Just to realize that big bass are swimming in between them in the water—unbelievable. I'm looking forward
to the time when I can be by the seashore and in the sun
chasing fish all year. Then if I take any vacation, it'll just be
from fishing. Right now, messing around with all that salt
water isn't the best thing for a bass player's hands. It softens
them up. But I'm always practicing, and I start rehearsing
seriously a week or two before we come back and my hands
are generally O.K. by the time we play our first gig.

Lewis

I met Mirjana, my wife, in Yugoslavia when the Quartet was on tour there. Her sister was going around with a Yugoslavian jazz pianist who worked in a group patterned after ours. I spent a lot of time with him and one night we went to Mirjana's house and I met her. She was going with someone else. I liked Yugoslavia very much. I liked it so much I went back every year to the jazz festival they have in June, and I'd spend most of my time with Mirjana's sister and her boyfriend. Then in the summer of 1962 Mirjana and her sister and the pianist—they were married by now—came to visit me in the South of France, where we were vacationing. They spent two weeks, and two weeks later Mirjana and I were married. You can only get married on Wednesdays and Saturdays in Zagreb, so we got married on a Wednesday, and on Thursday I had to leave for a South American tour, and it took two months to get all the papers so that Mirjana could join me. Both she and her sister are pianists, and their father is a voice teacher. He is a remarkable, great human being. He is teaching now at the New England Conservatory. Her mother was an actress on stage and in films and she worked in the Underground during the war. We have two children—Sacha, who is seven, and Nina, who is three. I think we live where we do, in an apartment looking over the Hudson back of Lincoln Center, because the view always reminds me of one in Yugoslavia.

Heath

June is one in a million, one in eighteen million. She comes from Philly, and when I met her she was working in a record shop. She had a falling-out with her family over things like having pictures of colored musicians on her walls. But she loved the music and she found the players were pretty human people. She'd stop by when we were practicing at my parents' house after the war, and I wouldn't even know she was there. She'd be sitting in the corner reading a book. It wasn't a matter of my choosing another race. It was a question of finding a good woman. I quit shaving back then— I couldn't stand all that scraping and chopping every day— and she didn't mind. She was willing to go to New York with me in 1949 and willing to take a gig as a nurse's aide at thirty dollars a week while I sweated out my union card. I guess what finally drove us out of Philly was one night when we were walking home from a movie or something and this cop pulled up beside us and says, "Are you all right, Miss?" June looked at him and said, "What do you mean?" "Well, I'm just doing my job," the cop says. "Of course I'm all right," June said, and we went on. And you know, that cop was a neighborhood cop and he knew who I was.

Kay

I still love to play, but it's not like when I was younger. I don't seem to see and hear that fire—that musical fire—that was all around us then. I don't seem to hear that kind of music anymore. Generally the people I like to play with just aren't around. They're in the studios or out of town or they have their own groups. But when I get the chance I like to play with Ray Brown and Bill Evans and Sonny Rollins and Jimmy Heath and John—John Lewis. To my mind, John plays very underrated piano. I like to play with Dizzy and Miles and I like Idrees Sulieman and Oscar Peterson. And Sonny Stitt and Cannonball, and I like Clark Terry and Sam Jones. I like to play with big bands, too. I don't think it's any harder. I play the same way as with a small group. A lot of drummers make the mistake with big bands of being louder and heavier, but all that does is bog things down. Playing with the Quartet can get a little monotonous, night after night, week after week. Sometimes you have to play the same numbers over and over to please the people. But no one in the group ever plays the same thing twice. It's always new, always different, and I have just about complete freedom. Sometimes John writes out a drum part to give me an idea of what he wants, but then I can change it around to the way I want it, and I'm absolutely free behind the soloists. I can feel by what they're playing when a solo is coming to an end. I can feel that they've just about run out of what they want to do. And I can feel when someone might want to change the rhythm or double the tempo.

Lewis

I think that the young primitive rock people have something going. There'll be new developments, some attractive ones. The music is getting better and better. A lot of their guitar players sound better to me than most of the thousand-note jazz guitarists. There are more good young jazz players in Europe than there are here—Jean-Luc Ponty, a French violinist, and a bass player from Copenhagen, Nils Henning Orsted-Pedersen. He's pretty terrific. He's only twenty-five, and he used to hang around Oscar Pettiford when he was a teen-ager. I've heard an eleven-year-old drummer in Yugoslavia with a great sense of time. And when you go to a festival in Europe it's not like it is here. Everybody *watches* everybody play, whether they're good or bad. Youngsters get up there on the stage, their faces as red as beets trying to play, and everybody watches. There's no question more is happening in Europe than here.

Heath

A group sound is one thing to work for and individual virtuosity is something else. I don't worry about the virtuosity thing. This recent bringing of the bass into the front melodic line is a mistake. Most bass solos, particularly if you don't know the tune, sound the same. The bassists figure out certain sounds and patterns and just fit them to whatever it is they're playing. I used to hang around with John Simmons a lot and then with Oscar Pettiford. O.P. and I would play bass-and-cello duets all night. Ray Brown showed me how to hold the bass properly. I always considered Ray the walker, the rhythm man, and Pettiford the soloist. But I'd rather be part of a group. I have to play certain parts as written, but you can hand a group of notes to ten different players and each one will read them differently. It's up to me to make those notes say exactly what they have to say, in a particular spirit. What we have over most groups is simple: We've played together for twenty years. Another advantage is doing exactly what we want to do by creating music and selling musical entertainment. We've taken jazz into the concert halls of the world, even into the Mozarteum, in Salzburg. We've performed with a lot of symphony orchestras, and respect for jazz has grown among symphony players. Some of them have even become jazz players. For a long time, white Americans only understood polkas and fox-trots and waltzes, but through rock they're beginning to understand the jazz feeling, even if it comes from listening to an imitation of Muddy Waters from England. Jazz has always been considered a dirty music, an evil music, a colored music, and the country is still ashamed of it.

Jazz is a funny thing. If you ever let the externals dominate—classical music or Eastern music or Brazilian music—you have something else. But as long as you can incorporate little bits and pieces from the East or Vienna or Brazil and still keep the special feeling of that dotted eighth, that pulse, that afterbeat, then it's fine. It's the same thing with the long solos, the Coltranes. I'd go hear Coltrane and after the set, which might be one long solo, I'd say, "Hey, 'Trane. How are you, man? You sound good," or some such, and I'd beat it out of there, so that I didn't have to say any more. That music was just one facet of existence; all it did was shout Help! But all you had to do was look away from the chaos Coltrane's music was staring at and you'd find the ocean still there, the beauty and peace still there.

The way you play has to do with the way you feel that
night. You hear that your kid was punched in the face three
thousand miles away or you're lonesome and haven't found
anybody to talk to or you're tired of the town and sick of
each other; it all comes out in the music. After all, those people up there on the stand or the stage are *men*. You have to
know how it feels to be miserable, how it feels to be sad,
how it feels to be in the dumps before you can project it.
When that slave cried out in the field, he wasn't just making
music, he *felt* that way.

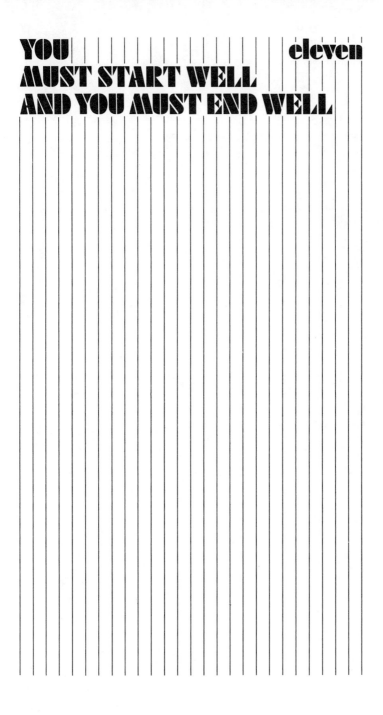

YOU MUST START WELL AND YOU MUST END WELL

Propelled by his brand-new Pulsar watch, which he resolutely kept set five hours ahead, at London time, Stéphane Grappelli, the formidable sixty-seven-year-old violinist, did not waste a second when he was in New York for his first real visit, and during his ten-day stay he went to West Forty-seventh Street and bought his Pulsar; kept an eye on Nigel Kennedy, a cherub-faced English prodigy who is a protégé of his friend Yehudi Menuhin and a Juilliard student ("You must laugh more, Nigel"); walked a league or two every day; delightedly spent most of an afternoon in Macy's; averaged four or five hours' sleep; drank an unaccustomed amount of white wine at the opening of Zoot Sims and Dave McKenna at Michael's Pub and grew quite jolly; attended the beginning of a typically thunderous Mahavishnu Orchestra concert; visited with his compeers Jean-Luc Ponty and Martial Solal (piano); gave a gentle and careful concert at Carnegie Hall ("The sound was a bit deesturbed. I couldn't hear myself, so I was not quite at home. If I can hear me, I'm safe. I didn't expect that ovation. I am always prepared for the worst"); played fourteen immaculate sets at Buddy's Place during his six days there; and confirmed what a good many people over here have long suspected because of his recordings—that he has pulled even with Joe Venuti, his consummate American counterpart and long the best of jazz violinists. All of which might seem akin to hailing the world's two finest unicyclists, there having been in the history of music only half a dozen first-rate jazz violinists. But adapting the violin to jazz at all is a feat, and doing it with the grace and skill and daring of Grappelli is a signal achievement. Grappelli's new preëminence has finally brought to a close the long evolution of European jazz musicians from ardent, self-denigrating copyists to unavoidably attractive professionals. Indeed, Grappelli, together with his noble colleague, the gypsy guitarist Django Reinhardt, initiated the trek in 1934, when the Quintet of the Hot Club of France, of which he and Reinhardt were nominal coleaders, made its first recordings.

Grappelli's style has changed little since then. As is true of all adventurous creations, its inspirations are diverse and subtle. They include the piano playing of Bix Beiderbecke

("It have a fantastic *psychologique* effect on me"); the buoyant, baroque dance music of the twenties and early thirties; the singing of Louis Armstrong; George Gershwin, both as pianist and as composer; Billie Holiday; Frankie Trumbauer; Art Tatum ("He was for a long time the only reason for me to come to this country. Then, when I am ready, he died, and—*incroyable!*—I miss him"); and Django Reinhardt, an extraordinary performer whose inventions have yet to be entirely absorbed. Grappelli's playing is often called "elegant," and so it is. But there is more to it than that. It has, at its best, a controlled ecstasy. It is fluid yet structured, flamboyant yet tasteful, lyrical yet hardheaded. Grappelli is a superb melodist; that is, he can play a song "straight" while subtly so altering its melodic line that its strengths double. And he is a tireless improviser. At fast tempos, he often gives the impression that he is carrying on two solos at once. He will start a chorus with a long, molten phrase in the middle register and, without warning, leap into the highest register; there, continuing his chain of thought, he begins solo No. 2 (while his opening middle-register passage still courses through the listener's mind); then, after flashing along almost above hearing, he will, again without pause, drop back to solo No. 1 (while No. 2 still seems to be sailing along), and close the chorus by plummeting into his lowest register for a fat double-stop. He is fond of rhapsodies, which he plays with a blueslike directness, and he is fond of the blues, which he plays rhapsodically. His tone is clear and measured; it doesn't go thin at fast speeds and it doesn't balloon at slow speeds. Grappelli has always swung. He often unwittingly made the ingenious Reinhardt sound chunky and heavy, and he does the same thing in a couple of recordings he made with Oscar Peterson. For a long time after Reinhardt's death, in 1953, one heard little of Grappelli, even though he worked almost steadily. A few years ago, he began to shine again. The reasons were many: Reinhardt was inevitably receding in memory; Grappelli had just spent the better part of five years at the Paris Hilton, which put him firmly before the public; the younger generation,

astonished by his joyousness and honesty and musical
aplomb, took to him; he began recording prolifically again,
often with startling results (marvellous collaborations with
Menuhin and the vibraphonist Gary Burton); and for the
first time he started travelling widely.

Grappelli stayed at the Americana when he was here, and
he made his trip to Macy's and back on foot. It was a cold,
blowing afternoon when he set off, and he went down Seventh Avenue at a near jog. He had on a tan sweater, a thin
tan safari jacket, and purple pants, and he said he was cold.
His white hair has receded, but it is long at the neck, as if
it had begun to slip off and been caught in the nick of time.
A block from the hotel, Grappelli pushed the time button
on his Pulsar and red numerals appeared: 7:26. "I do not
want to lose the London time," he said, in his soft, somewhat
high voice. "I love London, and it comforts me to always
have it with me. I must be back by five o'clock at the hotel
for an appointment, and since I am very nervous I must be
on time. Djangoo was always late, and often he forget to
appear at all at night, because his only watch was the sun.
He was taciturn and childish. He was illiterate, and he spoke
French—joost. He had the intelligence of the *paysan*. He did
not have the intelligence of the poet, except when he play.
He was not handsome and he often dressed badly, but he
have great personality. When he walked down the street,
people turned to look at him. Ah! The troubles he gave me!
I think now I would rather play with lesser musicians and
have a peaceable time than with Djangoo and all his monkey
business. One time, Djangoo and I were invited to the Élysée
Palace by a high personality. We were invited for dinnair,
and after dessert we were expected to perform. Djangoo did
not appear. After dinnair, the high personality was very polite, but I can tell he is waiting, so I say I think I know where
Djangoo is when I don't know at all. The high personality
calls a limousine and I go to Djangoo's flat, in Montmartre.
His guitar is in the corner, and I ask his wife where he is.
She says maybe at the *académie* playing billiards. He was a

very good player of billiards, very *adroit*. He spent his infancy doing that and being in the streets. His living room was the street. *Alors*, I go to the *académie* and when he sees me he turns red, yellow, white. In spite of his almost *double* stature of me, he was a little afraid. In the world of the gypsy, age count, although I am only two years older than him. Also I could read, I was instructed. He have two days' *barbe* on his face and his slippers on, so I push him into the limousine and we go back to his flat to clean him up a little and get his guitar. Djangoo was like a chameleon; *à toute seconde* he could change keys. He was embarrassed about everything, but his *naturel* self came back, and when we arrived at the Élysée and the guard at the gate saluted the limousine, he stick up his chin and say, 'Ah! They recognize me.' He disappeared again when we were playing a posh place in Biarritz named The Four Seasons. We were, for once, living just like customers in a good hotel. Djangoo says he is going fishing and I tell him I will go along to keep him company, even though I do not like to fish. Djangoo loved fishing! He would cut a branch and fasten some incredible string and find a worm and catch a big fish while people with *moderne* stick catch nothing. I go to his room, but he is gone—clothes, everything. I look and look and I finally find him in an abandoned caravan outside the town. I say to him, 'Now what have you done? For once, we have a good lodging. What push you to leave that hotel?' He say, 'Oh, I don't like all that carpet. It hurt my feet.'

"He was always trying to be something he wasn't. The first time we went to England, in 1937, the impresario made up a very good contrac'. We get travel by first class going and coming. When the impresario show the contra' to Djangoo, Djangoo studied it a long time—he cannot read, remember—and suddenly he banged his finger down on the page and said, 'I don't like that!' I looked where his finger is and it is the business about the first-class travel. I laugh and laugh and tell the impresario never mind, Djangoo is making a big joke, that's the way he always is. *Alors*, that same trip we play a concert at the Cambridge Theatre, and the master of ceremonies introduce me before Djangoo. Djangoo looked around and when the time comes he won't play. The other two guitarists in the group are terrorize of him and they just stare at him. So I started with the bass and finally after two or three choruses Djangoo started to play. I did not speak with him for one week, and always after that there was a little tension from him to me."

Grappelli stopped for a light at Fortieth Street. He looked up and down Broadway, and said rhetorically, "Why is this the only street that run diagonal in New York? Very strange." The light changed and he scuttled across the street, hugging himself to keep warm. The wind plumed his hair and made him squint, and his small, narrow face was fierce and hawklike. "When I first met Djangoo, it was 1931 and I am just coming back to the violin. Three or four years before, I had shut my violin box and *pouf!*—Stéphane Grappelli, pianist. I learn the piano the way I learn the violin and how to cook—from books and from watching others. I like the piano for two reasons: I discover I can play parties by myself in the Sixteenth Arrondissement for Madame This and Madame That and make a lot more money, and I discover I like the *harmonique* aspect of the piano. I am nineteen, and I play the piano in a French band at the Ambassadeurs, in Paris, for two seasons. *Voilà!*—one thousand dinnairs every night for five hundred men and five hundred women all covered with diamonds. Two or three maharajas. Clifton Webb singing Cole Porter's 'Looking at You.' Paul Whiteman playing. Bing Crosbee, who was one of the Rhythm Boys, asking me at the bar, 'Hey, man! Where can I get a *chasseur?*' Fred Waring and twenty girl singers going from table to table. Oscar Levant and George Gershwin playing 'Rhapsody in Blue' on one piano with two keyboards. I manage to congratulate Gershwin on his way out, near the kitchen. I grasp his hand and nearly kiss him. He smile and was very polite to me. *Alors*, after that I spend two seasons with Gregor and his Gregorians. Gregor was an Armenian who was picking up about ten languages and who arrive every night at the Palais de la Méditerranée, in Nice,

in a Renault with two black chauffeurs. Gregor was a tee-
totaller, but if we go to a night club after work he sometimes had a little drink, and it would go right to his head.
One night, he have a drink and he say, 'Hey, Stéphane, you
used to play the violin. Why do you not play it now?' Well,
by then I haven't played it in three or four years, but I'm
having a little drink myself, so I borrow a violin and play
and I play *gauche*. Just three days away from the violin is
like sitting in a chair with arthritis too long: it take the feet
a while to get going again. But Gregor stay after me and
pretty soon I am back with the violin, and I stay with it until this day. After Gregor, I go back to Paris, which was
marvellous then. I play violin and saxophone, which I learn
in the South of France in a little café where painters like
de Kooning come in in bare feet and short pants and where
the Prince of Wales sit in on drums with us. And I play accordion, too.

"One night when I finish work, this big, dark, funny-
looking man come in and say, 'Hey! I'm looking for a violinist to play hot.' It was Djangoo. But I lose contact with
him for two years until I take a job playing for tea between
five and seven in a hotel on the Champs-Élysées. There are
two bands, and Djangoo is playing rhythm guitar in the
other one. One evening, between sets, after I fix a new string
on my violin and am testing it, Djangoo starts to play, to ac-
company me. It go very well. 'Hey, tomorrow we do it
again,' he say, and 'Yeh! Yeh!,' I say. Soon Djangoo's brother
Joseph come in and *he* has a guitar and join us. He play
rhythm, and it was the first time I ever heard Djangoo take
a solo. Then Louis Vola, who is head of one of the bands
and plays the bass, come with us. *Alors*, Pierre Nourry, a
young businessman, say, 'Why not do a concert?' He rents
a small amphitheatre in an *école de musique*, and we give our
first concert. The place was filled up and they would not let
us get out. And that was the beginning. A few weeks later,
Djangoo bring in still another guitarist, and we decide we
need a name. Hugues Panassié, the *critique*, has begun the
Hot Club of France, so I suggest we call it the Quintet of

the Hot Club of France, and *voilà!*—it stick. We make our
first records on Ultraphone, and we do 'Sweet Sue,' 'Tiger
Rag,' and 'Lady Be Good.' Djangoo is like a child, he wants
so badly to hear how he sounds. The records are a success,
and pretty soon we start working together all the time. One
of the best jobs we get is at Bricktop's, in Paris, for four
months. The Quintet came in from ten until 6 a.m., and
during the intervals I play piano for a marvellous singer
named Mabel Mercer. Incredible clientele there, due to
Bricktop—the English gentry like Lady Mendl, the King of
Italy, the King of Belgium, Cole Porter. Every night, I ask
Mabel Mercer to sing 'I've Got You Under My Skin.' It
drive me mad the way she do it. So the Quintet compose a
tune in her honor called 'Mabel.' "

Grappelli charged through the Herald Square doors at
Macy's and came to a stop ten feet inside. His head moved
in a hundred-and-eighty-degree arc, and he smiled and lifted
one hand, palm up, as if he were asking a throng to rise in
honor of what he saw. "Iss *magnifique*," he said. "There is
absolument nothing like this in Paris or London. I wonder,
where are the gadgets?" During the next hour, Grappelli as-
cended gradually by escalator, giving off a rich "Ah" at the
top of each flight. He bought steadily but carefully, and by
the time he had reached the ninth floor he had acquired half
a dozen pairs of fit-any-size socks in white, red, and red-
and-black checks; a lined leather jacket, which he put on;
an aluminum measuring cup, and two adapter plugs to use
on his hot plate in London and Paris; a couple of wild, multi-
colored shirts and an equally blazing pair of bell-bottoms
("These colairs, they are very good for the stage"); and a
bottle of pear vinegar from Oregon ("If you brush your
teeth with this kind of vinegair constantly, they will get
very white"). From the ninth floor, he descended to the
basement, where he found a restaurant and had a leisurely
cup of coffee. He sat at the counter, and ceaselessly skated a
saltcellar back and forth while he talked. He suddenly wondered if he had double-locked his hotel room, for he had left

his violin on his bed. "That violin is from 1742," he said. "Nicola Gagliano was the maker. It is not as good as a Strad, but I am used to a smaller car, and to switch to a Rolls now would be difficult. That Gagliano is like a person, and I must be very careful not to let it get too hot or too cold. Coldness change the tone, and too much heat, like those terrible lights at Buddy's Place, make the glue melt, which is why I try and stand in a shadow there when I play. Before you play, you must prepare your way—first your violin and next yourself. If I'm doing a concert, I must have a good diet and I must be in the theatre at least one hour before. I must not be distract by anything—disease, chagrin, or too much sadness, although being sad is sometimes a great help to my playing. Not too long before I play, I take a large whiskey to give me courage. Fifty years ago, Maurice Chevalier told me, 'You must start well and you must end well. What is in the middle is not so important, because no one is listening then.' The alcohol make its effect. It liberate me and I'm free to improvise. Improvisation—it is a mystery, like the pyramids. You can write a book about it, but by the end no one still know what it is. When I improvise and I'm in good form, I'm like somebody half sleeping. I even forget there are people in front of me. Great improvisers are like priests; they are thinking only of their god. Sometimes I get an attack of memory. I have been playing 'Nuages' twenty-five years, and then one night I completely forget it. And once when I'm playing 'Lady Be Good' I think of the letter I just get telling me the water in the bathroom in the house I own at Chartres does not transport itself properly. Mostly, I improvise on the chords of the people playing behind me. The more good the chords, the better I play. I have made progress in the last four years since I stop smoking. My cerebral is clearer.

"The house at Chartres was a farm. I make the living room from the *grange*, the barn, and put a pavement in, and a huge red carpet. I would like to build an atelier, too. But I am almost never there. I have a flat in London, on Beaufort Street, where my grandson live, and I have a flat in Paris, on

Rue de Dunkerque, that an ex-drummer of mine take care of. I have a flat in Cannes, where my daughter live. But I love London. I live there during the war, and I think I will get rid of everything and take a place there that has a porter and service. When you get old, you must have protection. My daughter's mother was a very good-looking woman, younger than me, but very *difficile*. I can't retire. What shall I do? I have always work since I am twenty years old, because I must keep away the miseries that happen to me as a child. Also, when I'm not working two weeks, I'm *mélancolique*. The world stop. And I like different scenery. If I am offer a beautiful contrac' in the best place for a year I refuse it. I must fold up my blanket and my cot and move on. When I am at the Paris Hilton so long, I discover it is stupid to stay in one place so much."

Grappelli paid for his coffee, zipped up his jacket, and went out into Herald Square. The wind was blowing hard, and the streets were in shadow. It was four-thirty, and Grappelli headed up Broadway smartly. "This jacket is pairfect," he said. "It will bè very good at Chartres. But my head, it is still cold. I must find a hat. The miseries I have as a child started when I was three and I lose my mother. It was 1911. My father was a Latinist and a professor of philosophy, and he was always penniless. He had come from Italy when he was nineteen, and he could never go back because of his politics. Whenever he get a few francs together, he went to the Bibliothèque Nationale to work on his translation of Vergil, which he said would be the best ever made. He was not a gypsy, like Djangoo, but he live like one. He was the first heepie I met in my life. When my mother die, he had no choice, and he put me in a very strict *catholique* orphanage. When I was six and the war of '14 was breaking out, he realize that that *pension* was not right. We were unique together, my father and I, and he was very unhappy about what would happen to me. He find out that Isadora Duncan was looking for a young subject to personify an angel. I was hired, but I only was there about six months. I was not born

to be a dancer. I listen only to the music, which was a revelation to me and which was sometimes a pianist and sometimes a chamber orchestra. Isadora Duncan's school was in
trouble anyway, because she had so many Germans in it, so
when my father came on *permission* from the Army, he
took me out and put me in another orphanage. After Isadora
Duncan, it was not a pleasure to go back to a Dickens-type
pension. This place was supposed to be under the eye of the
government, but the government look elsewhere. We sleep
on the floor, and often we are without food. When my father came back from the war, I was in bad condition. Un-
dernutrition. Since then, all my life I have been *lymphatique.*
Feeble. Several times I nearly die. My father and I find a
room and life starts again.

"My father love music, and he would take me to the top
floor of the concert hall to hear the great orchestras. I became habitual to listening to music, and I was getting hungry to play something. My father found a little violin in the
shop of a shoe-repair man who was Italian, and finally he
bought it. There was no money for lessons, so, as with
everything, my father took a book from the Bibliothèque
and we learned solfeggio together. It was not very fast, but
I learn. I learn, too, from watching the street violinists.
When I was fourteen, I went to work in a pit band in a
cinéma—three hours for the matinée and three hours in the
evening. There were two violins and a piano and a cello, and
I manage. In fact, I remain there nearly two years, and it was
when I learn to play the violin. I also heard my first jazz in
a shop nearby that had a Victrola. One record was 'Tea for
Two' with a vocal, and the other was 'Stumbling,' by somebody called Mitchell's Jazz Kings, which I never discover
any more about. The pianist at the *cinéma* was a little illuminated, a little *fou.* He told me he had invent a way to play
Chopin better than Chopin himself. I took him to hear those
records. He was still living musically in the middle of the
nineteenth century, so the music explode in his head. After
that, whenever Charlie Chaplin came on, we play 'Stumbling' and 'Tea for Two.' When I was fifteen, I start divid-

ing my time between the *cinéma* and playing in the streets,
which my father never find out about. I work with an old
guitarist, and we play in restaurants, too, when they would
let us in. So things are getting better. My father and I get a
flat with two rooms and a kitchen. By this time, when I was
making a little bit, I get more power over my father and we
get a piano, and that is when I start to learn it."

Grappelli found a tiny Knox hat shop just off Seventh
Avenue in the Forties. He tried on a big white fedora but
settled for a narrow-brimmed maroon one. He punched his
Pulsar. It was five minutes to ten, London time, and he raced
out the door and up Seventh. "Djangoo have a hat like this
once," he said. "But, *naturellement*, he lose it. He spend the
war in France, and afterward we gave our first big concert
ever, at the Salle Pleyel, in Paris. We were together in and
out after that. Djangoo took up the electric guitar, but he
was playing it with the enormous strength he use on the
acoustic guitar, and it was no good. He retire more and
more in the late forties, for in the world of the gypsy it is
the women who get the money. Then, in 1953, someone arrange an American tour for Djangoo and me. I go to Paris
to look for him, but he is nowhere. Then, three months
later, I hear the news: His brains have burst and he is dead."

A block from the hotel, the wind seized a piece of paper
from the sidewalk and shot it into the air. Grappelli was
startled, and he stopped and shouted, "Look at that!" He
bent over backward and, holding his hat on with one hand,
pointed at the paper, which was dancing violently around
ten feet above him. "*Merveilleux!*" he shouted again. "What
city has so much beautiful commotion!" He righted himself, looked at his Pulsar, and ran the last block.

THE
ANSWER IS YES

Jane Hall, the wife of the guitarist Jim Hall, is a slender, gentle, intelligent woman in her thirties. When she talks about her husband, she reveals a nice mixture of devotion and objectivity, and when she talks about herself it is as if she were telling a fairy tale. "I was born an only child in New York and grew up in Harrison," she says. "My father was in textiles, and he was a self-made man, who never graduated from high school. He loved golf and business and piano players like Fats Waller and Erroll Garner, although he came to appreciate the subtler sounds, too. He had a good sense of humor and was sort of a ham, and all my friends always wished he was their father. He was very different from Jim. Dad always wanted him to have more—more records, more fame, more money. But he realized Jim didn't have that kind of push. Just before Dad died, he said he wished Jim would be nicer to himself. It meant a lot to me—his appreciation of Jim's kindness and gentleness. My mother complemented my father. She was from a large family and was more reserved. She designed children's clothes before she married and gave up her career. But my father always relied on her taste. They were a striking couple together, particularly when they were dancing, which they loved.

"I met Jim in 1960. At the time, I was going out with Dick Katz, the piano player, and one night when we were going to have dinner he brought Jim along. The only Hall I knew of in jazz was Edmond. I didn't see Jim again until the following winter. I was taking a night course at the New School, and I asked Dick if he'd babysit for Debbie, who's my daughter from a previous marriage. He brought Jim along again, and when I got home I discovered that Jim had somehow coaxed Debbie's dog out from under the bed, where she'd barricaded herself all day. We all sat around and talked for hours, and I fell in love. I'd never met anyone who *listened* like Jim. We started going out, but it was five years before we were married. Jim was very much against marriage. I went back to college in 1967 and graduated, and then I went to social-work school. I'm a psychotherapist at Greenwich House, and I have my own practice, too. Jim has been nothing but supportive and positive through it all. And that extends to my music. I write a couple of songs a year,

219

and I sing. Jim accompanies me, and he's even recorded some of my tunes. He's helped bring out my musicality. He's done the same with Debbie. She plays piano, and Jim works with her. He's been a father to her, which is what she never had.

"One of the things that impress me about jazz musicians is their camaraderie. There's a complete lack of narcissism, of competitive feeling. I don't think the same warmth exists even in sports. Jim has a great kinship for his fellow-musicians. The first time he took me to the old Half Note to hear Zoot Sims and Al Cohn, he said, 'You have to listen. You can't talk while they play.' After the first set, Al told me that not only could he *see* me listening, he could *feel* me listening. I've thought a lot about the pressures on jazz musicians, too. Jim was scared to death at his first job after he'd quit drinking. But since then his playing has grown and grown. He surprises me every time I hear him. I used to listen to him with my eyes closed, but now I don't. Just watching him concentrating and so in tune with his instrument and with his listeners is an experience."

It's not only an experience, it's a delicate, memorable event. Hall, though, doesn't look capable of creating a stir of any sort. He is slim and of medium height, and a lot of his hair is gone. The features of his long, pale face are chastely proportioned, and are accented by a recently cultivated R.A.F. mustache. He wears old-style gold-rimmed spectacles, and he has three principal expressions: a wide smile, a child's frown, and a calm, pleased playing mask—eyes closed, chin slightly lifted, and mouth ajar. He could easily be the affable son of the stony-faced farmer in "American Gothic." His hands and feet are small, and he doesn't have any hips, so his clothes, which are generally casual, tend to hang on him as if they were still in the closet. When he plays, he sits on a stool, his back an arc, his feet propped on a high rung, and his knees akimbo. He holds his guitar at port arms. For many years, Hall's playing matched his private, nebulous appearance. When he came to the fore, in the mid-fifties, with Chico Hamilton's vaguely avant-garde quintet (it had a cello and no piano), and then appeared on a famous pickup recording, "Two Degrees East, Three Degrees West," that was led by John Lewis and involved Bill Perkins, Percy Heath, and Hamilton, he had a stiff, academic approach. His solos were pleasantly designed, but they didn't always swing. But as he moved through groups led by Jimmy Giuffre, Ben Webster, Sonny Rollins, and Art Farmer, his deliberateness softened and the right notes began landing in the right places. Then he married Jane, and his playing developed a grace and inventiveness and lyricism that make him preëminent among contemporary jazz guitarists and put him within touching distance of the two grand masters—Charlie Christian and Django Reinhardt. Listening to Hall now is like turning onionskin pages: one lapse of your attention and his solo is rent. Each phrase evolves from its predecessor, his rhythms are balanced, and his harmonic and melodic ideas are full of parentheses and asides. His tone is equally demanding. He plays both electric and acoustic guitars. On the former, he sounds like an acoustic guitarist, for he has an angelic touch and he keeps his amplifier down; on the latter, a new instrument specially designed and built for him, he has an even more gossamer sound. This turning away from electricity may have a revolutionary effect on jazz guitarists, who have struggled for thirty-five years with faulty equipment, ignorance of electronics, and a cheap, strident sound. Hall is exceptional in another way. In the thirties and forties, Christian and Reinhardt put forward certain ideals for their instrument—spareness, the use of silence, and the legato approach to swinging—and for a while every jazz guitarist studied them. Then the careering, million-noted melodic flow of Charlie Parker took hold, and jazz guitarists became garrulous and arpeggio-ridden. But Hall, sidestepping this aspect of Parker, has gone directly to Christian and Reinhardt, and, plumping out their skills with the harmonic advances that have since been made, has perfected an attack that is fleet but tight, passionate but oblique. And he is singular for still another reason. Guitarists are inclined to be an ingrown society, but Hall listens constantly to other instru-

mentalists, especially tenor saxophonists (Ben Webster, Coleman Hawkins, Lester Young, Sonny Rollins) and pianists
(Count Basie, John Lewis, Bill Evans, Keith Jarrett), and he
attempts to adapt to the guitar their phrasing and tonal qual-
ities. In his solos he asserts nothing but says a good deal. He
loves Duke Ellington's great slow ballads, and he will start
one with an ad-lib chorus in which he glides softly over the
melody, working just behind the beat, dropping certain
notes and adding others, but steadfastly celebrating its melodic beauties. He clicks into tempo at the beginning of the
second chorus, and, after pausing for several beats, plays a
gentle, ascending six-note figure that ends with a curious,
ringing off-note. He pauses again, and, taking the close of the
same phrase, he elaborates on it in an ascending-descending
double-time run, and then skids into several behind-the-beat
chords, which give way to a single-note line that bobs up
and down and concludes on another off-note. He raises his
volume at the beginning of the bridge and floats through it
with edgeless, softly ringing chords; then, slipping into the
final eight bars, he fashions a precise, almost declamatory
run, pauses a second at its top, and works his way down with
two glancing arpeggios. He next sinks to a whisper, and
finishes with a bold fragment of melody that dissolves into
a flatted chord, upon which the next soloist gratefully builds
his opening statement.

When the Halls were married, he moved into her apartment,
on West Twelfth Street. It faces south and is at eye level
with chimney pots and the tops of ailanthus trees. Sunlight
fills the living room all day. The off-white walls are hung
with a lively assortment of lithographs, oils, and drawings.
A tall cabinet, which contains hundreds of L.P.s, is flanked
by full bookshelves. A sofa, a hassock, a fat floor pillow, a
couple of canvas Japanese chairs, and a coffee table ring the
window end of the room. An upright piano sits by the front
door, and Hall's electric guitar rests on a stand by the
kitchen door. Hall generally gets himself together around
noon. He will sit down on the sofa with his back to the

window and sip a mug of tea. Like many shy people, he is
a born listener and a self-taught talker. He weighs his words
as he weighs his notes. He speaks softly and has a mild
Midwestern drawl. He had, he said, been pondering improvisation. "Somebody asked me once, '*Why* do you improvise, why do you want to take a good song and change it?'—
and that stumped me. Maybe jazz musicians *are* egomaniacs,
as Alec Wilder claims. Maybe they feel they're above the
songs they play and that they have to improve them. I've always been of the notion—though most of my musician
friends disagree with me—that 'Body and Soul' would never
have been anything special if Coleman Hawkins hadn't made
his record of it. Yet I believe I treat the tunes I play with respect, and I know I always follow the gist of their lyrics.
Improvisation is just a form of self-expression, and it's very
gratifying to improvise in front of people. I feel I'm including them in what I'm doing, taking them someplace they
might like to go and haven't been to before. I like to draw
them in, and if you can get an audience on your side, then
you can finish a set with something abstract or different and
they'll come right along. I like my solos to have a beginning
and a middle and an end. I like them to have a quality that
Sonny Rollins has—of turning and turning a tune until eventually you show all its possible faces. Sometimes I'll take a
motif that I might have stumbled on while I'm practicing,
and develop it throughout a solo. It's a compositional approach, and it helps you get control over your playing. But
if a solo is going well, is developing, I let it go on its own.
Then I've reached that place where I've gotten out of my
own way, and it's as if I'm standing back and watching the
solo play itself.

"When I do the melody of a tune, I try to make it come
out mine. I also try sometimes to get the melody to sound as
it would on a wind instrument, as though I've got the air-
stream of a saxophone or trumpet to hang on to. I think of
the way Ben Webster played 'Chelsea Bridge,' with his fantastic sense of space and the way he'd let a note slide from
sound to the breathing just below sound, and I'll go after

that effect. I'm like Marian McPartland, I guess, in that I think of the keys in colors. A flat is reddish orange, G major seems green, E flat is yellow. I try never to bring distractions onto the bandstand, but if I do I know I always have a sort of floor to rely on. I know I won't ever really be terrible. Being tired doesn't seem to matter. I've seen guys on the road who were wiped out get up and play sensationally. Being tired seems to cut the fat and allow the musicality to come out.

"I've been playing a lot in duos with just bassists, and it involves a terrific amount of listening. I play off of the bass notes and try to make it always sound like a duet and not just guitar solos with accompaniment. All the accompanying I've done is a help, because accompanying is hearing the whole texture from top to bottom of the music around you and then fitting yourself in the proper place. When I was with Sonny Rollins, I found out right away he didn't like to be led, so I'd lay back a fraction of a second and let him show me where he was going and hope I could follow. When I was with Art Farmer, it was totally different. He liked the background laid down first, so he could play over it. And the whole timing was different, too. When I play behind Paul Desmond, it becomes a question-and-answer thing between us. But all you're trying to do is swing, and swinging is a question of camaraderie. You could be playing stiffly, but if everybody is playing that way the group will swing. But if one person is out of sync, is dragging, it feels like somebody is hanging on to your coattails."

Hall went into the kitchen to get another mug of tea, and when he came back a big gray-black cat appeared from the bedroom. It gave Hall three thunderous meows, sat down at his feet, and stared intently at him. It meowed three more times. Hall laughed and took a sip of tea. "O.K., Pablo. Cut it out. We didn't get him until he was a year old, and I think he was raised with dogs, because he's more like a dog than a cat. He greets me at the door when I come in and says goodbye when I go out, and he follows me around all day here. I was speaking of Ben Webster. After I finally left the Jimmy

Giuffre Trio, in 1959, I went back to the Coast, and I was in
a band Ben had with Jimmy Rowles and Red Mitchell and
Frank Butler. We worked for a while in a club on the Strip
called the Renaissance, and at first I didn't get paid. Then I
think everybody in the band chipped something in. Anyway, Ben and I hung out a lot. He didn't have a car, and he
lived with his mother and grandmother way over on the
other side of L.A., but he'd never ask me to pick him up.
What he'd do is call me whenever we had a gig and say,
'We'll meet at my house first.' I think his mother had been a
schoolteacher. One evening when I went to get him, he was
stretched out on the sofa snoring—the whole works. He
must have been up all night, and we couldn't budge him. He
had a reputation of taking a sock at whoever tried to wake
him. So his mother and grandmother would lean over him
and say, 'Ben, Mr. Hall is here and it's time to go to work,'
and then jump back about two feet. I finally suggested that
I get a wet towel or something, and they looked at me with
their mouths open, and said, 'Oh no, he don't like *any* surprises.' Ben was very melodramatic, and he talked in that big
voice just the way he played. Another time I went to get
him he had a washcloth on top of his head and he was shaving. Some Art Tatum records were on and he kept running
out of the bathroom and mimicking fantastic Tatum figures.
Then he started telling me what Tatum was like—he loved
to talk about the great ones he knew who were gone—and
the next thing I knew he was crying. I never saw any of the
meanness he was famous for, except once he fell asleep in the
front seat of my car and when I woke him he cursed me.
But the next minute he apologized.

"I had gotten to know John Lewis, and he called me about
this time—it was the early sixties—and told me I had to come
back to New York, that that's where it was at, and that I
could stay in his apartment because he was away on the road
so much. Well, I did for two or three months, and John
loaned me money and everything. Then I sublet Dick Katz's
apartment, and not much was happening. I felt I had a reputation by then, and I was too proud to call people about

jobs. I did work in a duo with Lee Konitz opposite Miles Davis at the Village Vanguard when he had Cannonball and Philly Joe Jones and Bill Evans, and the audience would listen to Miles as if they were in church, and then talk all the way through our set, which was about the way everything seemed to be going for me then. Suddenly, I began getting notes from Sonny Rollins. He didn't have a phone and I never answered mine, so he'd stuff them in the mailbox, and I think the first one said, 'Let's talk about music.' He was coming out of a two-year retirement and was putting a group together, and he wanted me, in addition to Walter Perkins and Bob Cranshaw. We rehearsed afternoons at the old Five Spot, and at first it was a little mysterious. Sonny would let me in the front door with one hand and continue playing with the other, and then disappear, still playing, into a back room and stay there maybe a half hour. We opened at the Jazz Gallery, and it was a great success. But I had to put *everything* into it. I was with him off and on for over a year, and wherever we went he brought the house down. There was something about the way he got himself across to an audience, as if he were right out there playing into its collective ear. It was a great experience, a turning point for me. Then, in effect, he fired me. There were two reasons. One was musical. He wanted to experiment with Ornette Coleman's trumpet player, Don Cherry, and that was beyond me. The other had to do with a cover of *Down Beat*. It was a guitar issue, and they had me in the front of the picture with Rollins set behind, and the talk began. 'Why does he need a white boy in the group?' and the like, and Sonny would tell me in various ways that people were putting pressure on him to get rid of me, and that was it. Then I ran into him one night a while ago at a club, and when he was leaving he leaned over and said, 'Sometimes I lose touch with myself,' and that made amends. I've always felt that the music started out as black but that it's as much mine now as anyone else's. I haven't stolen the music from anybody—I just bring something different to it. After that, I joined a nice little group Art Farmer had, with Steve Swallow on bass and

Pete La Roca on drums. But I was having trouble keeping things together. I had to concentrate on my work and I had to keep my drinking under control, which wasn't working too well. So finally, in 1965, I decided I had to get off the road after ten years and get things squared around. I came back to New York, started going to A.A., and Jane and I got married. I didn't want to go into night clubs again right away because of the atmosphere and the drinking, but I had to work, so I got a job in the band on the Merv Griffin Show. That was a shock. I'd felt, in my way, that I'd been doing something important all those years on the road, but suddenly I was like a stagehand. You're there in the studio but you're not there. It was very rare for any of Griffin's guests to acknowledge anyone in the band, and you'd think *some* of them would have known Bob Brookmeyer or Jake Hanna. I began to lose my identity. If I don't play what I want to play, improvise and all, I sink down. I forget I've ever done anything good musically at all. All the while, I was thinking about finally being a leader, and when I'd been with Griffin about three and a half years I got my courage up to go into clubs again, and I organized my own group. Clubs don't bother me too much now, but I only like to work two-week gigs and then regroup myself. I don't know why, but when I work it takes a lot out of me. I play every day here, I write some, and I have some students. With Jane working, we get along fine. Even so, I occasionally get in a panic. I wake up at night and think, What am I doing, what kind of a life is this? I've thought of giving it up and going into something else, but I know that would be crazy the minute I pick my guitar up again. So when I ask myself, Am I going to want to go into saloons and play guitar when I'm fifty or sixty or seventy, the answer is yes."

The telephone buzzed, almost inaudibly. "That was Jimmy D'Aquisto, out in Huntington," Hall said when he hung up. "He's a great guitar-maker, and he's made me my acoustic guitar, which is the first new guitar I've had since I was a kid. I got my old Gibson, over by the kitchen door, second-hand from Howard Roberts, on the Coast, in 1955. Jimmy has done some experimenting. The body, or box, of the guitar is a little thinner than usual, and, to compensate, the front and back of the box are arched a little more than usual and the f holes on either side of the tailpiece are bigger. He's strung it with lightweight steel strings, but I'm still experimenting with different weights. And he has kept the bridge low, which makes the strings more responsive. Most important, he hasn't put any electrical stuff on it. I've used it twice in public—at concerts at Yale and the New School. The Yale thing was a kind of shakedown cruise because the acoustics where I played—it was a church—were so strange. But I felt good about it at the New School. In that auditorium the sound creeps along the walls and gets everywhere, and even though I didn't use a mike, I think they heard me in the back. It's such a beautiful instrument. Unlike most guitars, it just doesn't have any bad spots. It's still strange to me. The dimensions are different enough so that it takes me a while to warm into it."

The telephone buzzed again, and Hall went into the kitchen, after he finished talking, to make a drink of one part grape juice and two parts 7-Up. The sun was. pell-melling in the window, and he lowered the venetian blind. "Jack Six just called. He played bass with Dave Brubeck three or four years, but we've been doing duets recently. We've got a gig coming up at Sweet Basil, so I thought it would be a good idea to practice some. He's on his way from Jersey right now.

"My mother gave me my first guitar for Christmas when I was ten. I was living with her and my brother in Cleveland. I was born in 1930, in Buffalo, but we only stayed there a few months and then came to New York for a while and moved out to Geneva, Ohio, where my Uncle Russell had a farm. He was one of my mother's brothers, and he had taught himself electronics. Her other brother, Ed, taught himself guitar and how to make blueprints. He'd play things like 'Wabash Cannon Ball.' I spent a year on Uncle Russ's farm. I was about seven or eight, and I remember the whole time as being dark. There was no electricity in the house, and one of my chores was to take the cinders out. I got some in my eyes once and for two weeks I couldn't see. Then I knocked over a kerosene lamp, which scared the hell out of me, but luckily it snuffed out when it hit the floor. Uncle Russ was married to a strange women then, and it was the old story of the wife upsetting the husband, who then takes it out on the kids. By this time, my mother and father had split up, and she and I and my brother moved to Cleveland. We lived in rooming houses and my mother supported us. She worked as a secretary at a tool company. It's funny how your perspective changes when you get older. It seems amazing to me now to be in your twenties—which she was then—and to be raising two boys by yourself. I don't remember much about my father, except that he played tennis and managed a grocery store for a time and was a travelling salesman in stainless steel. I never see him, but I think he's alive. My mother lives in Los Angeles. She's active and vivacious, a short, blond lady, kind of sparkly and with a lot of guts. Around 1940, we moved into a brand-new W.P.A. housing project in Cleveland, and we stayed there until I went to music school. It was the first place we'd lived in that no one had lived in before. It had an upstairs and a downstairs, and I think the rent was twenty-four dollars a month.

"It took a year to pay for my guitar, but I lucked up with a good teacher, Jack DuPerow, right away. He had me do scales and guitar arrangements of poptunes. My favorite was 'Music, Maestro, Please!' The accordion was big in Cleveland. In fact, the first group I worked in had accordion, clarinet, and drums, and we played dances on weekends. The clarinet player was into Benny Goodman, and he played Goodman's recording of 'Solo Flight' for me, with Charlie Christian featured, and I thought, What is *that?* It was instant addiction. I bought a 78-r.p.m. album of Goodman Sextet numbers even before I had anything to play them on. By this time, I was studying with Fred Sharp. He had played in New York with Adrian Rollini and Red Norvo, and he

introduced me to records by Carl Kress and Dick Mc-
Donough and Django Reinhardt. Taking Charlie Christian
and Django together, I've hardly heard anything better
since, if you want to know the truth. But a lot of my listening was not to guitarists but to tenor saxophonists and pianists. I had Coleman Hawkins' 'The Man I Love' and 'Sweet
Lorraine,' with Shelly Manne and Oscar Pettiford, and I had
the Art Tatum Trio. I'd listen to them in the morning after
my mother had gone to work, because she wasn't too much
on jazz then, and I'd think about what I'd heard on the mile
walk to school. George Barnes had an octet with a wood-
wind feeling that broadcast regularly, and all the bands
played the Palace Theatre there—Duke Ellington and Artie
Shaw, when Shaw had Roy Eldridge and Barney Kessel. I
began hanging out with older local musicians when I was
fifteen or sixteen—Tony DiNardo, a tenor player who
sounded like Lucky Thompson and who got me listening
to Lester Young, and Billy DiNasco, a piano player who
loved Mel Powell and Teddy Wilson and who worked out
a way of his own that was like Lennie Tristano. We had our
own group, and we called it the Spectacles, because we all
wore glasses. We sang four-part vocals, and they were my
first arrangements.

"I did well in high school, and when I graduated I decided
to go to the Cleveland Institute of Music. I thought learning
more craft would help. I went for four and a half years, and
I majored in music theory. I wrote a string quartet for my
thesis. I played guitar on weekends, but I wasn't all that involved in jazz. I thought I was going to go into classical
composing and teach on the side. Then in the mid-fifties,
halfway through my first semester toward my master's, I
began thinking two things: I was with people who did nothing but go to school and would probably do nothing else,
and I knew I had to try being a guitarist or else it would
trouble me the rest of my life. My decision was made for
me. Ray Graziano, a good local alto player, was driving a
Cadillac—a lavender Cadillac—out to the Coast for somebody, and he asked me if I wanted to go along. I had no

money, but I knew Joe Dolny, a Cleveland trumpet player, out on the Coast, and I also knew I could stay with my great-aunt. She was in her nineties, and had lived in Hollywood from the time it was clapboard houses and fields planted with peas. So I quit school, and there we were, driving through all these little towns in that lavender Cadillac, with me in the back seat playing and playing. I moved in with my aunt and got a job in a used-sheet-music store, and I studied classical guitar for a while with Vicente Gómez. Joe Dolny had a rehearsal band at the union hall, and I met a lot of people there like John Graas, the French-horn player. I'd go to his house, out in the Valley, and he recommended me to Chico Hamilton for his first quintet, which had Buddy Collette on reeds, Freddie Katz on cello, Carson Smith on bass, and Chico and me. I got ninety dollars a week, which was a fortune then. I was with Chico for a year and a half, and a lot of good things happened, even though that bass drum of his began getting in my dreams. I met Red Mitchell, the great bassist, and Herb Geller and Bill Perkins and John Lewis. When Chico's group went East for gigs at the Newport Festival and in New York, we worked opposite Max Roach's group at Basin Street, where I met Sonny Rollins. That was some experience—being up on the stand and looking out and seeing all your idols staring at you. Then we drove back to the Coast, and it was a weird trip. Chico was the only black man in the car, and he never got out of it. He stayed curled up like an animal in the back seat, and we'd bring him his food. What with one thing and another, but mostly Chico's bass drum, I left and went with Jimmy Giuffre's new trio.

"I was with this group for two different periods, the first starting in 1957. In between came a low point that matched my time with Merv Griffin. I went on the road with Yves Montand. What saved me was that Edmond Hall and Al Hall were both in the tour, too, and I had the chance to listen to them reminisce and to ask Edmond about Charlie Christian, because he had recorded with him. In fact, they were the only records Christian made on acoustic guitar.

Before I went back with Giuffre, I toured with Ella Fitzgerald all over South America. I finally jumped ship in Buenos Aires, where I stayed six weeks. The bossa nova was coming up, and one night I went to this big room filled with guitar players. They sat in a circle and passed a guitar around like a peace pipe, and everybody played. I didn't know what to do, so I played a plain old blues. One of the good things about being on the road in other countries is you're not just a tourist, you're something a lot better, something special, and I've made friends all over the world."

The doorbell buzzed, and Jack Six came in, carrying his bass and towing an enormous amplifier on wheels. Six is a big, cheerful man with a Southern accent, and he and his equipment filled one end of the living room. After Six unpacked, hooked up, and plugged in, Hall whacked one thigh with a tuning fork and rested its handle on the body of his old Gibson. Six tuned up to its silver hum. Hall spread sheet music on the dining-room table, and the two men bent over it in silence. They looked as if they were examining illuminated manuscripts at the Morgan.

"Let's play Janie's tune 'Something Tells Me,'" Hall suggested. "But we'll do it as she wrote it. She's got a couple of modulations in it which make it difficult to sing, so she sort of leaves them out when she's singing it around the house. Who would you say she sounds like, Jack?"

"A cross between Astrud Gilberto and Julie London."

Hall laughed, and sat down on a red kitchen stool. He played quiet, open chords as he went into the graceful, succinct melody. Six came in behind with offbeat notes. The music immediately transformed the room, filling it with motion and purpose. Hall improvised a chorus replete with silences, retards, and quick sotto-voce runs. Six soloed, grunting softly, and the two went out with some lilting counterpoint. A "Chelsea Bridge" reverberating with Ben Webster came next, and was followed by a fast, tricky Jim Hall blues, "Two's Blues." It has a complex, backing-and-filling melodic line, and the first run-through had many bugs.

"Anyway, that's the general idea of it," Hall said, laughing.

"My, those notes certainly go by fast," Six replied. "It's like Jake Hanna said to the new man on the band after he'd messed up at his first rehearsal: 'I didn't know you couldn't read.' "

After three more tries, the blues fell into glistening shape, and they played another Hall blues—a slow one, called "Careful." Hall said he had written it a long time ago as a "Monk thing." It has an ostinato bass, which the two musicians handed easily back and forth. They had just started "Emily" when the front door opened and Jane Hall came in. She was dressed in a blue pants suit, and she was carrying a bag of groceries, which she set down on the music. There was a round of pecks. She asked how everything was going, and Hall said good and that maybe it was time for a breather. He went into the kitchen to make some grape-juice-and-7-Ups. He set the drinks on the coffee table, put his arm around Jane's shoulder, and gave it a squeeze. Then he sat down next to Six on the sofa. He smiled up at Jane as she passed the drinks and said, "So, did you save any souls today?"

THE
WESTCHESTER KIDS

thirteen

In one form or another—big bands, small bands, trios, solo pianists—jazz was everywhere in this country in the late thirties and early forties. Five or six nights a week at 11 P.M., the three radio networks broadcast live music from Chicago, St. Louis, New York, Boston, and points between, and myriad local wires placed in clubs and roadhouses sustained the faithful for fifty miles around. Indeed, jazz of some sort could be heard in countless clubs and roadhouses as well as in hotels and ballrooms and theatres, and, before gas rationing and the wartime 30 per cent entertainment tax, it was simple and cheap to drive twenty or more miles to the Glen Island Casino or the Palladium Ballroom or the Bradford Hotel to hear Tommy Dorsey or Red Norvo or Count Basie. Every town of five thousand and over had a record store with at least one listening booth where you could sift the dozen or so new releases that came in every week, and there was no problem, as there is now, in ordering special records like the Jones-Collins Astoria Hot Eight's "Tip Easy Blues" on Bluebird or Albert Ammons' "Bass Goin' Crazy" on twelve-inch Blue Note. Nor could the neophyte get lost in this lovely new musical landscape, for there were plenty of maps—Ramsey's and Smith's "The Jazz Record Book" and Hugues Panassié's "The Real Jazz"; the little magazines of jazz, like *Jazz Information* and *The Jazz Record;* and the more commercial *Metronome* and *Down Beat,* with their news and gossip, their record reviews, which alternated between the ecstatic and the crabby (off-pitch third trumpeters beware!), and columns like "Lost Chords," which listed temporarily misplaced musicians. (Thus: "Where is Sal Bonso, the fine solo alto sax man last heard of two years ago with Bob Chester?" To which an answer would come a couple of months later, "My sister mailed me your Lost Chords column where who would have guessed it I am mentioned. Well, I left the music business and am selling insurance here in Topeka. P.S. The new Bob Chester record of 'Strictly Instrumental' is solid even without me. Ha. Ha.")

New York was Mecca, and the jazz in the air was dense and crackling. There were always six or eight jazz clubs on Fifty-second Street between Fifth and Seventh Avenues, and to the east on Fifty-eighth was Café Society Uptown. In the Village were the Vanguard and Nick's and Café Society Downtown. Harlem had Clark Monroe's Uptown House, Minton's, Small's Paradise, the Savoy, the Apollo, and a network of after-hours places. And there were at least half a dozen big bands on view at any given time in the hotels and movie houses. All this was garnished with radio shows, occasional concerts (still very much an innovation), and visits to the Commodore Music Shop, on East Forty-second Street, where musicians of the Condon persuasion were often on view, weighing their hangovers and putting the touch on Milt Gabler, who owned the place.

Every art needs its callow celebrants. Thirty-five years ago those surrounding jazz came largely from white middle-class families. Jazz loosed them from the neo-Victorian domestic regimens of their parents. More important, they revered the *music*, and the closer they got to it the better. To sit ten feet from Art Tatum's right hand at the Three Deuces was sublime. The careers of these adulators followed a predictable curve. They teethed on Glenn Miller and Harry James and Tommy Dorsey, and then one day, in a record shop or at the house of a slightly older acquaintance renowned for his record collection, they heard a 1926 Jelly Roll Morton or a Louis Armstrong Hot Five or an early Duke Ellington. The music sounded harsh and disturbing. But they went back again and again to these disagreeable records, and in six months they were also digging King Oliver and Fats Waller and James P. Johnson, and a year later, presuming they weren't snared by Moldy Figism, they were into contemporary Ellington and Billie Holiday and Count Basie. At the same time, to ease their enthusiasm, many of them took up instruments. Self-taught and highly imitative, they found their way into small dixieland bands patterned on Muggsy Spanier's Ragtime Band or Bob Crosby's Bob Cats or Sidney Bechet's New Orleans Feetwarmers. They played with passion and dedication until they were drafted or went to college, and then they gave it up. Many of them even disliked being reminded in later years of the feelings they had once bared. But a tiny number decided defiantly that they would not be firemen or policemen but would become jazz musicians. (Most of their parents were aghast at their decision, and one mother was heard to say to her eighteen-year-old son, "That's all right, dear. You'll outgrow it.") Probably the best and toughest of these admirable iconoclasts is Bob Wilber, who at forty-eight is a superb soprano saxophonist, a classic clarinettist, a gifted arranger and composer, and an invaluable preserver and enhancer of jazz tradition.

Wilber has wavy reddish-blond hair and a small pointed face, and wears glasses, and from the tenth row of Carnegie Hall he looks about seventeen or eighteen. Up close, though, his face reveals miniature signs of wear and his hair is misted with gray. He has intelligent, restless eyes. He is a small man, but he stands with his legs planted wide apart when he plays, and he has a surprising voice. It is deep and precise and deliberate. His manner gives pause to frivolity. Wilber loves Cape Cod, and when he can, he visits his father and stepmother in Orleans. One day last summer, he sat in a Boston rocker in the high-ceilinged living room of a renovated barn on his parents' place, and talked. The rocker has a good, if faded, townscape painted on its crest rail, and his head moved irregularly across it. "I first got interested in jazz when my father brought home the original Victor recording of Duke Ellington's 'Mood Indigo.' I must have been three. I remember the strange sound of the horns and the steady *bring bring bring* of the banjo. I heard my first live jazz when I was twelve and my father took me to Café Society Uptown to hear Teddy Wilson's band. I don't recall much about the band, even though it had Emmett Berry and Edmond Hall and Benny Morton and Sid Catlett—most of whom I'd play with one day. But I do remember the beautiful blue drapes behind the bandstand and the musicians' maroon jackets and the elegant atmosphere. We had constant music at home. My father had learned ragtime in college at its very height—he graduated in 1913—and he'd play every night when he came home from work. He also had a love for the musical theater and bought sheet music all the time. Several years after the Café Society visit, a bunch of us from Scarsdale, where I grew up, started sneaking down to Nick's in the Village when we were supposed to be at the movies in White Plains. There were three pianos in a row at Nick's, then a space, and then the bandstand, and we'd sit between the pianos and the stand, and only inches above us would be Pee Wee Russell's or Chelsea Qualley's or Brad Gowans's feet. Inevitably, one night we missed the last train. We sacked out in the waiting room in Grand Central and took the milk train, and there were plenty of 'Good Lords!'s and 'Where have you been?'s. We were hanging around Fifty-second Street when I was sixteen or seventeen. It was an incomparable education, and all the clubs seemed to tolerate underage kids. We'd go to Kelly's Stables to hear Coleman Hawkins, and he'd come out in a gray pin-striped suit and I guess we were expecting clarion bursts but all that happened was his piano player said, 'What you want to play, Hawk?' and Hawkins said, 'Body,' meaning 'Body and Soul,' which was his big thing then. After that, he'd do one of his riff tunes based on the chords of 'I Got Rhythm' or something like that, and you wouldn't see him again for a couple of hours. We heard Billie Holiday with Tiny Grimes, and Dizzy Gillespie and Charlie Parker and Milt Jackson. Jackson was playing the worst set of vibes I've ever heard; they literally clanked. Then every Sunday afternoon, from five until eight, there were jam sessions at Jimmy Ryan's. The most marvellous combination of musicians showed up—Pete Johnson, the boogie-woogie pianist, and Pete Brown, the huge alto player, and sometimes during the 'Bugle Call Rag' finale fifteen musicians squeezed onto that stand, and the trumpets alone included Roy Eldridge and Hot Lips Page and Sidney deParis and Bobby Hackett. Our other headquarters besides Fifty-second Street was the Commodore Music Shop. It had glass listening booths in the back, but best of all was standing around and waiting to see Pee Wee or Hackett come in.

"I was still in the Boy Scouts when I started playing the

clarinet. I wanted to be in the marching band at school because it was glamorous. I went to the band director and he gave me a trumpet and told me to try it over the weekend. I couldn't make a sound. He gave me a clarinet the next Friday, and by Sunday I was playing 'Row, Row, Row Your Boat.' The director was Willard Briggs, and he was an excellent clarinettist and my first teacher. I'd been listening to Benny Goodman and Artie Shaw, and I started playing jazz right away. A lot of kids in Scarsdale, and Larchmont, and even Greenwich were interested in jazz, but it wasn't like kids and rock today, which is social. We shared a passion for *music*. There was a nucleus of fifteen or twenty of us, and we were always on the lookout for somebody's living room to jam in. We also played at U.S.O. dances. Servicemen would be farmed out to various families for Sunday dinner, and then would be taken to a local country club for a late-afternoon dance. We'd get the gig because the U.S.O. couldn't afford anything better, and we'd jam the whole time, playing 'After You've Gone' and 'Sweet Georgia Brown' at way-up tempos, which the poor souls had to dance to. Dick Wellstood came over from Greenwich with Charlie Trager, the bass player, and with this little thin kid with spectacles named Johnny Windhurst, who was older and went to Brown and sounded like Bix. After school, we'd listen to Jelly Roll and King Oliver and Louis, and even to Red Norvo's 'Congo Blues,' which had Dizzy and Bird, along with Teddy Wilson and Slam Stewart. It was the first bop we'd heard, and we thought it was funny. We couldn't take it seriously. By the time I was sixteen, I had a sophisticated knowledge of all jazz.

"When I graduated from high school, in 1945, I was set on being a musician. My parents wanted me to follow the Ivy League route, but I couldn't see it. If you were into jazz then, you were auotmatically a kind of loner. It was a special music still. We compromised, and I went to the Eastman School that fall. There was very little jazz up there, and *everything* was happening in New York, Bunk Johnson had just come up from New Orleans, and Woody Herman was at the Pennsylvania Hotel with the first Herd, which was *the* band. But there I was in this chilling, inhospitable place, and at the end of the term I told my parents I didn't want to go back. I told them I wanted to study jazz, even though I had—and still have—an interest in legit clarinet. My father asked me how I proposed studying jazz, and I said by going to New York and hanging out on Fifty-second Street and in the Village. So I did. I'd play in sessions around Westchester and take off for the street or Nick's. Red McKenzie had a group at Ryan's called the Candy Kids, and he had Johnny Windhurst and Eddie Hubble on trombone. Hubble was a little older, and he had a Pierce Arrow convertible with isinglass windows, and after that he found a Rolls with an open cockpit for the chauffeur. We'd roar around Westchester in those cars and then down to Ryan's, and pretty soon we got to be called the Westchester Kids. Out of all this came our first real group, which a trumpet player, Bob Mantler, named the Wildcats. John Glasel was on trumpet, and we had Hubble and Wellstood and Trager. Denny Strong was on piano, and Eddie Phyfe on drums. We were the first band in New York, and maybe in the East, to do what Lu Watters and Turk Murphy had been doing on the Coast—playing music of the Hot Five and the Red Hot Peppers and the Creole Jazz Band. I moved into an apartment in New York with Wellstood in 1946. The first Eddie Condon's opened on West Third Street that winter, and Eddie Hubble waited there for a day or so before it opened, so that he'd be the first customer. He was, and he was underage, too. Jimmy Ryan gave us a chance to sit in at a Sunday-afternoon session, and he liked us and offered us a job. I already had a day job in the stockroom at Textron, and when *The New Yorker* did a story on the Wildcats, the president of Textron called me in and congratulated me on the fine public-relations job I'd done by mentioning the company. He also said he understood I was sometimes a little late for work and that, in view of what I did at night, the company would make allowances. I guess

I took him literally, because I came in later and later and pretty soon Textron and I parted ways.

By this time I had started studying with Sidney Bechet. I had got to know Milt Mezzrow, because he and Art Hodes played at high schools around New York. Mezz came into Ryan's one night and said, 'Bechet is opening a school of music, and he needs students.' Bechet lived on Quincy Street in Brooklyn in a house with tall French windows that reminded him of New Orleans. He had boarders upstairs and a girl friend who took care of him. I was his first student, and we got on from the beginning. At lessons, he'd sit at the piano and demonstrate. He was particular about form: give the listener the melody first, then play variations on it, then give it to him again. And tell a story in every tune you play. He also told me not to bother with the soprano, which I'd started fooling around with, but to stick to the clarinet. I was living in the Village and was short of bread, so after a couple of lessons I moved in with Bechet and slept on a couch in the parlor. He loved to compose at the piano. He even got hold of an early tape recorder and recorded his piano. His personality came through in his piano playing even more than it did on his horns. It was stark and strong, and he had a beautiful sense of harmony. But he had a beautiful sense of harmony on the soprano and the clarinet, too, and he liked to surprise people with it. He also had a great notion of passing on the traditions of jazz music. He felt that younger people weren't interested in the music's past. Sidney was a very intense man. If he took a dislike to something, he could be savage and dangerous. But generally he was charming and warm, and he had a good sense of humor. Like Louis Armstrong, whose success he had mixed feelings about, he spoke that special New Orleans argot, with its 'ders' and 'erls,' and he often got names wrong. Max Kaminsky was Mac Kavinsky, Brad Gowans was Brad Garfield, and Earl Hines was Earl Hine. I lived with Bechet six or eight months, and during part of that time he had a group at Ryan's, and I would sit in and we'd play duets. And we did shots together on Rudy Blesh's radio show with Baby Dodds and Pops Foster and Georg Brunis. Because of the duets, Brunis nicknamed us Bash and Shay, after the way Sidney pronounced his name. My style was naturally close to Bechet's, and when I started to change it, all he said was,

'That's all right, that's all right. He's finding his own way' "
Wilber got up and looked out the window. A tan field, recently cut, sloped toward a black pond—Ice House Pond. On the far right, abutting the road, was a white shingled 1825 house, and on the left, beyond the field, were pine woods. The old New Englanders loved small rooms, because small rooms kept the heat, and at the same time they loved doors, which let them escape from room to room. The Wilbers' house is a crowd of tiny rooms that eases through door after door on the ground floor, past the coffin door, or front door, up the steep front stairs and through the second floor, and down the backstairs. It is a handsome, cheerful house furnished with respectable American country pieces and fine hooked rugs, which float like islands on the painted, speckled floors. Wilber's father bought the house in 1943, for a "ridiculous figure," and Wilber must have been happy there. He was certainly relaxed. Whenever one of the Wildcats visited, they would take a canoe out to the middle of Ice House Pond and jam. One day, Mrs. Moore, who was august and in her nineties and lived on the north side of the pond stood outside her house and listened, and then gesticulated at the boys, and Wilber's heart sank: she was going to give them what-for for all the racket. They paddled over and Mrs. Moore cried, "You boys sound terrific, but you better come in now and have some milk and cookies."

Wilber sat down and talked again. "In 1948, Hughes Panassié organized a jazz festival in Nice and Sidney was invited, but he had taken a gig at Jazz Limited in Chicago and they wouldn't let him go. So he sent me. I was there a week and then took a six-week tour around Europe for the Hot Club of France. The most marvellous part of the trip was working with Baby Dodds. He was, in my way of

thinking, possibly the greatest jazz drummer. He was a per-
cussionist more than a drummer. He thought of drums in
terms of colors, and how to mix them. He was fanatical
about tuning his drums, and he'd be on the stand a half-hour
before showtime, tightening and tapping, tightening and
tapping. His time was superb, and his whole playing was
heavy and low. The tonality was down where it didn't get
in the way, as so much modern drumming does. He princi-
pally used his bass drum and powerful, accented press rolls
on his snare drum, and he didn't have a high-hat. But he had
a ride cymbal, and he played it in a way that young drummers think they invented—just four beats to the bar: *ting-
ting-ting-ting*, his head down low, and his right arm crooked
like a dancer's over his head and the cymbal, and his whole
body shimmying and shaking in time to the music. It was an
unbelievable experience to have Baby behind you. When I
went into the Savoy in Boston opposite a fine jump band led
by Tab Smith, I had Baby and Norman Lester on piano.
Then Kaiser Marshall replaced Baby, and Dick Wellstood
replaced Lester. We did an excellent business, and the owner
said expand, so I hired Henry Goodwin on trumpet, Jimmy
Archey on trombone, and Tommy Benford on drums. We
played Jelly Roll and Willie the Lion and early Duke and
King Oliver, and the band gathered momentum. The Savoy
had an all-black clientele, but white college kids began lining
up down the block on weekends. The musicians' union in
Boston was still split into a black union and a white union,
and I was the first white leader of a black group. The musicians didn't seem to mind. I guess my musicianship has stood
me in good stead. It was hard work at the Savoy—seven
nights a week plus a Sunday matinée and a couple of rehearsals. The guys in the band made about a hundred and a
quarter a week, and I got two hundred. It seemed like an
awful lot of money. We stayed at the Savoy for eight-week
stretches and would be spelled by someone like Ed Hall,
who'd bring in Ruby Braff and Jimmy Crawford. But I felt
we were getting stale, and between sets I'd run out to a
record store to listen to Charlie Parker or over to the Hi-

Hat to listen to Lester Young. We got an offer from Ryan's, but I turned the band over to Archey; he stayed at Ryan's on and off for a couple of years.

"I gigged around, spent a summer up here playing in a trio, and in the fall of 1950 took a band into George Wein's first Storyville, in the Copley Square Hotel in Boston. I had Joe Thomas on trumpet and Vic Dickenson on trombone and Big Sid Catlett on drums. Thomas and Vic left and the deParis brothers took their places. My playing was in a weird state of flux. You could hear Bird in it and Buddy deFranco. I learned a lot from Big Sid. He'd take a solo on a medium-slow 'Stompin' at the Savoy'—the kind of loose-elbows tempo most drummers fall apart in if they try and solo—and eventually get up from his drums and go into the audience, playing on the floor and on chairs and tabletops, and everybody would go wild. It was Sid's last gig. When the place shut down for a couple of weeks, he went back to Chicago, where he'd been working at Jazz Limited, and not long after that he collapsed backstage at the Chicago Opera House. But we had a forty-first birthday party for him at Storyville. Hoagy Carmichael sat in and sang, and Johnny Hodges and Sonny Greer stopped in. Hodges borrowed my soprano saxophone and put one of my clarinet reeds in it and played soprano for the first time since 1940. That was something. That summer, I came up here, and I listened a lot to Lee Konitz and Lennie Tristano. In fact, I studied with Lennie when I got back to New York. He had a concept of developing your intuition to the highest level, of getting your head and body together. He was intrigued with moving bar lines around, with using the higher intervals in chords, and with using two different rhythms at once. Tristano was a brilliant musician who was determined to do something different, but he had no interest in Louis Armstrong or in the past, and after three or four months I left him. The Korean war was on, and I got drafted and ended up on Governor's Island, playing solo clarinet in a concert band and feeling that it was time to stop being known as Sidney Bechet's protégé. So I took lessons from the great

Leon Russianoff. He said, 'Let's get an open sound,' and he started me from scratch. I studied with him five years. For a time, my jazz playing was destroyed, and it took a while to get back to playing without self-consciousness.

"Russianoff made me understand even more that the clarinet resists being played in a loose way, that it can only be pushed so far. The big temptation on the clarinet is to noodle, to play extraneous notes. Making the instrument sound like an extension of yourself is 100 per cent more difficult for a clarinettist than for a saxophonist or a brass player. Two of the best clarinettists we've had were Lester Young and Pee Wee Russell, and they were successful partly because they disregarded all the rules. For Lester, the clarinet was simply a different facet of his expression. He probably used a very soft reed to get that soft, wispy sound. And he certainly didn't disregard the microphone. Lester played the clarinet like a first-year student. Pee Wee had a nervous condition, of course, and he was subtle and devious in his thoughts and his playing, but he was a studied musician. He told me once, 'I only listen to three clarinettists—Benny Goodman, you, and me.' My favorite clarinettists are Johnny Dodds and Benny Goodman. Dodds had a surprising technique for his time. He'd weave beautiful melodies through a simple seventh chord, and he had a sublime way with the blues. He was very nearly the greatest blues player we have had. Goodman was perfect in his idiom. The marvellous relaxation he had with a pop tune—with everything, in fact! He could translate whatever came into his head directly onto the clarinet. He breathed and talked on it, and it *was* an extension of him. But he should have given Reginald Kell lessons, instead of the other way around. He started sounding like Kell, which is no drag, but it wasn't as good as Benny Goodman. I've loved other clarinettists. Irving Fazola was terribly simple, but he never made a mistake. Jimmy Noone was remarkable, although he had a sentimental streak in his playing and he had a faulty harmonic ear. Bechet always fought the clarinet, but he could fly on the soprano saxophone. Artie Shaw had a great lyric intensity. They say he worked his solos out beforehand. Certainly they are more like compositions than improvisations. He had a brilliant way of using sequential figures against the rhythm. He was very clever. I don't know why the clarinet has fallen by the wayside. Maybe Goodman set such high standards that he frightened everybody else away. Maybe it was because bop phrasing didn't transfer to the clarinet, because that constant stream of eighth notes didn't fall easily under the fingers. Maybe electronics washed it out. It's strange how fashionable the soprano saxophone has become. I suppose it's because John Coltrane put his blessing on it near the end of his life. Zoot Sims plays it right, and so does Kenny Davern, but most tenor players who have taken it up get a small sound—a bad-oboe sound. To me—a clarinettist, who thinks of his instrument as little—the soprano is big and should have a big sound. It should also be played in tune, but that's just about impossible. Trick fingering is the only way to correct, or come close to correcting, its endless pitch problems."

Wilber's clarinet is elusive. His playing is far more fluid than it once was. There are antithetical yet wholly comfortable hints of Goodman and Dodds in it, but above all is his mannerly tone and intense, thoughtful improvising. This intensity reaches passion when he plays the soprano. He *does* recall Bechet but he also recalls Johnny Hodges' streamlined version of Bechet's soprano playing: the vibrato has been cropped, the arabesques ironed, the where-to? noodling reined in. Bechet purposely tried to sound like a lead trumpet player in ensembles, and most of the time he succeeded, knocking aside whatever hapless trumpeter might be on hand. Wilber has mastered the trumpet style on soprano, too, and when he shifts into it in ensembles or in the closing chorus of a solo, the effect is electrifying. No one gets closer to the center of jazz than Wilber at such times.

Wilber talked about improvisation, which he considers as mysterious as speech. "How, after all, do people learn to talk?" he said. "If the musician thinks about improvisation for long, he won't succeed. The less he thinks, the more successful he's going to be. It's like swimming, which is an extraordinary combination of muscle and timing. If you think about each breath, each stroke, your arms and legs get out of sync, your breathing falters, and you sink. Swinging is swimming well, and it has a distinctive rhythmic feel. It's the contrast between a steady pulse and the syncopated figures against it. It's the excitement of simultaneously going with the beat and battling it. The rhythmic element is what releases the intuitive powers in great players. Intense swing sharpens their reflexes and carries them away. They might be thinking melodic lines and chords, but then the intuitive powers take over and it's like going on automatic pilot. The notes are ripping and they're totally free.

"During the past thirty or so years, improvisers have become too involved with harmonic possibilities—the passing chord, the altered chord, the note added to the high part of the chord. Often melodic beauty has been vanquished. Harmony has dominated melody when it should have been a servant to it. Harmony should decorate the melodic cake. What finally happened, of course, was the harmonic prison of bebop. Bebop was nothing but running the chord changes. The ensembles were not developable; all you had were chords. That's why the arrival in New York of old Bunk Johnson in 1946 at the time when bop was bursting forth was so refreshing. Bop was vertical and Johnson's New Orleans music was horizontal. There was no playing in thirds; the ensembles were all marvellous counterpoint. But the harmonic prison has been pretty much destroyed. Ornette Coleman revolted against it, and he opened the gates for free jazz, which ignores all the rules, musical and social.

"The resurrection of Bunk Johnson was a prime instance of the curious fact that all the museum work, the musical anthropology that has been practiced in jazz has been done by middle-class whites. Why? Whites have gone back and exposed the roots of what began as a black music, while black musicians have almost exclusively practiced the cult of the hip. We have been the conservatives and they have

been the revolutionists. I look at the New York Jazz Repertory Company, of which I'm a director, as an educational
thing. We hope when we play Ellington or Morton or Beiderbecke or the Savoy Sultans that the audience, black and
white, will get excited enough to go out and buy the records and listen some more. But repertory concerts are of
great benefit to the musicians who play them, too. It allows
them to get a glimpse of the inside of musicians who have
come before them. When I give a Tricky Sam Nanton solo
that I've transcribed to a trombonist in the Repertory Orchestra, I tell him to play it note for note first, so that he
can get a feeling for its beams and nails, and *then* play it his
own way."

Wilber began to look restless and said that in fifteen minutes he had to practice.
"I was born in New York on March 15, 1928. My mother
and father lived on Sullivan Street in a kind of development
of duplex apartments built around a courtyard. My mother
died of cancer when I was six months old, and my father
didn't remarry until I was four or five. Until then I was
raised mostly by a Miss Breed, a wonderful Boston lady.
We moved to Gramercy Park, and I went to Friends Academy, on Stuyvesant Square. My father said that one snowy
day he watched my older sister and me trying to slide
down the base of Edwin Booth's statue across from the
Player's Club, and decided it was time to move to the country. We settled in Scarsdale when I was seven. My father
was born in Mt. Vernon, Ohio, the son of a minister. He
was with Macmillan before the First World War, and when
he retired eighteen years ago, he was a vice president of
Appleton-Century-Crofts in their textbook division. He
loves tennis and fishing and sailing and camping, and he's
been terrifically civic-minded, as has my stepmother, who
came from California and whose father was in U.S. Steel.
I've always made a living playing jazz, but between the mid-
fifties, when I got out of the Army, and the late sixties,
when the World's Greatest Jazz Band started, I had my

share of scuffling. Right after the Army, the nucleus of the old Wildcats got together and we formed a coöperative band called The Six. Our intention was to bridge the schism between modern and traditional music. Our first job was at Child's Paramount on Broadway, but we were too modern for the audiences there. The same thing happened when we went into Ryan's. But when we got a gig at the Café Bohemia in the Village, where Cannonball Adderley and Bird played, we were too old-fashioned. Thank God most of that parochialism has disappeared! The Six lasted a year or two, and then I went into Eddie Condon's. I was studying with Russianoff and was getting facility all over the horn, and I guess I tried to make every solo imperishable, because one night Condon, a couple of sheets to the wind, said between numbers, 'Hey, kid! Make a mistake!' But the Condon style of playing had lost its freshness, and in 1957 I joined the superb band Bobby Hackett had at the Henry Hudson Hotel. It had Dick Cary and Ernie Caceres and Buzzy Drootin and Tom Gwaltney and everyone doubled on about six instruments. Hackett's band was ingenious, but the audiences at the Henry Hudson were only interested in dancing. When Capitol recorded it, they made Hackett play dixieland stuff, and the real, adventurous, funny flavor of the band was never caught. I went on to Benny Goodman after that. He had a big band, and in it were Herb Geller and Russ Freeman from the Coast, the bassist Scott LaFaro, who was killed in an auto accident, old Taft Jordan, nad Pepper Adams, whom I'd met at the Eastman School. Benny had commissioned all these up-to-date arrangements by Bill Holman and Shorty Rogers, and we rehearsed them for a month. We opened in Burlington, Vermont, and the audience was dumbfounded. They just sat there behind their faces, New England fashion. Benny was furious. He told us to take those damn things out of the book, and we went back to 'Sing, Sing, Sing' and 'Don't Be That Way.' I played tenor with Benny, and he gave me solos. He really felt like playing then, and it was a treat to hear him night after night. Then I went into the new uptown Condon's with Max Kaminsky, did occasional jingles, worked the band on the Jackie Gleason show, and did a Lester Lanin gig now and then. I was just floating, and what suddenly gave me direction was coming upon a curved soprano saxophone in the window of an instrument store on West Forty-eighth Street. I'd pretty much given up on the soprano in 1953, but I blew just one note on this curved one, and it was beautiful! It sang. I used it more and more with the World's Greatest, and it helped me through the dry times after Carl Fontana left and Lou McGarity died and the band began to play by rote."

Ricky Wilber, Wilber's wife, appeared, hunting for a book. Wilber seized his clarinet case and took off for the main house. A couple of minutes later, rigorous, piping clarinet scales floated across the lawn. Ricky Wilber found what she was after—a biography of Thornton Wilder—and perched on an arm of the sofa. She is Wilber's height and has a round face and round horn-rims and a full, round voice. She talks quickly. "He practices every day, sometimes for two or three hours at a time. Nothing gets in the way of his playing. Several years ago, he was up on a ladder cleaning a gutter on our house in New City and the ladder went over and he broke both wrists. They were set, and then had to be reset, after the mess the first doctor had made, by Dr. James Nicholas, who handles the Jets. But Bob was playing again in no time. He and I were married in 1948. I was in the theatre, and I lived on Sullivan Street, near where Bob was born, and I'd get taken to Nick's and Stuyvesant Casino and Ryan's. Sidney Bechet introduced us. We were married a year later, and off we went to the Nice Festival and what amounted to a six-week honeymoon in Europe. I came from Kutztown, Pennsylvania, a hundred miles west of New York. They had a lot of excellent craft fairs there, and people would come from miles around in broiling heat to watch them make soap and dip candles. I was an only child and was born Shirley Rickards—whence Ricky. My mother's family owned a restaurant, and I used to have to eat lunch there when I was a child. When I go into similar places now and smell that smell it just about does me in. My father was a nice man who had been very good-looking when he was young. He did clerical work most of his life. Rahn was my mother's maiden name. She is still very enthusiastic, and she kept us going by commuting a long distance to Bethlehem, where she worked for Western Electric. I've enjoyed being a part of Bob's life, partly because I sing and know something about music. Marrying into such a precarious profession has never frightened me. Bob has always supported me and our daughter, who's seventeen now. He's one of the few people in the performing arts who never questions himself. He has always lived from moment to moment, and has walked steadily forward into what comes next. He has an unconceited self-assurance. At times, I admit, I've felt ignored, but he *is* married to his music, and in a way I wish I didn't understand that so well."

INDEX